No Apologies

THE LIFE & WORK OF
SUSANNA NEWCOME

INCLUDING THE FULL-TEXT OF HER
SIGNATURE APOLOGETIC WORK:

AN

ENQUIRY

INTO THE

EVIDENCE

OF THE

Chriſtian Religion

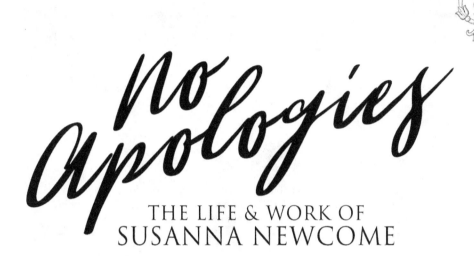

No Apologies

THE LIFE & WORK OF SUSANNA NEWCOME

SARAH R. ENTERLINE, M.A.

FOREWORD BY
DR. JOSEPH HOLDEN

Scripture quotations in PART TWO are taken from the ENGLISH STANDARD VERSION of the Bible while scripture quotations in PART THREE are taken from the KING JAMES VERSION, 1611 Edition.

Public Philosophy Press
www.publicphilosophypress.com

Cover/Interior Design & Author/Cover Photos *by* Matt Enterline

First Printing: November 2020

ISBN 978-0-578-67883-2

Dedications

To my parents:
For raising me as Susanna's parents did –
To love the Lord and pursue truth at all costs.

and

To Dr. Tim McGrew:
For introducing me to Susanna in the first place.

Table of Contents

iii   Foreword *by Dr. Joseph Holden*

v   Introduction

vii   Special Thanks

1   **Part One**:
The Life of Susanna Squire-Newcome

15   **Part Two**:
The Apologetic Arguments of *Enquiry*

161   **Part Three**:
An Enquiry into the Evidence of the Christian Religion
The 1732 original work by Sussanna Newcome presented in its entirety

All of the historical information, documents,
images, and sources referenced in the biography
portion of the book are organized into Appendices
and can be viewed at *noapologiesbook.com* along
with a list of hyperlinked footnotes.

Foreword

The Enlightenment period (c. 1688-1800) was a time of intense intellectual pursuit, when man was undergoing a rite-of-passage from ecclesiastical influence to independent secular thinking. During this time, human reason, scientific inquiry, biblical criticism, and natural theology ascended to new heights while divine revelation was relegated to spiritual matters and personal opinion. There were many precursors and catalysts for this shift in thinking. In the *Novum Organum*, Francis Bacon introduced Scientism, which set forward induction as the "new logic" which should be applied to the study of all things; Thomas Hobbes advocated in *Leviathan* a radical Materialism, and only the corporeal was viewed as the stuff of true reality; Benedict de Spinoza wrote the first systematic criticism of the Bible, dismissed the possibility of miracles, and rejected Mosaic authorship of the Pentateuch in his posthumous *Theologico-Politico Tractatus*; David Hume argued forcefully in his *Enquiries Concerning Human Understanding* for a radical Skepticism which virtually eliminated the Bible from the realm of meaningful truth, essentially making divine revelation worthy only of the flames; and in the *Critique of Pure Reason*, Immanuel Kant attempts to avoid Hume's Skepticism by joining two streams of epistemological thought (Rationalism and Empiricism) which resulted in hard Agnosticism. As a result, the tenets of traditional Theism were separated from the realm of objective truth and relegated to one's subjective opinion. This unfortunate dichotomy would form the worldview basis that fueled negative biblical criticism for centuries to come.

It was in this intellectually challenging environment that Susanna Newcome presented her arguments for God and the Christian faith. Unlike the critics, her arguments attempted to restore the tenets of the faith, using clear and systematic philosophical argumentation, as objective truth. Her uncompromising life and work stood in stark contrast to the apostates around her that relied on fallible human reason rather than the inerrant Word of God. Susanna's arguments for God reflected a clear understanding of His independent nature and the role causality played in the creation of the universe. In clear terms, she exposed the absurdity of the critics' logic by appealing to their common sense. In so doing, her thought foreshadowed many of the arguments used today in classical apologetics and classical theology, while at the same time drawing upon the those who came before her in the tradition of Augustine, Anselm, and Aquinas.

Susanna was a strong thinker and humble believer who served as a voice crying in the wilderness. With an uncompromising independent voice, incisive logic, strong arguments, and biblical truths, she stood against the prevailing critical thought of her day. For this reason, she is considered one of the unsung heroes of her time. Susanna's conviction and deep reflection gives hope to countless men and women today that God can still work in the darkest of times with hearts that are yielded to Him. We need more philosophers, pastors, and theologians that are willing to speak up as Susanna did, logically and unapologetically, in defense of the historic Christian faith.

Joseph M. Holden

Joseph M. Holden, PhD

President
Veritas International University

Introduction

In early 2016, when I first read *Enquiry* by Susanna Newcome, I was floored by her intelligence and how ahead of her time she was. I immediately dove into research to find out everything I could about her. There is not much, but what there is gives a clear picture of a very extraordinary woman. I felt an instant connection to her and knew it was my job to tell the world about her. The author John Green once said, "Sometimes, you read a book and it fills you with this weird evangelical zeal, and you become convinced that the shattered world will never be put back together unless, and until, all living humans read the book." Apart from the Bible, and anything by Lewis, Tozer, or Kreeft, I rarely get that feeling, yet that is exactly what happened when I read Susanna's book. In sharing it, I hope to inspire a new generation of female scholars who want to make their voices heard and their skill acknowledged in fields like philosophy, theology, and apologetics, which are generally dominated by men. It is time to change the culture, so that women in the future will be acknowledged in the field the way women like Susanna should have been in the past.

Many women throughout history have practiced the art of apologetics in their personal evangelism. Specifically, I think of Priscilla in the book of Acts, teaching Apollos how to give the case for Jesus being the long-awaited Messiah of Israel. Women engaging the fields of apologetics, philosophy, history, science, and logic - to tell others of Christ - is no new phenomena. However, Susanna's *Enquiry* appears to be the first time in history a woman published and publicly engaged in Christian Apologetics in a professional, scholarly capacity. Susanna showed the world that when it came to the mind, women were not the weaker sex but equally brilliant, as well as capable defenders of the historic Christian faith.

Why *No Apologies*? Susanna lived her life refusing to apologize for defending the truth and challenging the status quo of the day. She constantly kept those around her on their toes theologically, and openly critiqued any unbiblical ideology that crossed her path. In the introduction of her second book, a response challenging the author of *The Plain Account* (believed to be Bishop Hoadly[1]), she literally writes, "Sir, I make no apology for giving you this trouble..." Susanna had a passion for truth, and her deep faith compelled her to challenge those who would lead astray the consciences of sincere but unlearned Christians. She truly was a force to be reckoned with for the kingdom of God and we can learn much today from the spiritual courage of this formidable woman of the past.

Sincerely,

Sarah R. Enterline, M.A.

---

1   John H. Overton, *William Law: Nonjuror and Mystic*, London: Longmans, Green, and Co, 1881, p. 280. Susanna's younger brother John was Chaplain to Dr. Hoadley in 1730, which may explain her specific interest in his theology, (**Appendix 4**).

Special thanks to the following people for assisting in my research:

- MRS. KATHRYN MCKEE (Special Collections Librarian) and DR. ADAM CROTHERS (Special Collections Assistant) at St John's College, Cambridge, for gathering information about Susanna and assisting my husband and I on our visit to their beautiful library.

- MR. IAN STEVENS, Church Warden at St. Andrew's in Durnford, for sending me the pictures of the inside of Samuel's church, where Susanna grew up.

- MS. MARGARET MOLES, Archivist at the Wiltshire & Swindon Record Office, for getting me copies of Susanna's original baptism records.

- The team at the LONDON METROPOLITAN ARCHIVES, who were so helpful in getting me Susanna's marriage record.

- MICHELA BONARDI, Collections Manager at THE BRITISH MUSEUM for helping me obtain the rights to use Susanna's portrait in the book.

- The REVEREND ANNA MATTHEWS, Vicar of St. Bene't's in Cambridge, for letting us sneak in right before service to visit where Susanna was buried.

- PASTOR JAMES PEAT, Calvary Cambridge, for showing us around your beautiful hometown. I now know why Susanna was so happy there!

- The VICKERY FAMILY (Phil, Hannah, Steve, Amber, and kids) for hosting us and showing us around England. This research would not have been possible without your generosity!

- DR. JOSEPH HOLDEN for training and mentoring me in the discipline of apologetics, and for writing the foreword of my first book 15 years after that journey began.

And last but not least, my husband MATT ENTERLINE,
for all his love, support, photography, and graphic art skills.
I truly won the husband lottery with you!

🅵🅾🅾🅸🅽 @SarahREnterline

sarahrenterline.com
noapologiesbook.com

ARAH R. ENTERLINE is an apologist, teacher, pastor's wife, and mother. She has degrees in Biblical Studies, Christian Studies (Theology and Ministry), Social and Behavioral Science, and Philosophy; a CA State Credential in teaching History; and an M.A. in Christian Leadership.

In March of 2009, she founded The International Society of Women in Apologetics (womeninapologetics.com). In 2016, she handed the reigns over to two bright, upcoming female apologists, and is proud that Women in Apologetics is growing and still going strong to this day!

She has taught Apologetics, Bible, Philosophy, and History at both the secondary and college levels, speaks at churches and conferences around the country, and has frequently guested on numerous radio shows and podcasts.

She is also working as an apologist with the Library of Historical Apologetics, and was a writer and editor on the Special Divine Action Project.

Sarah is married to Matt, a Pastor and co-creator of Calvary Curriculum. She also has a 13 year-old son named Lochlann who loves learning about the Bible, animals, Legos, and superheroes.

No Apologies is her first full-length book, and she hopes to continue a series on women in historical apologetics, as well as other curriculum and works.

Part One

The Life of Susanna Squire-Newcome:
1684/5 – 1763

M.ʳˢ NEWCOME.

See pages 12-13 for portrait info.

Birth and Family

usanna Newcome[2] was born Susanna Squire late in the year 1684, in Durnford in Wiltshire, England. Two different St. Andrew Parish records show a baby girl named 'Susanna' was baptized there on February 11, 1685, by her parents, Samuel and Mary Squire.[3] Her father, Samuel Squire, was the Vicar of the St. Andrew's Parish at Durnford for fifty years, beginning in 1673 until his death in 1723.[4] Susanna's mother, Mary, appears to have given birth to nine children total – Mary (1674), Samuel (1675), Edwards (1677), Sarah (1678), Thomas[5] (1679), Francis (1681), Susanna (1684), Thomas (1685), and John (1691).[6]

Susanna seemed destined for a future at St. John's at Cambridge, given that three of her brothers (Edwards g.1700, Francis g.1715, and

2　Susanna Newcome's name has been spelled in many ways, and is spelled differently almost every time it is in print (Susana, Susannah, Newcomb, Newcombe, Newcomen, Newcomer, Comus, etc.). However, "Susanna Newcome" is the correct spelling as seen on all of her baptism and marriage records, her gravestone, and in her husband's own hand, inscribed in his copy of *Enquiry* left to St. John's College. (**Appendix 1**)

3　On one document, her baptism date was listed as 1684/5, so it was unclear which year she was born. Fortunately, Margaret Moles, an archivist at the Wiltshire Record Office, was extremely helpful in clearing up the matter: "In England the calendar year starting Jan. 01 was not formally introduced on documents until 1752 - prior to this date the year began on Lady Day (March 25th) – for the period 01 Jan. - 24 Mar. there was often a double indication on documents - for instance 1684/5. Susannah was baptized Feb 11th-this would have been regarded as towards the end of 1684 or the start of 1685 if using the 'new' calendar." On the other document, the date was listed as the "11th of February, in the first year of the reign of King James [II]" who took the throne of February 6, 1685, a mere five days before Susanna was baptized. (**Appendix 1**)

4　**Appendix 2**

5　This Thomas appears to have died as a young child, as there was a second child named Thomas born about 6 years later, and only the second one is mentioned in their father's will. Other omissions from their father's will are Samuel, and Sarah, who was recorded as being buried in the same year she was born.

6　**Appendix 3**

John g.1715), two nephews (Samuel g.1726 – son of Edwards, and Samuel g.1744 – son of Thomas), and great-nephew (Richard Beadon – son of her niece Mary), all attended and graduated from there. Most of her male family members ended up with careers in the church, except for her brother Thomas, who became an apothecary.[7]

Life

Having such strong connections to the school and the church, it should not come as a surprise that on December 5, 1727, Susanna married the Rev. Dr. John Newcome, a Professor of Divinity at St. John's College at Cambridge, at St. Giles, Cripplegate Church, in London.[8] It might seem odd that Susanna and John got married in London proper, being that neither one of them served at the church or lived in the parish. However, once it was learned it was the Reverend Thomas Bennet that married them, the oddity of it becomes clear. First, London city is ideally located between Salisbury where Susanna lived, and Cambridge, where John lived. This allowed both sides of the family to attend. Second, Reverend Bennet attended and was a fellow at St. John's College at the same time as Dr. Newcome.[9] Both majored in Divinity, so it would make sense that they would be acquainted. Third, if a couple did not live or serve in the parish, they had to apply for a license to married there. The record of their marriage on 05 December 1727 not only confirms this, but also that Rev. Thomas Bennet was indeed the Vicar in residence at the time.

---

7   *Admissions to the College of St. John the Evangelist in the University of Cambridge, July 1715-November 1767*, (Cambridge: University Press, 1903), p. 29, 49, 63, 133, 236, 343, 399, 427-429, 603, 627-628, 688-689; University of Oxford and Joseph Foster, *Alumni Oxonienses: S-Z*, (Oxford: Parker and Company, 1892), p. 1403. (**Appendix 4**)

8   **Appendix 5**

9   *Alumni Cantabrigienses: A Biographical List of All Known Students, Graduates– and Holders of Office at the University of Cambridge, from the Earliest Times to 1900*, John Venn/John Archibald Venn Cambridge University Press > (10 volumes 1922 to 1953) *Part I. Earliest times to 1752 Vol. iii. Kaile – Ryves*, (1924) p 246. *London Diocesan Clergy Succession From the Earliest Time to the Year 1898*, Reverend George Hennessy, London: Swan Sonnenschein & Co., 1898, p. 196.

Susanna married later in life, when she was forty-four years old, but only a year before she published the work for which she is best known, *An Enquiry into the Evidence of the Christian Religion* (henceforth referred to as simply *"Enquiry"*). The historians who recorded the shared life[10] of Susanna and Dr. John Newcome seemed to all share the same opinion, summed up well by Mullinger here - "It became almost habitual to attribute whatever was best in what Mr. Newcome did, to Mrs. Newcome's influence."[11] All of the Cambridge historians, with the exception of one, cast Dr. Newcome himself in quite an unfavorable light. Thomas Baker wrote that he was "a slow, dull plodding mortal whose talents were hardly above mediocrity. His parts were chiefly confined to a low cunning artifice and a desire to overreach, and had nothing liberal in his conversation, manner, and appearance."[12]

However, what is interesting is that every time he is disparaged, Susanna herself is praised and exalted in equal measure, as if they were afraid her stellar reputation would suffer for her husband's unsavory one. One historian, William Cole, goes so far as to call him duplicitous and even likens him to the pagan king Belshazzar that blasphemes against the God of the Old Testament.[13] This same commentator, however, writes the following regarding Susanna:

> Mrs. Newcome, his wife, bears the character, by everybody, of a most excellent and worthy woman; not to say learned: for she has given proof of her [scholarship] in more than one book which she has published... Some few years before [Dr. Newcome] died, he had the misfortune to lose his most amiable lady, who had everybody's good word... another writer[14] styles him 'the most pious and charitable

---

10   Appendix 6

11   James B. Mullinger, *St. John's College*. (London: F.E. Robinson & Company, 1901), p. 224

12   Thomas Baker, B.D., (1656-1740), Ejected Fellow, First Historian of Cambridge

13   John Nichols and Samuel Bentley, *Literary Anecdotes of the Eighteenth Century*, Vol. 1, (London: Nichols, Son, and Bentley, 1812), p. 556

14   Either Denne or Shrubsole was the one historian who favored the Doctor. Samuel Denne and William Shrubsole, *The History and Antiquities of Rochester and Its Environs*. (Rochester: T. Fisher, 1772), p. 197.

Dean' but reserves the chief part of his [public praise] for his wife, who, I believe, much better deserved it… I never heard anyone so universally well spoken of. She was one of the finest figures of any woman I ever saw of her age, and was esteemed a very learned lady.[15]

One wonders how a woman, described as Susanna was, dealt with her husband's questionable nature? Another such passage by Cole gives an insight into what kind of wife Susanna was, and how she reacted when her husband was acting in a way unbecoming of the Dean of a Divinity school. On one occasion, when Dr. Newcome had "committed a most indecent action very unsuitable to the dignity of St. John's", Cole was persuaded that if Susanna had "been at her husband's elbow, she would have [still] held his hand."[16] This faithfulness, exemplified by Susanna, was probably due to the fact that it was said of John, "He was happy many years in the strictest mutual affection of the conjugal state, with a most accomplished lady,"[17] and that "the Doctor did her all the justice that was due to so much merit."[18] Aside from Dr. Newcome's unfavorable reputation (regarding politics as well as a few character flaws), it appears as though Susanna and John had a happy marriage and a good life together.

Susanna had many other admirers as well, and in fact, not one description ever recorded about her is anything less than what would be considered an accolade. On another occasion, Cole reiterates his praises above, "Mrs. Newcome… being a woman of excellent parts and abilities; of sound sense and masculine judgment… had written a pamphlet or two on moral subjects, which I have heard much commended. She was as fine a figure of a woman when she was turned of sixty, as many are when they are twenty years younger; and she has often put me in mind of the person and character of that most

---

15   Nichols and Bentley, pp. 557 - 561
16   Nichols and Bentley, p. 556.
17   Denne and Shrubsole, p. 197.
18   Nichols and Bentley, p. 559

exalted and excellent woman, Madame de Maintenon[19], in a more humble style: for she was an accomplished one."[20]

Career and Influence [21]

Susanna Newcome did not have an official career as a writer, but still had considerable influence over those around her, which, at that time, is surprising for a lady constantly surrounded by male academics and clergymen. Linehan states,

> John Newcome was the only Master of St. John's in the eighteenth century who was already married when he was elected [in 1734]... It was surprising enough to see a wife in the Master's Lodge at all. What was amazing in that age was that she was not only an attractive and charming hostess, but also a learned, literary wife, who published more than her husband on the subject that he taught: Divinity. He mustered only a couple sermons in print. She wrote, anonymously but acknowledging her authorship when presenting copies, *Enquiry*, which went into three editions, and *The Plain Account of the Nature and End of the Sacrament of the Lord's Supper*, in two parts... The politically reactionary Baker[22]

---

19 A contemporary of Susanna's - the second wife of King Louis XIV of France who exercised quite a bit of political and religious influence on the court at the time, (1635-1719).
20 Nichols and Bentley, p. 559
21 **Appendix 6**
22 Thomas Baker, B.D., (1656-1740), Ejected Fellow, First Historian of Cambridge. He was not extremely close to the Newcome's, but was very fond of Susanna, even leaving her a ring of guinea in his will.

carefully transcribed into his copy of the *Enquiry*[23] that the book was 'By Mrs. Newcome' as well as this tribute from the German *Acta eruditorium* of 1734: 'She certainly deserves better than the lowest place among female philosophers, since she has treated an important theme, which has exercised the minds of serious scholars, with arguments both sound clearly expressed, with praiseworthy judgment and in a felicitous style.' Her writing was lively, she was determined to define terms properly, and she proved ready to modify the text of the *Enquiry* in a second edition to take account of further study.[24]

Even though she wrote anonymously, her knowledge and writing skills were an open secret among their close friends.[25] In fact, she became quite well known for them. McKitterick writes, "Those who were prepared to be impressed noted her theological abilities... In the eyes of many, her literary judgment seemed superior to that of her husband."[26] An example of this would be when a friend, Dr. Zachary Grey, asked Dr. Newcome to contribute to his published commentary on the satiric poem by Samuel Butler, *Hudibras*, but in the end, it was Susanna's personal notes on the translation that ended up in Dr. Grey's publication.[27] Dr. Grey writes regarding her contribution: "In the following note communicated to me by an admirable lady, who as she is endued with all the excellencies and perfections of her sex, is well known to the learned world for some

23   Baker's copy of *Enquiry*, with his notes, can be found today in the Special Collections section of St. John's College Library at Cambridge University, as well as another copy that states it was "Given to St. John's College Library by the Author Susanna Newcome." (S.11.7, Ee.17.16(1), O.10.58). John and Susanna did not have any children; therefore, 60 of their most precious books were donated to the College Library when he died, (**Appendix 6**).
24   Peter Linehan, *St John's College, Cambridge: A History*. (Woodbridge: Boydell Press, 2011), p. 185
25   David McKitterick, *A History of Cambridge University Press: Volume 2, Scholarship and Commerce, 1698-1872*. (Cambridge: University Press, 1998), p. 119; *Cambridge Journal* FN #30
26   McKitterick, p. 119
27   Nichols and Bentley, p. 481

useful and valuable tracts she has published and for her great and uncommon attainments in literature: her name, was I at liberty to mention it, would do a great honor to my notes."[28]

The volume he is referring to is a first edition of *Enquiry* (1728) that was included in a publication entitled *Divinity Tracts*, which was a collection of theological treatises by various authors. Cole notes that it was "a work which, in an age when female authors were not so frequent at present, conferred on her a greater share of literary reputation than many of her contemporaries would allow. Mr. Edward Clarke told [him] he had heard her speak upon literary subjects, when himself and many others dined at the Master's lodge."[29] Mullinger also writes that her *Enquiry* was "greeted with respect by the religious world at large"; while her charm of manner and gracious reception of her husband's guests at the Lodge "added much to his reputation for hospitality."[30]

One interesting account recorded that because Susanna wrote anonymously, their guests would constantly try to engage her in conversation, and deliberately bait her to get her to show her true self. One such guest, known only as T.F., reflects, "She had the character of being very learned. All that I know of that matter is, that as often as I have been in company with her, and when things were thrown out designedly to tempt her to speak, and [reveal] herself, as the armor produced to Achilles, it never took effect. So that I cannot speak of her learning from my own knowledge; but, if she was not that, she was something better; a very good woman."[31]

Being as learned as she was, it should come as no surprise that Susanna was also an avid reader. Her name shows up as a subscriber of multiple works at the time, most interestingly of *The Works of Mrs. Catharine Cockburn* (née Trotter) by the Reverend Thomas Birch.[32] Catharine Trotter-Cockburn was a religious female philosopher that

---

28   Samuel Butler and Dr. Zachary Grey, *Hudibras, Vol.1.* (London: Charles & Henry Baldwyn, 1819), p. 108, (**Appendix 7**).

29   Nichols and Bentley, p. 186

30   Mullinger, pp. 223-224

31   Nichols and Bentley, p. 559

32   Birch, Rev. Thos. *The Works of Catharine Cockburn.* (London: J. and P. Knapton, 1751), p. 19.

pre-dated Susanna by a few years, who had written a zealous defense of John Locke, a man whom Susanna was also quite influenced by. It is unclear if Susanna had read Catharine's work on Locke prior to publishing her own book, although it is unlikely since it was not officially published (and therefore not widely read) until 1751, and Susanna's was first published in 1728.

Susanna's literary influence even eventually reached across the Atlantic Ocean to America where it was noticed by a young, theologically-inclined preacher named Jonathan Edwards. Out of the hundreds of books listed in Jonathan Edwards' personal library catalogue, works by seven women appear – three anonymously – and among them was Susanna's *Enquiry*. Thuesen writes that, "her book garnered a notice in the *Republick of Letters*,[33] which brought the work to Edwards' attention." He continues, "All told, Newcome's book, in both its subject matter and its anonymous guise, anticipated attempts a century later by such American women as Catharine Beecher to enter the male-dominated sphere of philosophical debate."[34] The entry in the *Republick of Letters* states, "We have no performance on the same subject that is so short, and at the same time so strong, perspicuous, and convincing. It would be no dishonor to the greatest Divine[35] to be thought its author."

Susanna Newcome may have attempted to remain anonymous in her lifetime, but anyone who came into contact with her or her writing could not help but feel the way Samuel Denne and William Shrubsole did:

> Her modesty and humility always strove to conceal
> the great powers and extraordinary improvements
> of her mind. But no person of discernment could
> be long acquainted with that excellent woman,
> without esteeming her one of the most perfect
> pieces of human nature.[36]

33   Vol. 2, Article 24; and Vol. 9, Article 10, p. 128.
34   Jonathan Edwards, *The Works of Jonathan Edwards, Vol. 26: Volume 26: Catalogues of Books.* Edited by Peter J. Thuesen. (New Haven: Yale University Press, 2008), pp. 99-100.
35   18th century term for clergyman or theologians, most often from the Anglican or Presbyterian tradition.
36   Denne and Shrubsole, p. 197

Works

An Enquiry into the Evidence of the Christian Religion[37]

First Edition: Published in 1728 and 1729
　　　　　　　by Cambridge University Press
　　　　　　　and William and John Innys in London

Second Edition: Published in 1732
　　　　　　　　by William Innys in London.

A Response to: The Plain Account of the Nature and End of the Sacrament of the Lord's Supper

Part One: Published in 1737
　　　　　　by William Innys and R. Manby in London.

Part Two: Published in 1738
　　　　　　by Cambridge University Press
　　　　　　for William Innys and R. Manby in London.

Death [38]

Susanna died on the 18th of March 1763, at the age of eighty years old. She is buried at the St. Bene't Church in Cambridge, and shares a plot with her mother Mary.[39] Her tombstone reads: "A woman of an excellent understanding and an upright heart, who constantly employed her great talents to the honor of God and the good of

37　Appendix 8
38　Appendix 9
39　"Ecclesiastical Buildings: Parish Churches," in *An Inventory of the Historical Monuments in the City of Cambridge,* (London: Her Majesty's Stationery Office, 1959), 254-298. *British History Online,* accessed October 17, 2016.

mankind through the course of a long life."[40]

The Cambridge Chronicle records her death notice as follows:

"On Saturday morning last died, aged upwards of 80, universally admired, respected and beloved, Mrs. Newcome, wife of the Rev. Dr. Newcome, Master of St John's College, and Aunt of the present Bishop of St. David's. It is impossible for us to do justice to the memory of this incomparable Lady; how for the following Character will be found to resemble that of the Deceased is submitted to the Judgment of those 'Who knew her Worth, and must have leave to boast, they most admired because they knew her most.'"[41]

After her death, her husband asked a Mr. Lort to create a portrait of her from a picture done of her when she was younger.[42] Years later, in 1772, the Earl of Orford, Horace Walpole, who was a collector of portraits and a mutual friend of John Nichols and William Cole, as well as the Newcome's, saw the picture hanging in Bishop Beadon's home (Susanna's nephew, who inherited the majority of their estate and wealth), and decided he wanted one as well. He requested it in a letter to William Cole, who had a copy of his own.[43] In the end, Mr. Cole gladly gave his copy to the Earl, because he knew it would hang in a place of honor at the Earl's Strawberry Hill Estate.

Cole notes, "Dr. Newcome had a print scraped for Mrs. Newcome after her death, which he gave away: it is from a bad picture, and probably never was very like her. The young artist would not put his name to it... Mr. Lort told me, that he employed

40   Linehan, p. 185 and "Susanna Newcome", billiongraves.com, Accessed October 19, 2016.
41   *Cambridge Chronicle* 26 Mar 1763 No. 22
42   Thomas Baker and John E.B. Mayor, *History of the College of St. John the Evangelist, Cambridge*, (Cambridge: University Press, 1869), p. 1027.
43   Walpole, Horace. *Private Correspondence of Horace Walpole, Earl of Orford: Now First Collected, Vol. 3*, (London: Rodwell and Martin, 1820), p. 412.

him, after her death, to get an engraving of her picture: accordingly, a large mezzotinto is taken from a picture of her, which, I think, does not do her justice. As only Mrs. Newcome is wrote under it, being a private plate, it is in danger of being soon utterly forgot for whom it was engraved. Mr. Beadon was so kind to give me one of them, which I sent to my honoured friend, the Honourable Mr. Horace Walpole, to be reposited among his choice, valuable, and numerous collection of English portraits, designed by him for a public library, but which particularly, I am not at liberty to declare, where it will be safe, and known for whom it was designed, as I have written under it."[44]

It hung at Strawberry Hill for seventy years until it was sold to William Meriton Eaton, 2nd Baron Cheylesmore on Thursday, the 16th of June 1842, in an estate sale.[45] The listing can be found in Smith's catalogue, *British Mezzotinto Portraits*, published in 1884.[46] Today, it is a part of the British Museum's collection of portraits (bequeathed to the museum by Eaton in 1902),[47] and after almost three-hundred years, is finally being connected to the amazing woman for whom it was created.

44   Nichols, *Literary Anecdotes*, pp. 481, 559-560
45   Robins, George. *The Collection of Rare Prints & Illustrated Works, Removed from Strawberry Hill ... as Originally Collected by Horace Walpole ... Which Will Be Sold by Auction, by G. Robins, 13th June, 1842 and 9 Following Days. [With] Aedes Strawberrianae. Names of Purchasers and the Prices to the ... Catalogue of the Collection of Early Drawings [&c.].,*(London, Smith and Robins, 1842), p. 64.
46   Smith, John C. *British Messotinto Portraits; Being a Descriptive Catalogue of These Engravings from the Introduction of the Art to the Early Part of the Present Century, Vol. 4,* (London: H. Sotheran & co, 1883), p. 1740.
47   British Museum Online, www.britishmuseum.org/collection/ object/P_1902-1011-7289

Part Two

THE
APOLOGETIC
ARGUMENTS
OF
ENQUIRY

Table of Contents

Editor's Introduction   20

Susanna's Preface   22

Section I   *Definitions:* Truth, Evidence, and Belief   27

Section II   *Definitions:* Pleasure and Pain   29

Section III   *Proposition 1:* There is a Fit-ness and Unfit-ness of Things   31

Section IV   *Proposition 2:* We must have Reasonable Expectations of the Evidence   35

Section V   *Proposition 3:* To Examine Christianity is a Rational Pursuit   39

Section VI   *Enquiry 1:* What is the Evidence for God?   41

A. What do we know about the world?   42

     1. Things that exist are effects, therefore, they have a Cause.

     2. Moving requires a Mover

     3. Finitude cannot be Infinite

     4. Change requires a Changer

     5. The World is not Eternal

B. What is the Cause of the world?   50

     1. An Eternal First Cause

     2. Intelligent

     3. Omnipotent

     4. Omniscient

     5. Independent

     6. Immutable

     7. Content

     8. Benevolent

     9. Just

     10. Omnipresent

     11. Free

     12. Perfect

Section VII   *Enquiry 2:* After Happiness   67

    A. What are man's responsibilities?   67
       1. To Avoid Excess
       2. A Preservation of Self
       3. Do Justice and Love Kindness (Morality)
       4. Specific Duties to Honor God (Piety)

    B. Fulfilling these Responsibilities Leads to Joy   76
       1. In our Present State
       2. In a Future State
          a.) Argument from the Justice of God for the existence of an Afterlife
          b.) Argument from the Powers of the Mind for the existence of an Afterlife

Section VIII   *Enquiry 3:* Is it Rational that God would Reveal Himself   83
(beyond the creation of nature)?

    A. General Revelation was not Enough   83
       1. Ignorance of Duty and Virtue
       2. A Partial Revelation is not Enough
       3. Eternal Consequences Require Conclusive Evidence
       4. Answering Mr. Tindal, whose purported revelation is shown to be imperfect and unsuitable to God's attributes

Section IX   *Enquiry 4:* Is Christianity from God?   93

    A. What evidence do we have that the Christian religion   93
is a divine revelation?
       1. The Christian religion is worthy of God and suitable to His nature
       2. Examining the Evidence
          a.) An Argument for Miracles
          b.) An Argument from Miracles
          c.) An Argument from Historical Evidence
             1.) Eyewitness Accounts
             2.) Moral Testimony

          3.) No One Dies for a Lie they know to be False

          4.) The Growth of the Early Church

          5.) No Deception Could Be Found

          6.) The Highest Quality of Historical Evidence

Section X   Answering Objections to Christianity   113

  A. Objection: Jesus is an Imposter   113
    1. The Nature and Evidence of Prophecy
        a.) An Argument for Prophecy from Miracles
        b.) An Argument for Prophecy from Time
        c.) An Argument for Prophecy from Circumstance
        d.) An Argument for Prophecy from Concurring
          Events
    2. Did Jesus Claim to Fulfill Prophecies?

  B. *Objection*: Jesus is not the Messiah   123
    1. Jesus Fulfilled Messianic Prophecies

  C. *Objection*: Jesus abolished the Law   130
    1. The Creator of the Law can Change the Law
    2. The Law can (and should) be Interpreted in a
        Limited Sense

  D. *Objection*: Jesus and His Apostles Misapplied Scripture 133
           to Themselves
    1. Understanding the Jewish Covenant
    2. Did Jesus and His Apostles Misapply Scripture to
        Themselves?
        a.) Prophecies Intended to be Fulfilled Later
        b.) Prophecies with a Double Fulfillment
        c.) Matthew's Supposed "Nazarene" Mistake
        d.) The Elijah Challenge

Section XI   The Implications for the Jewish Scriptures if Jesus   145
          is not the Messiah

  A. God's Promise to Abraham is Unfulfilled

  B. Jacob is a False Prophet

    C. Moses is a False Prophet

    D. God's Promise to David is Unfulfilled

    E. Isaiah, Daniel, and Zechariah are False Prophets

    F. Malachi and Haggai are False Prophets

    G. The Implications for the Deist if Jesus is the Messiah

Conclusion of *Enquiry*   157

Editor's Introduction

usanna Newcome was born in 1684/5, and therefore had quite impressive contemporaries: John Locke, Matthew Tindal, Isaac Newton, David Hume, Immanuel Kant, and more. However, Susanna herself had a keen understanding of the world around her, and her peers declared her to be extremely intelligent with excellent literary judgment. She wrote *An Enquiry into the Evidence of the Christian Religion* because she saw the cultural tide turning, anticipated future Enlightenment criticisms of Christianity, and sought to succinctly answer them for a general audience. The first edition of *Enquiry* was published in 1728 and 1729, but when Matthew Tindal's book *Christianity as Old as the Creation* came out in 1730, Newcome purposefully updated and expanded her *Enquiry* in 1732 in order to answer his theories and challenge what became known as the Deist Controversy. Her answer to Tindal even predated (by four years) Bishop Joseph Butler's, whose reply was considered to be among the best.

However, *Enquiry* is not only an answer to the Christian Deism of the day, but is a valuable work of Christian Apologetics in its own right. In this small volume, Susanna manages to discuss - with clarity and understanding that is astonishing for that time period - the laws of causality, contingency, irreducible complexity, the Cosmological Argument, the Teleological Argument, the laws of thermodynamics, the unreasonableness of the Atheistic position, the argument from desire, the pursuit of happiness, the problem of evil, immortality (the case for the eternality of the soul), substance dualism, the case for special revelation, the value of and need for Christianity's moral code, the disciples' integrity and ability to be trusted as eyewitnesses, the case for miracles, and lastly, the case for Jesus as the promised Messiah of the Bible.

Newcome begins in Sections one and two by defining her

terms, and then continues in Sections three through five by offering propositions for consideration by the reader. In Sections six through nine, she argues the case for God, Special Divine Action, and Christianity. She then answers common objections to Christianity in Section ten, and concludes with the implications for the Jewish Scriptures if Jesus of Nazareth is not their promised Messiah.

Her original text of *Enquiry* was published in the early 18th century (1700's) and has not been published or updated since that time. Therefore, her language can be difficult to understand for those unaccustomed to the rules of 18th century writing. To that end, I have updated her arguments for a modern audience in Part Two, with my commentary, explanations, and observations in the footnotes. I have also preserved her original language in Part Three for the goals of research in academia, or for those laymen or women wanting to take on a challenge! Regardless of your reasons for picking up this book, please know that Susanna is very special to me, and I have spent years and taken special care to ensure her valuable insights are translated accurately to a modern audience. I hope as you read these pages, you too will realize just how amazing Susanna Squire-Newcome was, and be inspired by her boldness to speak the truth with no apologies.

Susanna's Preface to Enquiry
(1732)

I t being intended that a Second Edition of *An Enquiry into the Evidence of the Christian Religion* should be published, I thought it proper just to mention to the reader that I have made some few additions to it.[48] Particularly, I have added to, and strengthened my arguments, that the system of the universe did not always exist, but must have had a Cause of its existence that was external and existed prior to it.[49] And I have been more full and clear in my proof of the attributes of that Being who exists without Cause, and is the Author of the existence of this system.[50]

As I have been fuller and clearer in the proof of the attributes of the Deity, so have I in that natural religion, or the means to happiness, which is founded on them; and I will presume to say, that the natural religion which I advance, demonstratively follows from

---

48   The focus of Newcome's first edition published four years prior in 1728 was less on God revealing Himself to man and more focused on man's pursuit of pleasure over pain, and the evidence for Christianity based on prophecies of Jesus. When Matthew Tindal's work came out two years later stating that God would not utilize special divine action to reveal Himself to mankind, Newcome saw a need to expand her third enquiry to answer Tindal's claims.

49   The universe is not eternal and has a beginning, and the Beginner of it is outside of it and existed before it.

50   Based on the attributes or characteristics of the system of the universe, we can assert there are specific attributes or characteristics that the Cause and Author of it must have possessed.

the attributes.[51]

I have in one point gone higher than I did before; and as I had proved that if the Author of man's existence was a wise, good, and powerful Being, man must be made capable of obtaining happiness; so I now prove from the attributes of wisdom, goodness, and power, that his happiness shall be everlasting, and that he who by a right use of his powers shall obtain happiness, will enjoy it to all eternity.[52]

I have been more particular in an enquiry whether it was suitable to the attributes of God for Him to reveal Himself, because it has been lately advanced by a very considerable writer (Tindal), that the revelation of nature alone, given to all men, is a perfect revelation, and can have nothing added to it; from which it follows, (though Tindal does not admit it) that God cannot at all reveal Himself in special ways; and upon searching this point, I still find that it is very suitable to the attributes of God for Him to reveal Himself in special ways; and that the revelation of nature alone given to all men, is a

---

51   When Newcome uses the term 'natural religion', it is referring to the idea of general revelation, or the way God reveals Himself through nature. It is not to be confused with the later version of the term that is associated with Pantheism (God IS nature) and/or Deism (the idea that we do not need special revelation like the Bible, miracles, or Jesus). She is stating that as we observe nature and the universe, we can come to certain conclusions about God's attributes because the creation will somewhat resemble its Creator. God has created the universe in such a way that it allows us to know things about Him. Romans 1:19-20 states, "For what can be known about God is plain to them, because God has shown it to them. For his invisible attributes, namely, his eternal power and divine nature, have been clearly perceived, ever since the creation of the world, in the things that have been made. So they are without excuse," (ESV). Also, Psalm 19:1-4 declares, "The heavens declare the glory of God, and the sky above proclaims his handiwork. Day to day pours out speech, and night to night reveals knowledge. There is no speech, nor are there words, whose voice is not heard. Their voice goes out through all the earth, and their words to the end of the world," (ESV).

52   Here Susanna is explaining that she spent more time developing what I would consider an argument from desire in her second edition. This will be discussed more in depth when it comes up in later pages, but in general, it is the idea that if God is good and content in and of Himself, and humans are made in His image for the purpose of having a relationship with Him, humans will naturally desire goodness (morality) and happiness (satisfaction for their desires).

very imperfect revelation, and may have something added to it.[53]

I have not yet found reason to retract anything which I before advanced; still continue to assert there is no proof of a God *a priori*; and am ready to make good that assertion.[54] I have only to add, my sincere wishes, that, if I have delivered anything contrary to the truth, it may not be received.[55]

From Susanna's First Edition Preface

I have observed that what often confuses arguments, and makes them unsatisfactory, is using terms without determining meanings, and building on propositions not proven[56] but simply taken for granted. I have therefore in the following pages taken a different approach; and given definitions of all those terms whose precise meaning is necessary for the reader to understand in order to fully comprehend my arguments; and endeavored to go as in depth as one can go on my subject—built only on a claim allowed by everybody, which is that: pleasure is preferable to pain.

This method has been found to be most satisfactory to myself, so I hope it will prove to be the same for the reader as well, and that the setting of the evidence for the Christian religion before them in a short, plain, and easy light, will be a way to lead them to truth.

Some of my readers will, perhaps, be surprised to see me assert

---

53　This is referencing the idea that Tindal was pushing a form of Deism in his writings, that no special revelation is needed to truly know God. Tindal and Newcome both lived at the time where the focus on Christ and his free gift of grace in the Reformation was giving way to the Enlightenment and higher criticism of the Bible and other forms of special revelation, including the necessity of Jesus Christ himself. He also seems to imply that God is simply too transcendent and either cannot, or will not, reveal Himself to mankind in any way. Newcome finds it very suitable to God that He would utilize miracles as well as nature to reveal Himself to mankind.

54　It appears here that Newcome shares some ideas with philosopher John Locke, and these will be explored in more depth as they come up in her work. Her argument that there is no proof of God available to us before He reveals Himself to us is much more nuanced and needs to be read in full before being judged.

55　This statement right here is one of the reasons Susanna is one of my heroes. She is humble enough to know that she could be wrong, and if it is proved that she is incorrect, she requests to be ignored. Many humans today could learn from her example.

56　Unproven statements, concepts, or theories

that there is no proof of God a priori; *but I am persuaded, that if they think closely on the subject, they will find that I am not mistaken, and that we can only come to a knowledge of the existence of a Being who exists without a cause, from a consideration of the existence of things.*[57]

I have but one more thing to say by way of Preface, and that is, on behalf of Christianity, which upon the strictest examination, appears to me the true one. Let us hope that those who oppose Christianity, do it by reasoning and argument; by going to the bottom of the subject, and keeping close to the point in hand: and not let the arguing of church leaders, biblical scholars, and theologians, concerning the meaning of certain texts, be received as evidence that those texts are false to the reader; or that they add to the case of those who oppose Christianity. In short, let us not reject the Christian religion, until it is proven to be unworthy of God; or until it needs more evidence of being His revelation.[58]

57   Observation is the key to the scientific method, and therefore, the ability to gain knowledge about the world. God has revealed Himself in such a way that when we do look for Him, we can and will find Him.

58   The foresight of Susanna on the condition of the church here was remarkable. Her last statement is an encouragement for those who oppose Christianity to make sure they are doing so because they examined it closely in a reasonable manner, and not reject it because the leaders of the church argue over the truthfulness of the texts themselves. Often, unbelievers look at the church and all of the infighting and squabbles over the interpretation of texts, and decide that if the Christians cannot even agree on what they believe, why should they waste their time with it? Instead of fighting amongst one another, the church should be focused on evangelism to the unbeliever, and use reason and evidence to give the case for Christianity being a worthy endeavor.

Section I

DEFINITIONS:
Truth, Evidence, Belief

I. Statements which express facts (that is, statements which express things as they are) are called **Truth**.[59]

II. **Evidence** is the foundation of the mind's approval of truth, or the means or medium by which truth is communicated to the mind. There is:

   1. Evidence of **Sense** – our own senses give us proof of certain facts.[60]

   2. **Demonstration** – we can, by our own powers, find

---

59   This is the classical correspondence theory of truth dating back to the philosophers of ancient Greece. In his *Metaphysics*, Aristotle wrote, "To say of what is that it is not, or of what is not that it is, is false, while to say of what is that it is, and of what is not that it is not, is true; so that he who says of anything that it is, or that it is not, will say either what is true or what is false," (4.7). In modern vernacular, truth is that which corresponds to reality, that which corresponds to the facts, or that which portrays the way things actually are. Dr. Groothuis writes, "A belief or statement is true only if it matches with, reflects or corresponds to the reality it refers to. For a statement to be true it must be factual. Facts determine the truth or falsity of a belief or a statement. It is the nature and meaning of truth to be fact dependent… A statement is never true simply because someone thinks it or utters it. We may be entitled to our own opinions, but we are not entitled to our own facts. Believing a statement is one thing; that statement being true is another." (Douglas Groothuis. *Christian Apologetics: A Comprehensive Case for Biblical Faith*. Kindle Locations 1294-1298. Kindle Edition.)

60   Newcome's definition of 'Facts': the existence, nature, relations, powers, etc. of beings or things as they really are. Here she is giving three types of evidence that exists, beginning with the most obvious – observation: using our eyes, ears, etc. to gather facts about the world that surrounds us.

connections between truths; and from things known, discover other things that are unknown.[61]

3. **Moral Proof** – the eyewitness testimony of people that aligns with events, circumstances, or things.[62]

III. The highest degree of this last kind of evidence is called **Moral Certainty**.[63]

IV. A lower degree of it is called **Probability**

V. An agreement with unproven statements, concepts, or theories, for which we did not experience with our own senses, or that cannot be shown through demonstration, is called **Belief**, or opinion.[64]

VI. When our belief or opinion concerning things *agrees* with what they really are, then we are said to have a true, or right opinion or belief concerning those things.[65]

VII. When our belief or opinion concerning things *does not agree* with what they really are, then the mind has a false opinion or belief concerning those things.[66]

---

61   Experimentation: Scientific method, research, etc. This can include making connections between pieces of information or gathered facts, whether it be combining them, relating them to each other, or being inspired to produce abstract ideas in the absence of specifics (innovation).

62   Moral Testimony: Eyewitnesses, primary sources

63   If we did not experience the event ourselves, or prove it through experimentation, the most we can be certain of is the likelihood of someone's moral integrity, or a probability that something they said is true (the following point IV).

64   When someone agrees with a statement they have no evidence for, and cannot prove, it is a belief or opinion, not fact. Fact is something that is proven to be true by evidence or experimentation.

65   When what we believe reflects how things really are, or facts, then what we believe is true.

66   When what we believe does not accurately reflect how things really are, or facts, then what we believe is false. Evidence, not opinion, is the determining factor whether something is true or not, and finding evidence requires a careful examination of the facts.

Section II

DEFINITIONS:
Pleasure and Pain

I.   **Happiness** is a term for collected **Pleasure**, or a total amount of pleasure.

II.   **Misery** is a term for collected **Pain**, or a total amount of pain.

III.   The being that enjoys pleasure, without interruption of pain, may be called a happy being.

IV.   The being that suffers pain, without enjoyment of pleasure, is a miserable being.

V.   Every being, whose total amount of pleasure exceeds his pains, is considered to be happy.[67]

VI.   Every being, whose total amount of pain exceeds his pleasures, is considered to be miserable.[68]

VII.   Pleasure which brings pain to a being, is not to be considered part of their happiness, but misery.[69]

---

67   When a person has more pleasure than pain in life, they are considered (or are assumed to be) happy.

68   When a person has more pain than pleasure in life, they are considered (or are assumed to be) miserable.

69   Even if the original act brings pleasure in the moment, if it is bad for you in the long term, it counts as pain (e.g. eating junk food, smoking, etc.).

VIII. Pain which brings pleasure to a being, is not to be considered part of their misery, but happiness.[70]

IX. **Perfect happiness**[71] is enjoying the highest degree of pleasure that sensible beings are capable of, without any interruption of pain.

---

70   Even if the original act brings pain in the moment, if it is good for you in the long term, it counts as pleasure (e.g. getting an immunization shot, surgery, exercise, etc.).

71   This concept of 'perfect happiness' comes up later as the driving force behind Enquiry 2: After Happiness. It is the desire of mankind, the satisfaction of which can only be found in God. Newcome often uses the word 'felicity' in her original manuscript to describe it.

Section III

PROPOSITION 1:
The Fit-ness and Unfit-ness of Things

I.   To all sensible beings, pleasure is preferable to pain.

II.   If to all sensible beings, pleasure is preferable to pain, then all such beings must (and will) desire pleasure and avoid pain.[72]

III.   That which sensible beings prefer, will, and desire, is most **Fit** for them.[73]

IV.   That which sensible beings shun and avoid is most **Unfit** for them.

V.   Happiness is then most fit for sensible beings.

VI.   Misery is most unfit for them.

---

72   If pleasure is better than pain, then sensible beings (those in their right mind) will desire pleasure and avoid pain.

73   I have coined this particular concept, The Principle of Fulfillability. Rational humans only desire things that will positively satisfy them, and there must be a reason they desire those things in the first place. If humans were created by God to possess certain things, then it makes sense they would desire them. When they find that satisfaction, it 'fits' because it was meant for them to possess it in the first place. Rational humans (humans in their right mind) only have desires that are capable of being fulfilled (by things that exist), because if the objects of their desires never existed, they would not know to desire them in the first place.

VII.   If happiness is most fit for sensible beings, and misery is most unfit for them, then there are fit-nesses and unfit-nesses of things that were naturally determined prior to humans being given laws and rules by an authority.[74] The happiness of sensible beings is fit, and the misery of sensible beings is unfit.[75]

VIII.   It follows that if the happiness of sensible beings is fit, and the misery of sensible beings is unfit, that whatever is a means to the happiness for sensible beings, is likewise fitting, or fit, and that whatever is a means to the misery of sensible beings, is unfitting, or unfit.

IX.   All the actions of sensible beings (that add to their happiness) are most fit.[76]

X.   All the actions of sensible beings (that add to their misery) are most unfit.[77]

XI.   Right and true beliefs concerning facts and our moral inclinations are fit.[78]

        And,

---

74   Before there were laws and societal commandments, sensible humans realized that certain actions/consequences (those that brought pleasure) were better for them than others (those that brought pain) because happiness felt naturally right and misery felt naturally wrong. This was the process of humans learning what was good for them through trial and error, similar to a toddler who will never touch a hot stovetop after being burned by accidentally touching it once.

75   This idea of a fit-ness and unfit-ness of things is an assumption that there is a place for these things to fit, or not fit, into. It appears that Newcome's denial of innate ideas is similar to Locke's in that there is not a complete emptiness of the mind, but that God created us with a template of sorts for the later-acquired experiential content to plug into. "While the mind may be a blank slate in regard to content, it is plain that Locke thinks we are born with a variety of faculties to receive, and abilities to manipulate or process the content once we acquire it," (William Uzgalis. "John Locke", *The Stanford Encyclopedia of Philosophy*, Spring 2016 Edition. Edward N. Zalta, ed. URL = https://plato.stanford.edu/archives/spr2016/entries/locke/). That is, we are created with the potential to learn and innovate.

76   Actions that bring lasting happiness and pleasure are good or right.

77   Actions that bring lasting misery and pain are bad or wrong.

78   Truth 'fits' or feels right to a sensible being. Inclinations: the actions we tend toward.

XII. False beliefs concerning facts and our moral inclinations are unfit.[79]

XIII. An examination into the facts and our moral inclinations is fit.[80]

XIV. An assent to evidence is fit.

XV. And a dissent from evidence is unfit.[81]

---

79   False information does not fit and feels wrong to a sensible being.
80   If truth is right and brings happiness, and falsehood is wrong and brings misery, then a sensible human who desires pleasure over pain will try and figure out what is true in order to have lasting happiness.
81   If a human being wants lasting happiness, and truth brings happiness, they need to know what is actually true, and a sensible being would base their decision on evidence or proof, specifically: observation, experimentation, and moral testimony.

Section IV

PROPOSITION 2:

We must have Reasonable Expectations of the Evidence

I.   The power of the mind that discovers facts, and determines their fit-ness or unfit-ness based on what one already knows to be true, is called **Reason.**[82]

      Since reason is the power of the mind by which it finds truth, and determines the fit-nesses and unfit-nesses of things, it follows that whatever is **True** is also rational, **Reasonable**, or has some degree of reason.

Also that,

1. It is reasonable that sensible beings should be happy.[83]
2. It is unreasonable that sensible beings should be miserable.
3. Whatever is a means to the happiness of sensible beings is rational or reasonable.[84]
4. Whatever is a means to the misery of sensible beings is irrational, or against reason.
5. The actions of beings, which lead to their happiness, are rational.

---

82 To reason: to think, understand, and form judgments by a process of logic.
83 If one has any sense at all, they will pursue that which brings happiness, not misery.
84 The pursuit of whatever brings happiness (which Newcome has previously determined as 'truth') is a reasonable/rational pursuit.

6. The actions of beings, which lead to their misery, are irrational.
7. Whoever does not, as far as he has ability, search out the means to happiness, is irrational.[85]
8. Whoever does not make use of the means to happiness, when found, is irrational.[86]
9. An inquiry into, or pursuit after, truth is rational.
10. Agreeing with truth, once found, is rational.
11. When a proposition, that if true will affect our happiness to the highest degree, is offered for consideration, it is highly irrational not to examine whether it is indeed true or not.
12. It is reasonable and proper then to consider what kind of evidence propositions of that nature are capable of, and to consider by what means it needs to be obtained. Some truths can be supported with evidence of sense or demonstration, while others only by the eyewitness testimony of people that aligns with events, circumstances, or things.[87]
13. It is highly irrational to expect evidence supporting propositions, which the nature of such propositions will not admit. Suppose the question was concerning historical facts, professed to be before our own times — of these there can be no higher evidence than moral proof or the eyewitness testimony of people that aligns with events, circumstances, or things. It is then highly irrational to expect other kinds of evidence for such propositions. [88]

---

85 If one does not pursue truth, they lack reason/rationality.
86 If one does not assent to (or agree with) that truth once it is found, they are unreasonable/irrational (especially if it can bring lasting happiness and they refuse to even examine it – point 11).
87 What type of proof/evidence is needed (and can be sensibly expected) when determining the veracity (or truthfulness) of various claims and propositions? The same type of evidence (e.g. just experimentation) cannot be used as proof for all truth claims, as specific propositions need specific kinds of evidence to determine their truthfulness (experimentation *or* observation *or* moral testimony).
88 If an event happened before one's existence, they cannot utilize observation or experimentation to prove its actuality; they must rely on the historical records and sources that pre-date themselves.

14. When moral proof or probability is the only evidence propositions are capable of, this ought to be enough to convince one of its truth as truly as demonstration ought to convince one to agree with a truth that can be demonstrated.[89]

Agreeing with evidence is rational, and disagreeing with evidence is irrational. [90]

89   If moral testimony is all that is available (or possible) based on the specific event, it is irrational to expect to be able to use experimentation or observation.

90   One who agrees with the evidence (that is actually available or possible) is rational, and one who disagrees with the evidence (because they desire evidence that is unavailable or impossible) is irrational.

Section V

PROPOSITION 3:
To Examine Christianity
is a Rational Pursuit

If the Christian religion is a revelation from God, and will affect our happiness in the highest degree;[91] it is highly irrational not to

---

91   If Christianity is true, then joy (a feeling of great pleasure and happiness) is attainable. Also, if Christianity is true, the fact that man pursues happiness and pleasure makes sense considering he was created in God's image. Groothuis writes, "Given the Christian hypothesis that humans are 'deposed royalty' – both image bearers of God and fallen from grace – this desire for and limited sense of the transcendent must be viewed as marred by sin. The desire to transcend one's situation, to experience glory or joy, are not pure desires, but rather a mixture of the soul desiring its proper divine fulfillment and the flesh desiring to transcend a fallen world in any way possible," (Douglas Groothuis. *Christian Apologetics: A Comprehensive Case for Biblical Faith*. Kindle Locations 3923-3925. Kindle Edition.) We inherently know there is something more, something better. This could be a better state of being – one that is free of sin and includes immortality/eternal life. We were created in an absolutely perfect and moral state of being, and to live eternally in that state. The Fall of Man (in Genesis 3) tarnished that perfection and immorality, but we still yearn for it because God has put eternity in our hearts, (Ecclesiastes 3:11, HCSB). If we are beings somehow imbued with an innate sense of the hope of eternal life and we lost access to it in the Fall, it would make sense that we would desire it. Gregory of Nyssa wrote that, "The more we believe that 'the Good', on account of its nature, lies far beyond the limits of our knowledge, the more we experience a sense of sorrow that we have to be separated from this 'Good', which is both great and desirable, and yet cannot be embraced fully by our minds. Yet we mortals once had a share in this 'Good', which so eludes our attempts to comprehend it," (McGrath, Alister E. *The Christian Theology Reader*. Malden MA: Blackwell, 2007; p. 412). Humans need God to attain true joy and eternal life, for no other being besides a Supremely powerful, benevolent, Creator God could bestow those particular wants on humanity. Dr. Geisler states, "Few theists would rest their case for God on any one argument…But if there is a real need for God, it is far more reasonable to believe that there is a real God who can really fill this real need," (Geisler, Norman L. *Baker Encyclopedia of Christian Apologetics*. Grand Rapids, MI: Baker Academic, 1999; p. 282).

consider whether it is true or not.[92]

If the Christian religion is true, and the happiness of all those to whom it is shared with must consist in believing this religion and obeying its commands (which is evident from the nature of this religion and its repeated declarations[93]), it is highly irrational not to examine whether it is true or not.

However, in order to determine whether the Christian religion is a revelation from God, we must first consider whether we have good reason to believe that there is really such a God.[94]

---

92   Here Newcome is offering an earlier version of C.S. Lewis' argument that either Christianity is the most important thing, or it's not important at all. If Christianity is the way to perfect happiness, then it is unreasonable to not examine it at the least.

93   Newcome explains that there are conditions on attaining pure joy. If Christianity is true, then belief is required to obtain its blessings, as stated in the Scriptures. If pure joy and perfect happiness are only obtained through Christ, and one truly wants to be happy, it is unreasonable for them not to examine Christianity.

94   After defining her terms and offering propositions for consideration, Newcome begins her argument in Enquiry One with the case for the existence of God, then later in Enquiry Three, answers Tindal's book by giving the case that it is reasonable that God would reveal Himself to mankind.

Section VI

ENQUIRY 1:
What is the Evidence for God?

In the first place then, we find the mind empty and void, without any innate ideas, or notions of a God, until it ascends to the realization by that which is the basis of all knowledge, ideas of sensation, or experience.[95]

As there are no innate ideas of a God, we can have no proof of such a Being *a priori*; and if there is really such a Being, we can only come to a knowledge of His existence after a consideration of the existence of things.[96]

We observe that certain things do exist, and those things must exist either with, or without, a cause. If they exist without a cause,

95   Again this is not a complete emptiness, just an assertion that we are not born with an inherent knowledge of proof for God. The template for processing information and potential for humans to reason and be creative is there. This idea of 'ascending' is that the mind will believe in God once one uses their experience to examine the evidence that exists for God. Once they experience this process, and reason through it, it will 'fit' in their mind.
96   This is the point of Christian apologetics – to get man to look around and wonder why there is something rather than nothing.

then it follows that they must have existed eternally[97] - *it being certain that nothing can have a beginning without a cause.*[98] If they exist with a cause, then we must consider, what could be the cause of their existence?

A. What do we know about the world?

The question then is, whether we have reason to think that the things that exist which we observe, existed eternally without a cause or whether there is a Cause of their existence? The most likely method to obtain satisfaction in this point is to consider the things which do exist, and, what we already know to be true about their existence.[99]

1. Things that exist are effects, therefore, they have a cause.

Within the system of things that exist, we find chains of causes and effects. Many parts of this system (the 'effects') owe their existence to a pre-existing cause, therefore, we cannot reasonably assert that the whole system (made up of those dependent parts) exists without Cause.

If X produces Y, and Y produces Z, there still must be a cause

---

97   Once man observes that there is something rather than nothing, the existence of a material world begs the question of how it all got here. There are three possible ways something can exist: self-caused, no cause, or caused by another. The notion of self-causation is illogical and self-refuting due to the fact that nothing can exist outside of itself long enough to do the causing. It cannot exist and not-exist at the same time. Therefore the only two options left to explore are: no cause, or caused by another. If there is no cause, it must be eternal as Newcome states, meaning it was always here. If it has no cause, it cannot have a beginning because there is no beginner accounted for, therefore it must have always existed. The only option left is that it was caused by another.

98   Here Newcome makes one of the earliest known (after Aristotle and Aquinas) arguments for causation. She appeals to the idea of Aristotelian physics in that if the universe is not infinite/necessary/eternal, it has to have a cause (an unmoved mover). In his *Metaphysics*, Aristotle writes, "It is obvious that there are principles and causes which are generable and destructible apart from the actual processes of generation and destruction; for if this is not true, everything will be of necessity: that is, there must necessarily be some cause, other than [an] accidental [one]," (*Metaphysics* VI, 1027a29).

99   Does what we observe have evidence of being eternal? Or did it have a beginning, and therefore a Beginner (a Cause)?

of X, otherwise there would be a beginning without a cause, which is impossible. And if there must be a cause of X, that is, if there must be a cause of every link in a chain or series of causes and effects, then the whole chain or series of causes and effects cannot exist without an initial cause. From observing and considering what we already know to be true about the existence of this system — that many of the parts of it, in every period of time, have a cause — it is a contradiction to assert that the whole system exists without an initial cause.

To assert that certain parts of a system have a cause, but that the whole system exists without an initial cause, is the same as asserting that the parts do not belong to the whole — that A is not a letter, B is not a letter, C is not a letter, and yet all three are letters. Those who assert that this system exists without an initial cause, assert that this system eternally existed the same way it does now. Therefore, those who assert that this system exists without cause must either admit that every part of this system this moment existed eternally, which they know to be false (they being able themselves to tell the cause of the existence of many things in this system), or that the parts do not belong to the whole, which is a contradiction.

When we observe that many of the parts of the system do have a cause (and the contrary opinion that this system exists without cause is unsupported), we must, if we consider ourselves people who determine things according to evidence and reason, determine that this system does have a cause, and consequently has not existed eternally.

Also, if we take any species of beings, and we observe that no one individual of that species exists without a cause, then we cannot justify the claim that the whole species — composed of those individuals — exists without a cause. If every link in a certain chain has a cause, then the whole chain of individuals must have a Cause.[100]

They may reply: Even though every link in a chain, or every individual in a species, has a cause, the cause is only within the chain itself, or within the species. A succession of such individuals as a

---

100   If everything that has ever existed (every "effect") has been observed to have a cause, then it is unreasonable to say that if one goes back far enough into the past, there will cease to be a cause in that chain. If A caused B, and B caused C, and so on and so forth throughout the entire alphabet, then ultimately A caused Z.

whole can be infinite, and consequently, without cause.

I answer: A succession that depends on something external to it for its continuance (which is the case of all the chains in our system) must have a Cause external to and that pre-existed it. For, whatever has existed always, and without cause, must always exist; and there cannot be a ceasing of that which had no beginning, nor cause. If a succession of beings like men has always existed without a cause, there can be no end to the succession of men.[101]

But a succession of men is liable to come to an end from several causes. It may cease by external accidents; and it is also possible that those things which have often been partially destructive to mankind, may become universally so, and the whole species could be destroyed by them.

It may cease from a lack of support and assistance from other beings and things; and mankind could go extinct from a lack of sustenance. A succession of beings then, which is dependent on something external to it for its continuance, may end and if it may end, then it could not exist without a cause; since you cannot end something that never began in the first place.[102]

2. Moving Requires a Mover

There is no motion except what is the effect of a previous motion; therefore, there is no motion in a system that has existed from eternity, or has not been caused. This is because the cause of motion in a material system cannot be in the material system itself, it being impossible for matter to begin motion.[103] To suppose that matter begins motion is to suppose a beginning without a cause.

---

101   If man has no cause, then he is eternal, and therefore immortal and indestructible. However as Newcome goes on to point out, we know that is not true, as humans die all the time, occasionally in massive numbers.

102   Therefore, mankind is contingent in that it relies on something 'other' and outside of itself to continue its existence. If it can cease or end (through death), then it also had a beginning.

103   Here Newcome shows a keen understanding of Newton's laws of motion considering that Newton himself had just published on the laws of motion a mere thirty years prior. There's a possibility that her long relationship with the University of Cambridge gave her access to Newton's writings earlier than others.

Consequently, there must be a cause of motion in a material system prior to, and distinct from, such a system. [104]

If it should be said, that matter may begin motion, (though I suppose very few will venture to say this) then I say again, that motion in a material system must have a Cause external, and antecedent to it, in the same way that all the changes in a material system, must have an external Cause, that exists prior to them,[105] otherwise there would be a beginning without a cause.

3. Finitude Cannot be Infinite

Man is not only a being dependent on some being or thing for happiness, but also for his physical existence, therefore, he could not exist without a cause. We find man cannot live at all without the support and assistance of other beings and things, and that there is something outside of himself, which is necessary to his very existence. A succession of beings, each of which cannot exist but in finitude[106], without the support and assistance of something external to the succession of mankind (which is the case of all the successions in this system), must have an external Cause, that exists prior to it.

If there is contingency[107] in an individual of a succession, there is cause of that contingency; otherwise, there would be a beginning without a cause.[108] The cause of contingency in such an individual, must be in the succession, or not in it. But there cannot be a cause

---

104   A First Cause/Actuality/Energy. Aquinas enhanced Aristotle's argument for an unmoved mover in his *Summa Theologica*: "Now whatever is in motion is put in motion by another.... For motion is nothing else than the reduction of something from potentiality to actuality.... It is therefore impossible that in the same respect and in the same way a thing should be both mover and moved, i.e., that it should move itself. If that by which it is put in motion be itself put in motion, then this also must needs be put in motion by another, and that by another again. But this cannot go on to infinity, because then there would be no first mover, and, consequently no other mover.... Therefore it is necessary to admit a first efficient cause, to which everyone gives the name of God," (19:12,13).
105   Law of Inertia: an object in a state of rest or motion tends to remain in that state of motion unless an external force is applied to it.
106   The condition of being human and limited.
107   Finitude, dependency, not necessary.
108   Impossible – a beginning must have a beginner, a cause.

of contingency in that which exists without cause.[109] Therefore, a succession of beings, each of which cannot exist but in contingency without the support and assistance of something external to the succession, could not exist without cause;[110] and that cause must be external, and pre-exist it.

If beings cannot exist but in finitude, without the support and assistance of other beings or things; then it fits that they will suffer pain if there is a lack of that support and assistance,[111] and it also fits that they receive pleasure from receiving it;[112] and a fit-ness in the assisting beings and things, to give them that pleasure. For parts to fit for certain ends, the fit-ness of different beings and successions of beings to each other; and all these things to fit to one grand goal (which is the preservation of the whole species), must have an external Cause, that exist prior to them.[113]

There is through all inanimate nature a fit-ness of certain things to others, and a dependency of some parts of this system on other parts of it. Particularly, all vegetables and plant species depend on something external to themselves for being what they are, and for their continuing to exist. There is a fit-ness in the inanimate part of nature to give pleasure, or preserve the existence of the animate, for which it seems alone to exist.[114] The whole system of beings, and things, is as one grand machine composed of a vast variety of parts, each part depending on other parts,[115] and all concurring to certain uses, or ends, which is the preservation or the existence of the whole.

⧫⧫⧫⧫⧫⧫⧫⧫⧫⧫⧫⧫⧫⧫⧫⧫⧫⧫⧫⧫⧫⧫⧫⧫⧫⧫⧫⧫⧫⧫⧫⧫⧫⧫⧫

109   Something that is eternal cannot have contingency; infinite-ness and finite-ness cannot co-exist in the same being/thing.

110   A succession or chain of finite beings cannot exist infinitely.

111   If a being is finite, it makes sense (the concept fits in one's mind) that it has to rely on something else (something infinite) for its existence.

112   If a finite being needs a cause, the cause must desire to give existence to the finite being, and it brings the finite being pleasure (life/happiness) to receive it.

113   An infinite regress of finite beings is impossible.

114   Example: humans and animals need things that nature provides (plants/crops for food, spring water to drink, trees for oxygen, etc.) to continue a healthy existence. If there existed nothing that needed oxygen or water, it would be strange for them to exist themselves, as they would have no purpose.

115   Irreducible complexity: "a single system, which is composed of several interacting parts, and where the removal of any one of the parts causes the system to cease functioning." Michael J. Behe, *Evidence for Intelligent Design from Biochemistry*; from a speech delivered at Discovery Institute's God & Culture Conference, August 10, 1996.

Such a variety of fit-nesses[116] then, in order to the preservation or existence of a whole system of beings, must have an external Cause, and that exists prior to them.[117]

4. Change require a Changer

A material system which is composed of parts that are changeable, must have an external Cause, which is distinct from and exists before, all the changes in such a system.[118] Whenever there is a change, there must be a cause of that change; otherwise, there would be a beginning without a cause. Now the cause of change in a system must already exist within the materials of the system, or not. If it *is* in the materials of the system already, then the materials must exist prior to all the changes in the system[119], and likewise, itself must exist without Cause.[120] If the materials of the system exist without a cause, they cannot possibly have a cause of change in them[121] for then there would be a cause of change in that which exists without cause,[122] which is a contradiction. And, if the cause of change in a material system cannot be in the system, then it follows that it must be distinct from, and prior to, all the changes in such a system.

If the cause of change was not in the materials of the system, and the materials had a cause of their existence, then that cause would

---

116   Intelligent design

117   This Cause itself cannot have parts either. This is known as the doctrine of Divine Simplicity: "God is not made up of a conglomeration of pieces. He certainly has no physical parts. And in that sense [He] is remarkably simple." (William Lane Craig on Divine Simplicity) However, while not separate, God does have distinctions within His being (e.g. the Trinity).

118   I would add here that the Cause not only needs to be external and preexisting to the changes, but unchangeable itself as well (the latter criteria being one the God of the Bible fits as well as the two former). This is known as Immutability, the doctrine that God cannot change. Leftow, Brian, "Immutability", *The Stanford Encyclopedia of Philosophy* (Winter 2016 Edition), Edward N. Zalta (ed.), URL = https://plato.stanford.edu/archives/win2016/entries/immutability/.

119   It must be a pre-existing cause to the entire system.

120   It must also be a First Cause (eternal).

121   You can't go from Actuality (fully simple with no possibility of changing/eternal) to Potentiality (the possibility of or potential to change/temporal).

122   If humans were eternal (no cause), they would not be finite (able to change from the state of living to a state of death.)

be the original cause of all the changes in the system; and then, our proposition would be proved.[123]

5. The World is not Eternal

From the frame and constitution of the system of our world, it is evident that it did not exist without Cause.[124] A system that never had a beginning, never can have an end, and if it has always existed, it must always exist; otherwise (as has been observed) there could be a destruction of that which exists without cause, and has always existed, which is impossible.[125] But from the nature and constitution of things, the decrease of fluids in the planets,[126] of the light and bulk in the Sun, and fixed stars, and from the resistance that is made to the motions of the heavenly bodies, it is evident that this system cannot

---

123   This pre-existing, First cause necessary to the system of the universe is exactly the point she is trying to prove.

124   This is known as the Cosmological Argument: Everything that begins to exist has a cause, the universe began to exist; therefore, the universe has a cause.

125   A thing that is eternal cannot be destroyed (that which has no cause to its existence can have no end to its existence).

126   Here Newcome references Dr. Cheyne's *Philosophical Principles of Religion* (1st ed. 1705, 2nd ed. 1715) in a footnote. After reading both side-by-side, the editor can confirm that she relied quite heavily on this work of his. In it, he himself also quotes Newton extensively, which is not all that odd considering they were acquaintances. In *Never at Rest: A Biography of Isaac Newton*, the biographer, Richard S. Westfall, recounts the nature of Newton and Cheyne's relationship. "Some years ago, Newton had loaned out a manuscript with some general theorems about squaring curves, and was later met with some things copied out of it in the writings of George Cheyne, and so he decided then to make it public. According to David Gregory, this was what provoked Mr. Newton to publish his *Opticks, Quadratures*, and *Light & Colors, etc.* When Cheyne came to London from Scotland, Dr. Arbuthnot introduced him to Newton and told him about a book Cheyne had written but could not afford to publish [*The Inverse Method of Fluxions*]. Newton thought Cheyne's manuscript was "not intolerable" and supposedly offered Cheyne a bag of money to publish, but Cheyne refused. After this, Newton refused to see him anymore," (Cambridge: University Press, 1980, p. 639). Also interesting to note is that Cheyne was the doctor of Newton's close friend, Alexander Pope.

last forever[127]; and if it cannot last forever, then neither has it always existed; that is, it did not exist without Cause.

As for the argument, that has the world lasted from all eternity as it is now; it is altogether impossible.[128] If we can show, as we certainly can, that the whole appearance of nature, agrees with this system's beginning to exist at a certain time,[129] we have evidence that it is not eternal. If we have a History that informs us that this system did actually begin to exist at that time; then our argument against the eternity of this system is strengthened.

From the whole appearance of nature and the History of the Creation, it is evident that this system did not exist eternally, and consequently, did not begin to exist without Cause.

B. What is the Cause of the World?

We have then full evidence, and have proved several particulars, that this system did not exist eternally, and consequently did not exist without Cause. Come we then to consider, secondly, "What is the cause of its existence?"[130]

---

127 Law of Entropy: everything tends toward disorder. The amount of usable energy in the universe is getting smaller and smaller. If the universe were eternal, it would have an unlimited amount of energy, or have reached an equilibrium where everything stops breaking down. Many new theories are popping up (flat/open universe, string theory, multiverses) that disagree that we live in a closed universe because of the fact that material heavenly bodies keep moving further and further away from each other. However, just because things are still moving apart, it does not mean that there is a limit for that movement to be reached sometime in the future. It just means we have not observed it being reached yet.

128 While Newcome did rely heavily on Cheyne's understanding of Newtonian physics, it is clear here that she did depart from Cheyne and had her own mind regarding Newton's theories. While Cheyne argued that life cannot be created from non-living matter, and stated that life "must have existed from all eternity", Newton and Newcome both assert a First Cause.

129 Cosmic microwave background radiation, or the "Big Bang Echo" was discovered in 1941 by Andrew McKellar, and confirmed by Arno Penzias and Robert Woodrow Wilson in 1964.

130 Now that she has proven that the universe did not exist eternally and had a cause, it is time to argue what type of cause that must be.

1. An Eternal First Cause

As this system, which began to exist, must owe its existence to a prior cause; so likewise must that cause, if it began to exist, owe its existence to another cause; and so must all beings, and things, until we ascend to a Being, who never began to exist. That Being, who never began to exist, can have nothing that came before it, and therefore, can have no cause of its existence.[131]

As we are sure then that the material world does exist, and that it does not exist without cause; but owes its existence to something that pre-existed it; we are sure also, that if the cause, to which the material world owes its existence is not eternal, then it derives its existence from something that *was* eternal. Therefore, the Being to whom this system owes its existence, is a Being who exists absolutely without cause, and is eternal.[132]

Our knowledge of such a Being wholly arises from a consideration of the existence of things, as we can have no knowledge of Him farther than the existence of things will lead us.[133] Things which exist with a cause cannot lead us to a knowledge of the manner of existence of a Being, who exists absolutely without cause, and is eternal.[134] Neither will they lead us to a knowledge of the substance of this Being; there being no connection between the substance of a Being; and His works.[135] In these particulars then is our Enquiry to stop.

2. An Intelligent Cause

However, though the things that exist cannot lead us to a

---

131   A First Cause: an eternal being to which every chain of causes must ultimately go back (the unmoved mover).

132   The universe could have started with some event (a Big Bang perhaps), but the cause of that event must still be eternal (a First Cause). Again, if A caused B, and B caused C, then A caused C. Otherwise, you end up with an infinite regress (a sequence of reasoning or justification that can never logically come to an end).

133   We should only make assumptions based on evidence.

134   Just because we can reason to a First Cause, the evidence presented thus far does not tell us who or what this Being is.

135   Knowing the effects (the material world) or actions (creating the material world) of a First Cause does not tell us who or what this Being is.

knowledge of the manner of existence, nor to the substance of a Being, who exists absolutely without cause, and is eternal; they can lead us to several of His attributes.[136] Then, from an effect (attribute) we can justly argue to its cause[137] and we may find certain attributes (effects) connected with others. Thus, secondly, we can prove that the Being who framed, and fitted up this system, is an intelligent Being.[138]

When we see a machine composed of a vast variety of parts, which regularly, and constantly do distinct offices, and all concur to one grand use, or end, we pronounce it to be the effect of intelligence; having observed like effects to be owing to intelligence, and not knowing any other Cause that is capable of producing them.[139] When we see the grand machine of the Universe composed of a vast variety of parts, all suited, and fitted to each other, and each part regularly, and constantly doing distinct offices, in order to the preservation of the whole, if we pronounce not this to be the effect of intelligence, we are inconsistent with ourselves, and with constant experience; we judge differently in this case, from what we would do in all others of a like nature.[140]

We have reason to believe the universe is the effect of intelligence, or we have no reason to believe any machine, that we did not observe the forming of, the effect of intelligence. Again, not only does the nature of things which do exist, and the manner of their existence, lead us to an intelligent Cause; but the existence of intelligence in this

---

136   However, even if we cannot determine who or what this Being is, we can ascertain (figure out) some things about it (its attributes).
137   By studying creation (the material world/effect), we can learn (or make assumptions) about the Being that caused it.
138   Teleological Argument: the argument for the existence of God from the evidence of order (design) in nature.
139   Fine-Tuning: "According to many physicists, the fact that the universe is able to support life depends delicately on various of its fundamental characteristics, notably on the form of the laws of nature, on the values of some constants of nature, and on aspects of the universe's conditions in its very early stages." (Friederich, Simon, "Fine-Tuning", *The Stanford Encyclopedia of Philosophy* (Spring 2018 Edition), Edward N. Zalta (ed.).) Basically, the world is fine-tuned for life.
140   Common sense dictates that effect implies Cause, design implies Designer, and fine-tuning implies a meticulous Tuner. To deny common sense in these situations simply because of the implications of where they might lead (a supernatural God) is to not behave consistently as a seeker of truth.

system, it is evident, that the Cause of this system is an intelligent Being.

It is impossible for a Being to give a perfection which He possesses not Himself; for then there would be an effect without a cause, or a beginning without a cause, which is impossible. And to assert that an unintelligent Being can give intelligence, is to assert that there may be an effect without a cause.[141]

3. An Omnipotent Cause

We find that the Being, who framed and fitted up this system, and gave it its present form and appearance, must be a Being of great power.[142] We are sure that the power of this being must be equal to the effects of it; that is, that He must be capable of making and sustaining a world, because in fact He has done it: we are sure likewise, that His power must be unlimited by any Being which derives its existence from Him;[143] that none of His own creatures can successfully resist His power;[144] for then He would give a perfection which He possessed not Himself; there would be an effect without a cause, or a beginning without a cause, which is impossible. And this is full enough for us at present under a general consideration of His power.

4. An Omniscient Cause[145]

The Being who framed, and fitted up this system, must be a wise Being. Wisdom lays down the best end, and pursues it by the best means; that is, by means most effective to the proposed end.[146] The best end that any Being can propose is the existence of beings. If then sensible beings are capable of happiness, if existence is better

---

141   Non-information cannot give rise to information. Intelligence cannot come from non-intelligence. This would be an effect without a cause.
142   The First Cause must be omnipotent (all-powerful)
143   2 Peter 1:3, 2 Cor. 3:4-6, Heb. 1:3, Col. 1:17
144   Meaning able to create and sustain themselves apart from His power.
145   Omniscient: knowing everything
146   The First Cause must also be all-knowing and completely wise, choosing the best scenario or most effective solution in every situation.

than non-existence to them, (and our desire to continue our existence is important to us, which it is[147]) then the Supreme Being, when He determined to make such beings, laid down the best end.[148]

That He makes use of means most effectual[149] to this end, and to the preservation of all kinds of beings, not only their continuing existence is evidence; but also, these means are everywhere visible. Thus, we find instincts, or desires in all beings, which push them on to preserve existence.[150] Different beings are wonderfully framed, and constituted,[151] and fitted to each other, as has been observed in order to the continuance of existence,[152] and all things work for the preservation of the system.

If any then should doubt the wisdom of the end; that is, whether existence is better than non-existence to sensible beings; they must wait for further evidence, which will appear in due time. But the wisdom of the means, in order to the continuance of existence, cannot be questioned, they being, through all nature most obvious.[153]

5. An Independent Cause

The Being who exists without cause, must be an independent Being.[154] Independency is included in existing without cause, and as a Being who exists without cause does not get or need anything from another; so can nothing be taken from Him by any other. There can be no cause of the destruction of that, which has no cause of its

---

147   One of our main priorities as a human is self-preservation or a continuance of life.

148   He gave us life, the potential to have a joyful one, and the ability to preserve it (i.e. not die).

149   Able to produce a desired effect

150   Humans prefer life to death.

151   Composed, made up of

152   God made it so that even with the incredible variety of different human beings in the world, they would still desire to have relationships with each other in order to continue the existence of the human race.

153   Whether existence is better than non-existence is unable to be proven with the evidence we have because no one who has ceased to exist has come back to tell us if it is preferable or not. The wisdom of God in continuing our existence seems obvious to a sensible being.

154   This is known as Aseity: the quality or state of being self-derived or self-originated; specifically: the absolute self-sufficiency, independence, and autonomy of God (Merriam-Webster).

existence.[155] And a Being who derives nothing from another, and can have nothing taken from Him by any other, is an independent Being.

6. An Immutable Cause

The independent Being, who exists without cause, must be unchangeable;[156] that is, He must always exist with the same powers, attributes, and qualities, and consequently must always act by the same motives and reasons. If a Being with certain powers, attributes, and qualities, has no cause of its existence, then these powers, attributes, and qualities have no cause. If powers, attributes, and qualities in a Being have no cause, they can never cease to be in that Being; for then there would be a cause of the ceasing to be of that which never had a beginning, which is impossible.

Again, wherever there is a change, there is a cause of that change; otherwise, there would be a beginning without a cause. The cause of change in a Being, must be either external, or internal. But there can be no external cause of change in an independent Being, who exists without cause; for then He would be a dependent being, dependent on other beings or things for powers, attributes, and qualities, which had no cause; which is a contradiction.[157]

And for a Being, who exists without cause, to have in Himself a cause of change;[158] that is, a cause of not being what He is, is likewise a contradiction. It follows then that a Being who exists without cause, must always exist with the same powers, attributes, and qualities. And if a Being must always exist with the same powers, attributes, and qualities, then He must always act by the same motives and reasons, and be an unchangeable Being.

---

155   If God is eternal, He cannot end/die (See. Gen. 21:33; Deut. 32:40, 33:27; Is. 40:28, 41:4, 44:6; Ps. 90:2; Heb. 1:12; 1 Peter 1:23; 1 Tim. 1:17; Rev. 1:8, 10:6).
156   The doctrine of Immutability: not capable of change (See Ps. 55:19, 102:27; Mal. 3:6; Heb. 1:12, 13:8; Jas. 1:17).
157   God cannot be contingent (unnecessary) and a First Cause (necessary) at the same time.
158   God cannot have the potential to change either (see previous footnote on the topic of Actuality v. Potentiality).

7. A Content Cause

The intelligent, independent Being, who exists without cause, and is Author of this system, must be perfectly happy.[159] There is no misery without cause. The cause of misery in a being must be either external, or internal. It cannot be external to an independent Being; for then He would be a dependent Being that is dependent on other beings or things for His happiness.[160] A Being who exists without cause, cannot have a cause of unhappiness in Himself. Then it follows that an intelligent, independent Being cannot be unhappy.[161] An intelligent, independent Being, is not only incapable of suffering misery, but likewise He must enjoy pleasure, or be a happy Being.

A Being who communicates pleasure to other beings, must enjoy pleasure Himself; otherwise, He would give a perfection which he did not possess and there would be an effect without a cause, which is impossible.

Again, a consciousness of possessing powers, capable of being exerted to certain ends, and a real exerting of them to those ends, must give great pleasure to the Being who possesses, and exerts these powers. And the greater the powers, and the more certain their effects, the greater is the pleasure to the Possessor of them.

A power then of making and sustaining of a world; or forming beings and things, and the suiting of them to each other in order to the preservation or happiness of the whole; and the real exercise of this power, must give great pleasure to the Being who possesses it.

Further, the intelligent, independent Being, who exists without

---

159   Divine contentedness: the Triune God is self-content (a Being in communion with Himself) and does not need beings outside the Godhead to feel content. God always has been, currently is, and always will be, perfectly happy (John 1:1, 17:13).
160   Acts 17:25
161   This naturally raises questions about those passages in Scripture where God/ Jesus feels grief/sadness. John Piper explains it well here: "God's heart is capable of complex combinations of emotions infinitely more remarkable than ours. He may well be capable of lamenting over something He chose to bring about. And God may be capable of looking back on the very act of bringing something about and lamenting that act in one regard, while affirming it as best in another regard... God is able to feel sorrow for an act in view of foreknown evil — foreknown pain and sorrow and misery — and yet go ahead and do it for wise reasons." (www.desiringgod.org/interviews/ why-does-god-regret-and-repent-in-the-bible)

cause, must not only be a happy Being; that is, enjoy pleasure without any interruption of pain; but He must likewise be perfectly happy; that is, He must enjoy the highest degree of happiness, that any being is capable of.[162]

As He is the fountain of joy to other beings; that is, of all that rational pleasure which does not produce pain, He must Himself enjoy the highest degree of it; otherwise He would give more than He possessed, and again there would be an effect without a cause.

Again, as the powers of a Creator vastly exceed the powers of His creatures, so must His joy from a consciousness of such powers and from the real exercise of them, vastly exceed any joy which His creatures can have from a consciousness or exercise of their own powers.

Further, there is great joy in communicating pleasure, in a consciousness of bestowing on beings that which they always must prefer and choose; a Being then who communicates to other beings all that true joy or happiness which they possess, must have pleasure from a communication of happiness, which no created being can be capable of.

Lastly, as the Supreme Being is an independent Being, He has joy that no dependent being is, or can be, capable of. He must have great pleasure from reflecting that the joy He has is un-derived, held by no other, nor can it possibly be taken from Him; that He is self-sufficient, and His joy everlasting.

---

162   God does not lack anything, nor does He need anything outside of Himself. As a compound unity, or Tri-unity (three persons in one nature), He is a Being in communion with Himself throughout eternity. He did not create humans because He was lonely or lacked relationship. He was, is, and always will be a perfectly happy Being, otherwise He would not be God because He would lack something. This begs the question of why God created humans at all. Isaiah 43:6b-7 states, "…bring my sons from afar and my daughters from the end of the earth, everyone who is called by my name, whom I created for my glory, whom I formed and made," (ESV). Genesis 1:27 states that we are made in the image of God. The point of an image is to project the essence of the original. The earth is filled with billions of images of the living God, it is literally filled with His glory, (Is. 6:3). Also see Romans 1:20-23, Eph. 1:5-6.

8. A Benevolent Cause

The perfectly happy, independent Being, who exists without cause, must be a good Being.[163] A good Being is one who always wills the happiness of beings, and promotes it as far as He has power. Now a happy, independent Being, *must* will happiness to other beings.

First, because pleasure is in itself a motive to the will. All beings must prefer it in other beings, as well as in themselves. What they must *prefer*, they must *will*, when there is not a motive to the contrary.[164]

A perfectly happy, independent Being, can have no motive to will pain, as motives to will pain, come from weak, dependent beings (beings liable to injuries and want, or from a sense of dread or pain); but a happy, independent Being can neither fear nor suffer, and therefore can have no motives to will pain. If a Being can have no motive to will pain, and has always motives to will pleasure (that is, happiness), then He must always will happiness. Again, the perfect happiness which a Being Himself enjoys, is a motive to will happiness to other beings; and a Being always pleased and happy, always wills happiness.[165]

Further, as the Supreme Being is a Creator, He must always will happiness to His creatures, He must will them that which they must always prefer; otherwise He would will in opposition to Himself, He

---

163   Here Newcome is referring to Omni-Benevolence, the idea that God is all-loving or infinitely good. If He were not perfectly good, He could not be God.

164   Again, this harkens back to the idea of God temporarily allowing painful things if it is for the eternal good. Romans 8:28 states, "All things *work together* for the good." It does not say that everything is good all of the time. We live in a fallen world, so pain is to be expected, but God has an ultimate plan for the good of the world. Also see 1 Peter 1:3-5, 5:6-10.

165   God must will happiness for His creatures, otherwise He would be acting out of character which is the one thing He cannot do, because if He willed anything but happiness, He would not be perfectly happy Himself, and therefore, not God.

would will the imperfection of His own works, which is impossible.[166]

It is abundantly evident then, that the Supreme Being must always will happiness to other beings. And, as He must always will the happiness of beings, so must He always act agreeably to His will, and to promote their happiness as far as He has power.

Dependent beings, subject to pain, may often change their mind regarding potential actions by a dread of danger or consequences, but a happy, independent Being has nothing to suffer or fear; therefore, nothing can stop Him from executing that which He wills, when He has power to do it. It is evident then, that the happy, independent Being, who is the Author of this system, is a good Being; one who always wills happiness to other beings, and promotes it as far as He has power.

It follows then, that His end goal in creation was to communicate happiness and that whatever pleasure He might Himself take in the performance, He could have none in opposition to the happiness of His creatures;[167] for then (as He always must will their happiness) He would will in opposition to Himself, which is impossible.

We find then, the attribute of goodness in the Author of this system connected with His happiness, and particularly we find, that His end goal in making sensible beings was to communicate happiness to them.

But secondly, we not only find simply the attribute of goodness in the Author of this system connected with His happiness, but we likewise find that He is a good Being, and can prove it directly *a posteriori*,[168] from His works.

Whatever helps preserve our life, is created to give us pain. As things good for us grow hurtful when used immoderately, pain is added to the immoderate use of them in order to stop us from the evil,[169] and this is evidence of the wisdom and goodness of the Supreme Being.

Again, as He has made us capable of contributing to the happiness or misery of those of our own species, so has He added pleasure to a consciousness of promoting their happiness; and pain to a consciousness of promoting their misery; and from hence we have

---

168   Not only can we show that God is a good God because He Himself is perfectly happy and therefore wills it for His creation, we can also prove that God is good by examining His works. *A posteriori* basically means "after the fact". It is a method of gaining knowledge about something by observing its characteristics as an effect, and then attributing those same characteristics to its cause. To borrow a phrase, 'the apple does not fall far from the tree.'

169   Newcome is referring here to the earlier mentioned concept that we live longer the more we avoid things that are bad for us. God made the things that will hurt us, hurtful, so we would not continue to pursue them. This is similar to the also earlier mentioned idea that once a child burns their hand by touching a hot stove, they will likely never do it again. Similarly, while something like medicine may be good for us, if we abuse it, it will harm us, and that pain is a warning that we have not utilized it in the way it was intended to be used and we should stop. Many people do not believe in God or refuse to follow Him because this wisdom can make Him seem like a cosmic killjoy. However, God does not give us laws for no reason; He instructs, chastens, and corrects us because He loves us, not unlike our parents who force us to eat our veggies instead of candy for dinner, and tell us to look both ways before running over to our friend's house across the street. It is because they love us and want the best for us that they give us boundaries and teach us to make good choices. Proverbs 3:11-12 (NIV) states, "My son, do not despise the Lord's discipline, and do not resent his rebuke, because the Lord disciplines those he loves, as a father the son he delights in." The author of Hebrews expands on this proverb by writing, "Endure hardship as discipline; God is treating you as his children. For what children are not disciplined by their father? If you are not disciplined—and everyone undergoes discipline—then you are not legitimate, not true sons and daughters at all. Moreover, we have all had human fathers who disciplined us and we respected them for it. How much more should we submit to the Father of spirits and live! They disciplined us for a little while as they thought best; but God disciplines us for our good, in order that we may share in his holiness. No discipline seems pleasant at the time, but painful. Later on, however, it produces a harvest of righteousness and peace for those who have been trained by it," (Hebrews 12:7-11, NIV).

demonstrated that He is a good Being.[170]

No man can create happiness, but he secretly applauds it when it occurs; no man plans goodness that does not get pleasure from it, even if it is simply the intention of goodness. No man chooses to inflict misery, but does so to gratify some passion or desire which stands in opposition to the happiness of others; and every man suffers remorse and anguish, when the gratification which stirred the evil action ceases.[171] No man sees the misery of others without feeling pain, unless he feels the misery is justly deserved.

Therefore, God adding the feeling of pleasure to a soul that plans and promotes the happiness of others, and pain to a soul that designs or promotes the misery of others; and the giving of compassion,

---

170   Here is the evidence that God is a good Being: He created pleasure to bring happiness, and pain to bring misery, so that they could act as signals to teach us what is good, and what is bad for us. He designed the world so that it inherently teaches us how to pursue and obtain ultimate happiness, and avoid misery. He was considering us and anticipating our fallen human nature from the very beginning of Creation, and therefore built in safeguards to help us find happiness and pleasure even in a fallen world. He also built in a sense of pleasure that is to arise when we plan or bring happiness to others, and a sense of pain when we plan or bring misery to others. It is an inherent moral compass to tell us to be good to our fellow man.

171   Here Newcome is referring to the idea of guilt and conscience. Of course, this cannot apply to those who are not of sound mind, and therefore psychopaths and sociopaths can be excluded. However, any human of sound mind (or what Newcome refers to as 'sensible beings') is going to applaud an action that brings happiness or pleasure, and will always feel remorse over an action that brings misery.

which is naturally in all men[172], we have demonstrated that God is a good Being.

Now that we have proved God is a good Being, our Argument is complete: that He is a wise Being, and that when He made sensible beings, He laid down the best end, which was, their happiness.

9. A Just Cause

If God is a good Being (that is, as He wills and promotes the happiness of all Beings, so far as He has power) so is He also a Being, who in all His interactions with sensible beings, acts according to reason and a fit-ness of things; that is, He really promotes their happiness.

Beings may will happiness to other beings, and promote it as far as they have power, and yet fall very short of their end; of which we ourselves are sad instances. They may want the ability to discern, or power to execute, that which is the best for the happiness of beings. But in neither of these cases can the Supreme Being be imperfect, as He always must know first — the fit-ness and unfit-ness of things, second — what tends to cause happiness and misery in His creatures,

172   C.S. Lewis called this The Law of Human Nature. He writes, "If we do not believe in decent behavior, why should we be so anxious to make excuses for not having behaved decently? The truth is, we believe in decency so much–we feel the Rule or Law pressing on us so–that we cannot bear to face the fact that we are breaking it, and consequently we try to shift the responsibility. For you notice that it is only for our bad behavior that we find all these explanations... human beings, all over the earth, have this curious idea that they ought to behave in a certain way, and cannot really get rid of it... Supposing you hear a cry for help from a man in danger. You will probably feel two desires–one a desire to give help (due to your [social/relational] herd instinct), the other a desire to keep out of danger (due to the instinct for self-preservation). But you will find inside you, in addition to these two impulses, a third thing which tells you that you ought to follow the impulse to help, and suppress the impulse to run away. Now this thing that judges between two instincts, that decides which should be encouraged, cannot itself be either of them... [In musical terms] the Moral Law tells us the tune we have to play: our instincts are merely the keys. Another way of seeing that the Moral Law is not simply one of our instincts is this: If two instincts are in conflict, and there is nothing in a creature's mind except those two instincts, obviously the stronger of the two must win. But at those moments when we are most conscious of the Moral Law, it usually seems to be telling us to side with the weaker of the two impulses. You probably want to be safe much more than you want to help the man who is drowning, but the Moral Law tells you to help him all the same." (*Mere Christianity*, Harper San Francisco: 2001, p. 26-29)

and third — must possess the power to act in accordance with His will.

A Being who is Creator (who has wisdom sufficient to form a world and suit and fit all beings and things to each other in order to the preservation of the whole, and who has fitted a variety of things to give pleasure to His creatures) must know whether beings could be made capable of happiness — that is, whether existence would be better than non-existence to them. He also must know the best possible state of existence for all ranks and orders of beings; that is, the state which would produce the most happiness to the whole creation.

Since He must know whether existence would be better than non-existence to sensible beings, and also the best possible state of existence for all ranks and orders of beings, so must He always know what is best for His creatures in all stages of their existence, and what will tend to the happiness or misery of the creatures whom He has formed. He must also always have the power to act agreeably to these fit-nesses — that is, to do that which will most contribute to their happiness.

As He is an independent Being, His powers are independent, and consequently, cannot be limited or restrained by any being whatsoever.

As He is an Infinite Creator, His power cannot be limited by His finite creatures. Those whom He has formed cannot successfully resist Him.

It is evident then, that as the Supreme Being always wills happiness to other beings, knows the fit-nesses and unfit-nesses of things, what will contribute to the happiness or misery of His creatures; and has power to act agreeably to these fit-nesses, that is, to really promote their happiness; He must therefore, in all His interactions with such beings, act according to reason, and a fit-ness of things; that is, He must do that which brings the utmost happiness for such beings.

Having proved all of the above, all the other moral attributes, which are generally ascribed to the Deity, as justice, holiness, faithfulness, etc. are included.

For example, a Creator can only be said to be unjust to His creatures one of these ways; either,

- By making them incapable of happiness,
- By ruining any happiness He has made them capable of,
- By not making them happy in proportion to what they deserve.

However, a Being that knows the fit-nesses and un-fitnesses of things, what will contribute to the happiness or misery of His creatures; who always wills their happiness; and in all His interactions with them acts according to reason, and a fit-ness of things, could not make them incapable of obtaining happiness, nor ruin the happiness they were made capable of; nor so order things that they should not be happy in proportion to what they deserve.

As justice is included in the attribute of goodness, so is holiness and faithfulness — and as a Being who never swerves from reason is holy, so neither can He deceive, nor promise and not perform what He promised; that is, He is faithful and true.

10. An Omnipresent Cause[173]

That is, as He always governs His creatures in the best manner, He is at all times so far present with them, as to be able to do this. By omnipresent I mean that He is at all times *so present* with His works as to have a perfect view and knowledge of them, and as a wise being, He would not make a system which He could not at all times supervise, govern, and direct.

11. A Free Cause

He is a free Agent, and does not act by necessity, but choice. That God is a free Agent, I prove by one single argument: Every man naturally thinks himself a free agent, and blames or applauds himself after certain actions; and while blaming, or applauding of himself is an effect of consciousness, as a free agent it was in his power to have done otherwise.

173　Omnipresent: present everywhere at the same time.

Now then, if man is *not* a free agent, but is obliged in the circumstances he is at any time in to do that one thing he does and he cannot possibly do otherwise[174], then he has faculties given him upon the exercise of which he is necessarily deceived, and the Author of his existence, by giving him such faculties, has forced him into error[175]; and therefore, acted contrary to reason, and a fit-ness of things in His creation.

If the Author of man's existence is a Being who always acts according to reason and a fit-ness of things, and consequently, cannot force him into error or deceive him; then it follows that man *is* a free agent.

Also, if man is a free agent, God must be one; otherwise, there would be an effect without a cause, or a beginning without a cause; or a perfection in a creature which is not in the Creator, which is an impossibility.[176]

There are many other arguments which prove man a free agent, and all these prove that God is a free Agent. There are many arguments taken from the nature of God, and His works, which prove Him a free Agent; but these having been fully explained by others already, I leave them out, determining that what I have said is sufficient to prove my point.

12. A Perfect Cause

Now, having proved that the Author of this system is an eternal, intelligent, wise, powerful, independent, unchangeable, good, just, holy, omnipresent, omniscient Being; and a Being who always acts according to reason and a fit-ness of things; we include all these attributes in one general word, and call Him a **perfect** Being.

Perfect is a relative word, and signifies the agreement of

---

174   Similar to a pre-programmed robot

175   We must be free because if God controlled us, He would be to blame for our sin and error. This is impossible if He is in fact God, because to be God requires complete and perfect holiness, which cannot be near sin. Newcome goes on to explain that the idea that a holy God could cause us to sin is illogical.

176   If man has free will, then God is a free agent as well, because you cannot have an effect without a cause, and freedom had to originate somewhere, or with Someone.

something to a certain measure, or standard in our minds. Thus, a Being, who always lays down the best end, and pursues it by the best means, is perfectly wise — that is, wise without any failure or end.

Beings may be counted more or less perfect if they possess powers which are capable of being means to happiness, and if they really exert them to that end.

The Being who possesses all those powers, attributes, and qualities, which are capable of being means to the happiness of Himself and other beings, in the highest and most perfect degree they can be possessed, and who really does employ them to the end, is the best of all beings, and a perfect Being.

We have then full evidence that the Being who framed and fitted up this system, is an eternal, intelligent, powerful, wise, independent, unchangeable, good, holy, just, faithful, omnipresent, free Being, and a Being who in all His interactions with sensible beings acts according to reason and a fit-ness of things; *or*, that He is a perfect Being.

Whoever believes that there is no such Being must likewise believe there may be a beginning without a cause, or an effect without a cause — that is, he must believe impossibilities or contradictions. Whoever does not act agreeably to the belief of the existence of such a Being, acts contrary to reason and a fit-ness of things.

Section VII

ENQUIRY 2:
After Happiness

A. What are Man's Responsibilities?

Supposing there is really such a Being who is the Author of man's existence, how must man act in order to act according to reason and a fit-ness of things? How must he act in order to obtain happiness? An enquiry after happiness is highly necessary before we dive into whether it is rational that God would reveal Himself — for if the revelation put forth should require any practice of us inconsistent with the attributes of the Deity, we are to reject it.[177]

1. To Avoid Excess

Man is formed with certain mental and physical abilities, which were given him by his Maker, in order to bring happiness to himself or other beings. It is necessary then, that he keep all these mental and physical abilities unimpaired, so that he may be able at any time to be happy. If he impairs his mental and physical abilities, he loses the means to his happiness. He also loses the pleasure which would naturally arise from the exerting of unimpaired powers and he would

---

[177] The next section is on whether or not God has actually revealed Himself to humankind. This section explains that if God did indeed reveal Himself to mankind (in the form of His Son and His Word) and that message included prescriptions for or instructions in righteousness, and is proven to be the Truth, then any contrary belief or practice "revealed" afterwards should be rejected as false.

displease that Being who gave them to him.

Whatever then tends to weaken the powers of either the mind or body of man (that lessens his ability to perceive, apprehend, reason, judge, will, or act), directly tends to make man miserable. Therefore, all excessive eating and drinking beyond what tends to health and refreshment, an indulgence in inappropriate sensual gratifications, and all those vices which could be categorized similarly, are contrary to man's happiness.[178]

2. A Preservation of Self

As it is man's duty to keep his abilities unimpaired, it is also his duty to preserve his existence. If God has made man, and given him means to preserve his existence, He wills that they be made use of to that end. Whoever then neglects the means of self-preservation, to the injuring of his health, acts directly contrary to the will of God, and consequently to his own happiness. If a man injuring his health is contrary to the will of God, then who willfully deprives himself of existence (takes his own life) does so to much greater degree. This is direct opposition to God, is throwing Him back His favors, and is the highest degree of rebellion against Him.[179]

3. Do Justice and Love Kindness (Morality)

With regard to his own species, it is evident that happiness must arise to man from his being a just, or righteous being, that is, one

---

178   Simply stated, sinning is not good for us and if we chose to engage in activities that impair our judgment, we not only displease God, but we will also make ourselves miserable because as mentioned before, if God says something is not allowed, it is probably not good for us.

179   In the Psalms, David writes how God skillfully wrought him in the womb similar to the way an embroiderer designs and weaves a tapestry. God designed and created humans in His image and our bodies are meant to be a house for the Holy Spirit to dwell in. Therefore, while we are free to harm ourselves and even take our own lives, it is an act of blatant rebellion against God and His marvelous work, (Psalm 139:13-16, NKJV). 1 Corinthians 6:19-20 states, "Or do you not know that your body is the temple of the Holy Spirit who is in you, whom you have from God, and you are not your own? For you were bought at a price; therefore glorify God in your body and in your spirit, which are God's," (NKJV). Also see Proverbs 11:17.

who violates the rights of no man, and renders to all their dues. Also, from his being a good being, that is, one who wills and promotes the happiness of all mankind, as much as it is in his power.[180]

Every man possesses rights or property which cannot be violated without pain and injury to him, and God wills that this right or property not be violated — that every man be left uninterruptedly to possess that which belongs to him.[181] Therefore, murder, adultery, theft, oppression, tyranny, slander, backbiting, deceit, lying, treachery, insolence, flattery, etc. which are all instances of injustice, are consequently opposite to the will of God.[182]

All of mankind stands in certain relations to each other, from which there arises rights which cannot be withheld from those to whom they are due without pain and injury to them. God wills that they be not withheld, but that every man has that which belongs

---

180   This concept of acting justly and doing what's right comes from Micah 6:8, "He has told you, O man, what is good; and what does the LORD require of you but to do justice, and to love kindness, and to walk humbly with your God?"

181   Here, writing about individual rights, Newcome is once again clearly influenced by John Locke, the very same man that influenced Thomas Jefferson when writing the Declaration of Independence more than 50 years after Susanna's book was first published. In his *Second Treatise of Government* (1690: Ch. 2, Sect. 6), Locke writes, "But though this be a state of liberty, yet it is not a state of license: though man in that state have an uncontrollable liberty to dispose of his person or possessions, yet he has not liberty to destroy himself, or so much as any creature in his possession, but where some nobler use than its bare preservation calls for it. The state of nature has a law of nature to govern it, which obliges every one: and reason, which is that law, teaches all mankind, who will but consult it, that being all equal and independent, no one ought to harm another in his life, health, liberty, or possessions: for men being all the workmanship of one omnipotent, and infinitely wise maker; all the servants of one sovereign master, sent into the world by his order, and about his business; they are his property, whose workmanship they are, made to last during his, not one another's pleasure: and being furnished with like faculties, sharing all in one community of nature, there cannot be supposed any such subordination among us, that may authorize us to destroy one another, as if we were made for one another's uses, as the inferior ranks of creatures are for ours. Every one, as he is bound to preserve himself, and not to quit his station willfully, so by the like reason, when his own preservation comes not in competition, ought he, as much as he can, to preserve the rest of mankind, and may not, unless it be to do justice on an offender, take away, or impair the life, or what tends to the preservation of the life, the liberty, health, limb, or goods of another."

182   To know the will of God, we must always refer to the Scriptures. For this specific issue, see Galatians 5:13-26 and Exodus 20:1-17.

to him.[183] Here it might particularly be shown that children who fail to honor their parents, parents who neglect their children,[184] all disturbances of the peace of society, and of families, all breach of contracts (particularly all breach of marriage contracts),[185] breach of promises,[186] etc. are withholding of dues to others,[187] and are therefore, opposite to the will of God.

As God wills that the rights of no man be violated, and that all have their dues, so must He order things that happiness must be the effect of righteousness, and misery of unrighteousness. For if just and righteous actions produced misery to man, and unjust, cruel, and tyrannical ones produced happiness, God would have ordered things contrary to reason, and a fit-ness of things, and would not be a good Being; or He would act in opposition to Himself.[188]

As happiness must be the effect of righteousness, it must also be an effect of goodness; and every man must be happy in proportion to his goodness, and miserable in proportion as he is evil.[189] God always wills happiness to the whole creation, and has made man capable of willing and promoting the happiness of his species. This shows that God wills that man always will happiness, and promote it as far as he is able.[190]

Man may not always be able *to do* that which tends to the happiness of others — he may not have the ability to discern what is best for them or the power to execute it. However, he always has the

---

183   "Do not withhold good from those to whom it is due, when it is in your power to do it," Proverbs 3:27, ESV.
184   Ephesians 6:1-4, "Children, obey your parents in the Lord, for this is right. 'Honor your father and mother' (this is the first commandment with a promise), 'that it may go well with you and that you may live long in the land.' 'Fathers, do not provoke your children to anger, but bring them up in the discipline and instruction of the Lord'," (ESV).
185   Malachi 2:16, Matthew 5:31-32, 19:6-9
186   Numbers 30:2, James 5:12, Matthew 5:33-37, Ecclesiastes 5:4-5.
187   Romans 13:7-8, Luke 6:38.
188   If doing that which is right makes man miserable, and doing what is wrong brings man happiness, it could indeed be said that God acted illogically when He ordered things and it would be a contradiction to His character. However this is not the case.
189   Simply stated, if you are good, you will be happy. If you are evil, you will be miserable. Even if this is not the case materially, it will at least be true metaphysically (i.e. you may not be rich, but your conscience will be clean. See 1 Peter 3:17).
190   Proverbs 3:27, Psalm 37:3, Galatians 6:10, Luke 6:27-28, 1 Thessalonians 5:15, Ecclesiastes 3:12.

ability to will happiness,[191] and God always wills that he do this and be a benevolent being. He also wills that man promote it as far as he has power. Man may say he wills happiness, yet not want to give up what he possesses, so he falls short in the actual doing of it. However, because God not only wills happiness, but in all interactions with sensible beings actually does it, so consequently man must, if he would be acceptable to God, promote happiness whenever he has opportunity.

He must save from evil or deliver out of it, feed the hungry, clothe the naked, visit the sick, deliver the oppressed, protect the fatherless, the stranger, and the widow: these are actions which God wills that man perform as often as he has opportunity, in consequence of benevolence or willing good.[192] That is, God always wills that man be a good being. If doing no ill and not withholding that which is due is pleasing unto God, how much more pleasing to Him is doing good? This is joining with our Maker in the great work in which He Himself is employed; and is resembling of the Deity.

Man is also placed among creatures of much lower powers than himself, who are fitted to serve him with their labor, or to be sustenance for him. They are not free agents, but determined by instincts to preserve themselves, and their species; which is certain evidence that they were formed for the use of some other beings.[193] Some of these creatures are useful in the creation and to man in particular instances, but would be destructive to him if their species were too numerous; these, then, he has a right to cull from his higher duty of self-preservation. Others of them which can assist him with their labor or serve him for food,[194] we presume that God wills that he

---

191   Man may not always have the ability or wisdom to do the right thing or do good in every situation, but regardless of his limitations, he should always have good will, the desire or want to do good, and possess a charitable heart and spirit towards others. This is how we reflect Christ and embody what He would do, and ultimately glorify God with our lives: to simply love others with a pure heart and want the best for them.
192   James 1:26-27, Matthew 25:35-40.
193   Here Newcome switches to discussing man's relation to animals, and how they are to be treated. See Genesis 1:26-28, 2:19-20, and Psalm 8:6. We need to reflect God in how He manages and never misuses or mistreats His creation (Psalm 36:6, 145:9, 147:9, Matthew 6:26, Luke 12:6,).
194   At first, man was not to eat animals, but instead God provided plants for them to eat, (Genesis 1:29, 9:1-3).

should make use of.[195] However, he is to remember that when he makes the creatures labor, to do it with mercy. He is to lay no overbearing burden on them (what is not proportioned to their strength), or to be severe with them, but to be as compassionate towards them, as is consistent with their being serviceable to him.[196] Further, when he takes away their lives, he is to do it in that manner which is least painful to them. This is behaving towards the creatures acceptably to the Creator, who wills the good of the whole creation.

4. Specific Duties to Honor God (Piety)

With regard to the Supreme Being, who is the Creator, the Preserver, and the Bestower of happiness on man, it is evident that certain duties arise from man to this Being, in the performance of which, he will find joy. Man has the ability to discover the relation in which he stands to God, so God must will that he discover this relation, and to perform towards Him those duties which arise from it.[197]

God is not like man, to be hurt if we do not pay Him that which belongs to Him; but still it is man's duty to render to God that which is due to Him, whether the withholding it affects Him negatively or not.[198] And, it is man's duty to God:

    a.   To *acknowledge* with all humility: the power, wisdom, and goodness by which he was formed.[199]

    b.   To *give thanks* to the divine Majesty for his existence, his preservation, and his capacity for happiness; for all that

---

195   Genesis 3:21

196   Proverbs 12:10, 27:23, Exodus 23:5, Deuteronomy 22:4, 25:4, Numbers 22:32, Isaiah 66:3, 32:20.

197   If God is real, and our Creator, and is the satisfaction of our desires and can bring us pure and ultimate happiness, but requires of us certain tasks - such as learning about Him and knowing Him intimately – then it is His job to make them known to us, and our job to complete them. Newcome follows this up with 13 different tasks that the Christian should pay heed to and obey.

198   It does not affect God negatively or cause Him harm if we do not worship or even acknowledge Him. However, as Creator He still deserves our praise and obedience.

199   1 Peter 5:5-6

he possesses that is desirable and good.[200]

c. As the Supreme Being is the most powerful of all beings, it is man's duty to *fear Him* more than all other beings; that is, to fear offending Him.[201]

d. As all things are under God's sovereign control, it is man's duty to God to *be patient* under whatever befalls him, and *never complain* about the will of the most High.[202]

e. To *trust* in God. As God always knows what is best for us, as He constantly wills our happiness, and has power to execute what He wills, we are to trust that He will deliver us, when a deliverance is best for us.[203]

f. To endeavor to *know His will.*[204] As the divine will is that rule by which we must act, if we would obtain happiness, we ought to pursue a knowledge of it,[205] which is to be obtained by a consideration of His attributes.[206]

g. To *perform His will.* Better is it not to know the divine will, than to know it and not conform to it. To know the divine will, and not to conform to it, is stating to be wiser than God, and is a rebellion against Him.

h. As man is an offender before God, as he is conscious of not always conforming to His will, it is his duty to *acknowledge his sin*, and to beg of God to forgive him.[207]

---

200   Psalm 100:4, Philippians 4:6-7, James 1:17.
201   Proverbs 15:33, 22:4
202   Psalm 27:14, 37:7; Proverbs 14:29, 16:32; Isaiah 30:18, Ephesians 4:2, Romans 8:25, 12:12; 2 Peter 3:9, Matthew 6:25-34.
203   Proverbs 3:5-6, 16:9; 1 Chronicles 5:20, Psalm 56:11, 62:8; Isaiah 25:9, 48:17; Romans 4:5, 15:13; Genesis 18:19, Jeremiah 10:23.
204   1 Thessalonians 5:18, Ephesians 5:15-17, Hebrews 10.
205   Hebrews 13:20-21, Micah 6:8
206   He is Infinite (Col. 1:17, Ps. 147:5), Immutable (Mal. 3:6, Jas. 1:17), Self-Sufficient (Jn. 5:26), Omnipotent (Ps. 33:6, Job 11:7-11, 2 Cor. 6:18, Jer. 32:17), Omniscient (Is. 46:9-10, 55:8-9), Omnipresent (Ps. 139:7-10, Jer. 23:23-24), Wise (Rom. 11:33, 1 Cor. 2:7), Faithful (Deut. 7:9, Josh. 21:45, 2 Tim. 2:13, Rom. 3:3, Ps. 33:4, Rev. 19:11), Benevolent (Ps. 25:8, 34:8, 106:1, 145:9, 1 Chr. 16:34, Luke 18:19), Just (Deut. 32:4, 2 Chr. 12:6, Job 9:19, Ps. 11:7, Is. 30:18), Merciful (Eph. 2:4, Rom. 9:15-16, Neh. 9:31, Is. 63:9, Micah 7:18, Lk. 1:50,78), Gracious (Ps. 145:8, Eph. 2:8, Ex. 33:19), Loving (Ps. 36:7, 86:15, 136:26, John 3:16, 15:9-17, Rom. 5:8, 8:37-39, Gal. 2:20, Eph. 2:4-5, 1 John 4), Holy (Is. 6:3, 1 Peter 1:15-16, Rev. 4:8, 15:4), Glorious (Ex. 24:17, 1 Chr. 16:29, P s. 72:19, Hab. 3:4).
207   1 Kings 8:46, Eccl. 7:20, Rom. 3:10, 23, Ps. 14:1-3, Lev. 5:5, Ps. 32:5, Prov. 28:13, Rom. 10:9-10, 1 John 1:9.

i. To *love God*. When we have pleasure in the happiness of a Being, we are said to love Him. If we have pleasure in the happiness of a Being, or if we love a Being, His pleasure is a motive of action to us. When then we consider the Supreme Being as the Author and Fountain of our existence, and of all that we possess that is desirable and good, we are justly excited to love Him, that is, to have pleasure when His will is conformed to. His will is a motive of action to us separate from the consideration of our own interest.

j. It is our duty to God to *worship Him*. As we are to acknowledge God's attributes and our dependence on Him, to thank Him for what we possess, and to implore His pardon for our offenses against Him; and as our bodies, as well as souls, are His; it is proper that these duties be accompanied with such bodily postures, as custom has made expressive of our mindset. Thus, as kneeling is the posture of a supplicant, we ought then to *fall on our knees* when we approach the great God of Heaven.[208]

k. To worship Him in public. When we have discovered the Being and attributes of God, and the relation which we stand in to Him, we ought to *publicly testify* to others that we acknowledge Him as our God. This has purpose for other men as well as for God, that they may be emboldened also to worship Him.[209]

l. To *set apart time* for His service. As all our time, that is, our whole lives, are given us by Him, it is our duty to set apart some portion of our life for His worship.[210]

m. To resemble Him in His attribute of goodness, and to *be a good being*. In what better state could a being be formed, than to have powers given him by which he is capable of resembling his Maker? How undutiful, then is man to God, how ungrateful, how unworthy of what he possesses, if he does not employ them to this end?

208 Eph. 3:14-21, Ps. 95:6
209 Mt. 10:32-33, Lk. 9:26, 12:8
210 Rom. 12:1, Ex. 20:8-10, Lev. 19:30, Ps. 92:1, Heb. 10:25, Col. 3:16, Eph. 5:19, 2 Tim. 2:21.

All these are immediate duties from man to God which arise from the relation in which he stands in to Him. As God gives man powers to discover the relation which he stands in to Himself, so must God will that if man acts agreeable to it, happiness will be the consequence. Thus I have traced out the conduct of man by which he is to obtain happiness; that is, I have shown what actions of man are agreeable to the belief of an eternal, intelligent, powerful, wise, good, just, etc. Being. And if there really is such a Being, who is the Author of man's existence, it is the practice of that which I have been describing, that is his way to perfect happiness.

I call this practice **natural religion**[211] or **virtue,**[212] and a contrary behavior, **vice.**[213] The part of our duty[214] which relates to ourselves and other created beings is called **morality,**[215] and that part of it which relates to God is **piety.**[216] When we consider *all of our duties* as the will of God, every breach of morality is opposition to Him — this also is a part of natural religion.[217]

---

211   The *natural religion* Newcome is referring to here is actually *natural theology*, or the argument for God's existence from an observation of natural facts, it does not refer to the Pantheistic doctrine that adheres to the idea that nature itself is divine. At this time, Deism had not become popular yet, and therefore, Newcome used the former term before it became associated with Pantheism or Deism. Chignell and Pereboom write, "In contemporary philosophy, however, both *natural religion* and *natural theology* typically refer to the project of using the cognitive faculties that are 'natural' to human beings — reason, sense-perception, introspection — to investigate religious or theological matters. Natural religion or theology, on the present understanding, is not limited to empirical inquiry into nature, and it is not wedded to a pantheistic result...In general, natural religion or theology (hereafter *natural theology*) aims to adhere to the same standards of rational investigation as other philosophical and scientific enterprises, and is subject to the same methods of evaluation and critique," (emphasis mine.) Chignell, Andrew and Pereboom, Derk, "Natural Theology and Natural Religion", *The Stanford Encyclopedia of Philosophy* (Spring 2017 Edition), Edward N. Zalta (ed.), URL = <https://plato.stanford.edu/archives/spr2017/entries/natural-theology/>.

212   Virtue: behavior exemplifying high moral standards, or goodness.

213   Vice: Evil, wicked, immoral or bad behavior.

214   Responsibility

215   A system that discerns between right/good and wrong/bad behavior, or more specifically, a preference for good behavior over bad behavior.

216   Devout, reverent, faithful – specifically to God.

217   When we mistreat others, or lack in our morality, we are sinning against God as well, because man is made in His image. It is His will that we treat others well, so to not do so is to directly disobey Him.

B. Fullfilling these Responsibilities Leads to Joy

1. In our Present State

Now having, from the attributes of God, traced out man's way to happiness and what is the means to it, I proceed farther, and would examine how far happiness is the effect of the practice which I have been describing, by the order and composition of things:

First, we find that keeping our powers unimpaired is a means to health, cheerfulness, and the ability to think and reason. And that on the contrary, all excess produces pain.

Second, we find that it is the nature of men to esteem virtue; however he may be tempted to forsake it. On the other side, vice is sure to meet with contempt; a thing terrible to man.[218]

Third, doing no injury to any, rendering to all their dues, and doing good, is a natural means to the good offices and friendship of men.

Fourth, virtue fills us with pleasant reflections, while vice with painful ones. It is not in the nature of man, as has been observed, to prefer vice to virtue, however he may be tempted to embrace the former, and abandon the latter. When, then, the pleasure which invited to vice ceases, and man looks back on his past conduct, a consciousness that he has abused his powers, acted unworthy of his nature, and below other beings, must fill him with shame, remorse, and anguish.[219] On the other side, a remembrance of virtue, a consciousness of having acted right, worthily, and according to the dignity of his nature, must give him pleasure inexpressible.

Fifth, we find ourselves capable of great pleasure or pain from expectation; we hope for good or fear evil before it arrives, depending on which we deserve.[220] When we are conscious that we have acted

---

218 Humans naturally esteem or praise goodness. Rarely does mankind dislike virtue or good behavior, however, evil is almost always sure to be met with contempt or dislike.
219 A guilty conscience always follows an evil action once the pleasure of the instant gratification fades away.
220 Expectation of future consequences, i.e. rewards and punishments for past actions.

a righteously, that we have done ill to no man, and extended our goodness to many, that we have joined with our Maker in His great work of doing good, and that we resemble Him, we are full of just confidence and expectation of good from both God and man; we have a joyful hope and expectation of happiness. On the other side, when we have injured and oppressed others; been malevolent, tyrannical, and unjust, and shut our ears to the cries of the needy, we are full of fear and dread of evil; have shame and anguish at looking backward, and horror at looking forward. We find then that the practice I have been describing, the practice of virtue, is naturally productive of happiness.[221]

2. In a Future State

But though it seems natural according to the constitution of things, yet there are many facts on the other side, and frequently do we see the good and the evil, just and unjust, involved in the same calamity.[222] Evil men raise themselves to prosperity, by injustice, cruelty, and oppression. They rise even upon the miseries of the good, and the good perish by the evil.[223]

These are frequent facts, and they put us upon searching farther into the acts of sovereignty by God. This we are never to depart from — *that by righteousness and goodness shall man obtain happiness.* This is as certain as the attributes of God.

We also find that if virtue does not procure us happiness in this world (if righteous and good men are not happy), that this life is not

---

221   If doing good leads to future rewards, it is a contributing factor to our potential happiness.
222   Even though doing good naturally leads to happiness, and evil to misery, there is also an argument to be made for the fact that people who do good or are virtuous are not always happy, and those who do evil are not always miserable. Newcome then goes on to answer this particular challenge.
223   Many have questioned why bad things happen to good people and vice versa. Psalm 73 answers this: "I was envious of the arrogant when I saw the prosperity of the wicked...Behold, these are the wicked; always at ease, they increase in riches. It seems that I have kept my heart clean and washed my hands in innocence in vain...When I thought how to understand this, it seemed to me a wearisome task, until I went into the sanctuary of God; then I realized their end," (ESV, Paraphrase mine).

(and cannot be) man's best and final state, but that he shall exist after the dissolution of his body, in order to future happiness.[224]

The question then is, whether happiness is always the effect of virtue in *this* world? Whether happiness is constantly in proportion to righteousness and goodness? If it is, then the point, which I have been laboring, has been proven — virtue is the way to happiness. If it is not, the righteous and good are sometimes miserable (a fact few will dispute), then we are sure that happiness is ahead; that man shall exist in a future state, when his present sufferings shall be followed with great felicity.[225]

If existence is extended beyond this life, eventually the righteous and good cease from suffering, and the evil from oppressing. The righteous will be happy in their own reflections,[226] and the evil miserable in theirs (without any positive rewards or punishments from God), as it is rational to expect that there shall be rewards and punishments from Him.

---

224 This is essentially the argument from desire: If, for man, goodness ultimately leads to happiness, yet that is not the case in this world at all times, then this world must not be all there is. If being good does not lead to happiness in this life, according to God's attributes of benevolence, love, and justice, there must be an afterlife in which a virtuous man can obtain bliss. Otherwise, the natural law would not be fair, and God would be unjust. This idea of an afterlife proves that man's soul is immortal. This would make sense given the fact that humans pursue immortality and fear death and suffering. If we were originally created to live forever with God, then we would naturally desire it. C.S. Lewis wrote, "Creatures are not born with desires unless satisfaction for these desires exists. A baby feels hunger; well, there is such a thing as food. A duckling wants to swim; well, there is such a thing as water... If I find in myself a desire, which no experience in this world can satisfy, the most probable explanation is that I was made for another world. If none of my early pleasures satisfy it that does not prove that the universe is a fraud. Probably earthly desires were never meant to satisfy it, but only to arouse it, to suggest the real thing." (Lewis, C.S. *Mere Christianity*. New York, NY: Macmillan, 1960; p. 120). If man desires happiness, it must exist and come from somewhere, or from Someone. Therefore, a Being capable of fulfilling man's desire for ultimate happiness must exist.
225 Intense happiness
226 Consequences of actions perpetrated in their past lives, i.e. the result of heaven or hell.

a.) Argument from the Justice of God
for the existence of an Afterlife

Premise 1:   God always wills happiness to His creatures, acts according to reason and a fit-ness of things

Premise 2:   God has made man capable of obtaining happiness (as virtue is the way to happiness)

Premise 3:   The virtuous are not always happy in this world, or in proportion to their amount of virtue.

Conclusion: Therefore, that their existence shall be prolonged after the dissolution of their bodies, in order to their future happiness.

So, we have proven man's future existence from the attributes of God and the miseries which often befall righteous and good men in this world.[227]

b.) Argument from the Powers of the Mind
for the existence of an Afterlife

Besides proving man's future existence from justice of God, we also consider it reasonable to expect an afterlife based on the reasoning and thinking powers of man.

We cannot accept that reasoning and thinking are properties of physical matter because we have great experience with the properties of physical matter, and have never found that it had any of these sorts of properties. They must be of a different and superior substance, because as far as we know anything of physical matter, it is utterly

---

227   If God exists, and is just and good, then there must be some happiness waiting for the virtuous at the end of this life, since the good are rarely rewarded in this fallen, temporal state.

incapable of such powers and properties.[228]

If reasoning and thinking are not properties of matter, but of a different and superior substance, then the dissolution of the physical composition of matter (the ceasing to exist of the body of man), is no reason why a different and superior substance should cease to exist.[229]

If two substances have the same nature, powers, and properties, then the dissolution of the one gives us reason to expect the dissolution of the other. However, if they have different natures, powers, and properties, we have no reason to accept that what happens to the one, will also to the other. We, in fact, have reason to expect the contrary.[230]

Lastly, it seems absurd to suppose that such powers as man is possessed of (his powers of reasoning, thinking, judging, etc.) should be given for so short a time as the physical life of man, and to so little purpose as only to provide temporary pleasure.

---

228   Here Newcome discusses the idea of substance dualism: that the mind (including its faculties of thinking and reasoning) and body are of two separate substances: physical and metaphysical, or material and immaterial. As J.P. Moreland points out, there are things that are true of the mind that are not true of the brain. In his paper on Substance Dualism, he writes, "For example, thoughts cannot be a physical state of the brain. Why? Because there are things true of my thoughts that are not true of a physical state of my brain. It does not make any sense to ask how many inches long is my thought that lunch is in an hour and a half. How much does it weigh? Is that thought closer to my left ear or closer to my right ear? What geometrical shape does that thought have? Is it sort of weird shaped or is it a square or a rectangle? That is all nonsense. However, while I am thinking, the state that is going on in my brain at that time does have a shape. It is located in, say, my left or my right hemisphere, so it will be closer to my left or right ear. It will have a certain mass and chemical composition. And there is something true of a thought that cannot be true of a brain state. Thoughts can be true or false. Brain states are neither true nor false, they just exist. So there are things true of my thoughts that cannot be true of my brain state, so thoughts cannot be the same thing as my brain state," (http://www.sebts. edu/faithandculture/pdf_docs/naturalism_and_the_crisis_of_the_soul.pdf). If the mind and the brain are not the same thing, then it follows that the mind is of another substance, that of the immaterial. Therefore, man is not just a physical being, he is spirit as well.

229   Because man is also immaterial, or spirit/soul, then it follows that just because his physical part (body) dies, it does not automatically mean that his immaterial part will as well. Especially if, as Newcome asserts, it is a superior substance.

230   If Substance Monism is true, then the body and mind/spirit are the same substance, and both will perish at the same time and an individual's complete existence will simply decompose and fade with time. If Substance Dualism is true, and the fact that the mind (thoughts) and brain (physical body) are of different properties, then the immaterial part of man will exist far longer than the material part, therefore there is an afterlife of some sort.

It is rational then, to expect man's future existence, from a consideration of his nature and powers, but also from the goodness and justice of God we depend on it. We depend that God will equally proportion happiness to virtue,[231] and that the Judge of all the earth will do right.

Now, having from the attributes of God proven that man must be capable of obtaining happiness, and that *virtue* is the means by which this happiness is to be obtained; I will proceed a step further, and prove that this happiness shall be everlasting.

I prove it from God's goodness and power:

- God always wills happiness to his creatures.
- He has power to continue the existence of beings He has formed.
- Therefore, He will always continue existence, to those who by a right use of their powers have obtained happiness, to all eternity.

Whether then the virtuous obtain happiness on this, or the other side of the grave, the difference is but of small importance to them. This is certain: they shall obtain it; and when it is obtained, they shall enjoy it to all eternity.

Everlasting happiness to the righteous and good is a consequence of God's justice, goodness, and power. If it is asked, "Who is equal to the task which He has set? Where is the man who lives and falls not short of his duty?"

I answer, "God is no hard Taskmaster; He knew what we would be capable of before He formed us; saw our necessary failings and imperfections, and would not have formed us if we had not been capable of obtaining happiness, regardless of these failings and imperfections. These then, are not a bar to our happiness."

But so far as man willfully shuts his eyes against his duty, yields to present pleasure in opposition to reason, is unjust, cruel, and tyrannical, a spreader of unhappiness, is malevolent, and a

---

231   To give everyone the amount of happiness they deserve in relation to their virtue.

disposition hateful to God; then he must take the consequence, and fall short of happiness.

The most rational feeling, after such behavior, most certainly is to be very sorry, and to ask God forgiveness for the offense against him; and to be very diligent for the future; and we hope God will forgive it; but still we cannot say that this man is in the same condition with him who has always walked uprightly. God may forgive him, but he hardly will approve of himself.

Section VIII

ENQUIRY 3:
Is it Rational that God would Reveal Himself beyond the creation of nature?

An enquiry into whether a special revelation would come from God is highly necessary before we get into the evidence of the Christian religion — for if it is not agreeable to the attributes of God for Him to reveal Himself beyond His natural creation, a farther search will be to no purpose.[232]

Now if we consider the before-mentioned attributes of God, there arises no argument against revelation; and if it was not unworthy of the divine Being to create (general revelation), it appears not to be unworthy of Him to direct, take care of, and govern that creation (special divine action).

A. General Revelation was not Enough

Is there any objection against God needing to reveal Himself (beyond the creation of nature) after considering the sinful nature of man? Surely there appears none. We find mankind often falling short of happiness, ignorant of natural duties and of virtue (the means to happiness), and even of not practicing what they do know.

---

232   In Newcome's first edition of *Enquiry*, this section was only one page. However, after Tindal's book came out, she expanded it in her second edition to more thoroughly answer his arguments that God would not supernaturally reveal Himself to man (Deism).

1. Ignorance of Duty and Virtue

First, we find a great part of mankind ignorant of several natural duties and of virtue (the means to happiness).

If we consider mankind in the beginning, having just come out of the hands of their Maker, we shall find them (unless divinely instructed) entirely ignorant of almost all natural duties and of virtue without reason to guide them (there being no reasoning before experience), nor any motives to act by except learning through the results of pain and pleasure from their actions.

They were indifferent to the distinction of good or evil, having no ideas or notions of either,[233] nor instincts to direct them to what alone was good for them, nor to the quantities of those things which would add to their health and life. They would have to learn moderation by excess; truth by error; and to search after the greatest good by experiencing how certain degrees of pleasure produce pain.

Such would have been the condition of mankind at first, if left to themselves without a revelation; their first guides would be pain and pleasure, and these would be very insufficient ones as they could not lead them all the way to the level of happiness which they were naturally capable of, nor so much as secure them from doing things immediately destructive to them.

2. A Partial Revelation is Not Enough

Second, after mankind has had the experience of their forefathers to build their conduct on, after some knowledge has been transmitted

---

233   If God did not give Adam explicit rules for how humans were to act, he would not have known what was good or bad for him (physically or morally) except through trial and error, and could have destroyed himself in the process. However, this is not the case. God did spend time with Adam, teaching him how to live. Many people will say that there is no evidence for this, but in Genesis 3:8 it says that Adam and Eve heard the Lord God walking in the garden, and hid from him. It does not say they saw Him and hid, it says they heard Him. They recognized the sound of the Lord's steps because it was familiar to them. They knew the sound of His steps from experience. He also gave Adam explicit rules for what was allowed and what was not (i.e. everything *except* eating from the Tree of the Knowledge of Good and Evil was okay), in order to show him there was such a thing as right (God's way requiring humility) and wrong (man's way involving pride), see Genesis 2:15-17.

to them from others, yet we find great numbers not able by their own powers to find out all natural duties, and very few the greater motive (eternal happiness) for carrying them out.[234]

Some want to say that natural abilities are enough to discover all natural duties. It is true, after mankind has subsisted some time, the duties of morality must end up becoming obvious to even those with very mean capacities,[235] but this is not so regarding our immediate duties to God. Fear may cause us to mistake the Deity, and consequently not to worship Him in a manner suitable to His nature and attributes.[236]

Many have the mental faculties to discover the above duties, yet do not have the opportunity to trace out *all* of their natural duties and the obligations to them. Many people have to get their bread by the sweat of their brow and do not have leisure time to search after all that knowledge which may be beneficial to them.[237]

Multitudes are also kept from truth by the craft of interested deceivers. Such is the misfortune of mankind that they have not been left to follow the dictates of their own reason, but have been led backward from truth.[238] Religion in many ages and nations has been calculated to serve some private views and then imposed universally on mankind as divine. Morality has been corrupted and the grossest absurdities put in its place. This has been a damaging blow to natural religion, and to our discovery of truth by reason.

---

234   This is referring to the saints of the Old Testament who, even though they knew right and wrong from their forefathers, were not able to discern God's preference until He gave them the Law.

235   After man has existed around other humans a while, his natural responsibility in society would become clear to even those of the most inferior mental understanding. How he "ought" to act would become obvious eventually due to the reactions of his peers.

236   While man would have eventually figured out how to act appropriately in society, he would not, on his own, ever naturally figure out how he ought to act in relation to God. He would need some help so as to not mistake the Creator of the world for a different deity and worship a false god.

237   Many people want to learn what's right and wrong, and spend time researching religions and to learn their obligations to the Creator, but simply do not have the time given their station in life.

238   There are many charismatic false prophets out there that have led people astray from the truth, and have deceived them into thinking they do not need to reason through their own personal belief, but to simply trust that what they have been told by the prophet is the truth.

It is evident then, that if all humans have entirely been left to themselves without a revelation, particularly if God did not reveal Himself to mankind as soon as He had formed them, some part of them must have been ignorant of several natural duties, and consequently must have fallen short of happiness which they are naturally capable of.[239]

It follows then, as there is no objection against a revelation from a consideration of the attributes of God, so there is none from a consideration of the nature of man — on the contrary, instruction in our natural duties seems highly beneficial to man and therefore, we hope that God would impart it to us.

Particularly we hope and trust that God, when he formed mankind, did not leave them to grope in the dark in a worse condition than the animals (who at least have instincts to guide them to what alone is good for them and never excess in it). We hope that divine wisdom filled in the gaps of man's lack of experience, and showed them their way to happiness.

We further hope that God, who sees the many constant limitations on mankind to the discovery of all their natural duties, the weaknesses of their natures, the necessity upon them to get their bread by labor, and the prejudices which they lie under from the impositions of deceivers; either has interposed, or will interpose, to guide them to truth.[240]

3. Eternal Consequences Require Special Revelation

Mankind often fails in another particular, a particular where a failure is of much more fatal consequence to them than simply a lack of knowledge of their duty, and that is in the actual practice of it, so

239   If God had not instructed Adam and Eve at the beginning, they would have eventually figured out some morality through trial and error, but would still be missing other important knowledge/instruction that they could not discover on their own. For example, if Jesus is the only way to obtain eternal life, how would one know that if God did not reveal Himself through His Son or His Word? Humans may have figured out there was a Creator God, but which one He was would have been obscured.

240   We trust that God, knowing that He is the path to ultimate, eternal happiness, and knowing the fallen nature of man, the lack of time humans have, and abundance of deceivers present on earth, He will intervene supernaturally to guide us to the truth.

we also in this case hope for divine assistance.

If man falls short in the knowledge of his duty, he loses a happiness he is naturally capable of; however, if he falls short in the practice of it, he exposes himself to the displeasure of God, and to his own severe regrets lasting as long as his existence. In the first case he loses happiness, in the second he adds to himself everlasting misery.

As then it does not appear disagreeable to the attributes of God for him to instruct mankind in their natural duties, neither does it appear disagreeable to Him to assist them in the performance of them and to help them in a case where a failure is of most fatal consequence to them.

God may even make further manifestations of Himself to more quickly reveal to mankind their duties: He may give new reasons for us to obey Him, find means which may help to secure our virtue, or contrive methods for our happiness which human reason could not invent.

We cannot say God cannot, or will not, do this or more; and as it does not appear unsuitable to His nature for Him to assist us, we from His goodness hope that He will do it.

4. Answering Mr. Tindal

And now, having found that a revelation does not appear unsuitable to the attributes of God or nature of man, we should next proceed to examine into the evidences of an asserted revelation, the Christian religion, but first think it proper to consider what has been lately delivered by Mr. Tindal, which if true, will overthrow what I have been advancing under the two last particulars, which was:

1. That if humans are entirely left to themselves without a revelation, a great part of them must be ignorant of several duties and consequently fall sort of the happiness which they are naturally capable of; and it appears agreeable to the attributes of God for Him to instruct them in their natural duties.

2. If there is no argument to be made from the attributes of God or the nature of man, why wouldn't God reveal truths to mankind that human reason can't discover on its own?

<u>Mr. Tindal's argument is as follows:</u>

- God has from the beginning given mankind some kind of revelation, and if they observe it, they can obtain happiness or be acceptable to Him.[241]
- He has given all men, at all times, sufficient methods to know this revelation.
- This revelation cannot be too difficult for man to understand.
- The only means of knowing this revelation is the use of those higher mental powers that differentiates man from animals; and that using these powers after the best manner they can, they must answer the end for which God gave them, and justify their conduct.
- This revelation is perfect.
- Nothing can be added to it.

If the *revelation* includes all the means to happiness, it follows that God will not reveal to mankind[242] any natural duties which all men by their reason cannot discover to be such; nor truths that cannot be discovered by human reason.[243]

In answer to Tindal, I say that the *revelation* cannot be a perfect *revelation* unless we give up the attributes of God. For if the Creator of man is a just, good, and powerful Being, and a Being who, in all His interactions with His creatures, acts according to reason, and a fitness of things, it demonstratively follows, that every man has several duties to himself, to God, and to mankind, from the performance of each of which must arise happiness; that every act of moderation, righteousness, goodness, and piety, produces happiness; that it

---

241   *Christianity as Old as Creation*, Ch. I, page 3, 4, 5.

242   "This first conclusion, *that God **will not** reveal to mankind any natural duties which all men by their reason cannot discover to be such*, is not this gentleman's: he supposes God may reveal to mankind all natural duties; but such a supposal is inconsistent with the perfection of the law, rule, or religion, given to all mankind; and if the law (etc.) given to all mankind is perfect, and can have nothing added to it, then God **cannot** *reveal to mankind any natural duties not discoverable by the reason of all men*." – Newcome's note

243   To Tindal, there is no need for special divine action, or God interceding to give a supernatural revelation to man. He asserts that the 'natural religion' (the ability to discover everything we need to know due to the faculties God created us with naturally, and without God's interceding later on in time) is all humans need to be right with God.

recommends to God's favor, and secures to us pleasant reflections[244] lasting as long as our existence.

It follows then, that the more our duties are known to us and practiced, the greater our happiness is; and where there is a lack of knowledge of our position in relation to God and man, and an ignorance of the duties arising from our position, there would be a falling short of happiness. Also, it is an undoubted fact that not all men are equal in their faculties, and therefore cannot obtain equal happiness with others, nor can they obtain what they could be capable of obtaining if they had clear instruction on how to do so.[245]

Tindal would answer that what is the duty of some men is not the same as the duty of others, but that all have knowledge sufficient for the circumstances they are in. [246]

I respond that all men, in the circumstances they are in, should be capable of some degree of happiness and that no man shall ever suffer (receive punishment) for not doing that which he did not have power to do. All men cannot obtain equal happiness with others because it is impossible for those who never had it in their thoughts to do certain actions to have the same amount of pleasure which would naturally and necessarily attend the performance of them.

It is evident then, that if the Creator of man is a just, good, and powerful Being, and a Being who in all His interactions with his creatures acts according to reason, and a fit-ness of things, that the revelation offered by Tindal is a very *imperfect* revelation. For if Tindal is correct, the justice of God should be impeached for not letting all men have equal opportunities or capacities for happiness; and for constructing things so that some men by the use of their natural powers can obtain that happiness, and others cannot. I return, it is undoubtedly certain, and a consequence of God's attributes, that He has constructed things in the best possible manner for the good of the

---

244　Consequences of actions perpetrated in their past lives, i.e. the result of heaven or hell.

245　Some people are not born with the same mental faculties as others, and cannot reason to the same extent as others. Therefore, it is inconsistent with God's attributes to let those wander in ignorance their whole lives and suffer the eternal consequences of actions they did not know to be wrong.

246　*Christianity as Old as Creation*, Ch. I, p. 5.

whole. Where there are generations of beings who are free agents, there *must* be different opportunities or capacities for happiness, since vice (sin) naturally impairs the powers and faculties of beings.[247] God would not have to reward a man who is forced to do His will, but He does reward those (in this life or the next) who freely choose to do His will in whatever capacity they can.

We find then, upon a review of our argument, that:

- All mankind cannot, by the use of those higher mental powers that differentiates man from animals, obtain all that happiness which they are naturally capable of. Also, not all have equal opportunities or capacities for happiness, consequently, Tindal's revelation is an imperfect revelation.

- As it is imperfect, it is suitable to the attributes of God for Him *to add to it,* and to *reveal to mankind all the duties by which they may obtain happiness by practicing.*[248]

Tindal's argument does not overthrow what I advanced in the first place so we will proceed to see how far it affects what I delivered in the second, which is:

First, it does not appear disagreeable to the attributes of God for Him to reveal to mankind truths not discoverable by human reason.

Second, the reason given by Tindal why God will not reveal to man any truths not discoverable by human reason is because his revelation, as he has defined it, is perfect. But we have proved that his revelation is very imperfect; and that it does not include all the means to happiness.[249]

There is, then, from Tindal's book, no proof that God *will not*

---

247   Because he is fallen, every man is not physically perfect. Due to sin, by which death came into the world, there is the Law of Entropy. Man's DNA is not perfect, and can occasionally break down, and be mutated or deformed. If every person is not born with the same abilities but is held to the same standard of righteousness, it would make God unjust. However, because we know He is just, otherwise He would not be God, we know this is not the case.

248   Here Newcome gives the case for special divine action and asserts that Deism is inconsistent with the attributes of God. If He is just and loving, He would not leave His created beings wandering around imperfect in the dark, but would reveal and illuminate that which will lead to their perfection, specifically, salvation through Jesus Christ.

249   Human reason is not enough because not everyone has the same mental faculties or ability to reason.

reveal to mankind truths that he could not discover on his own. Also, if it is suitable to the attributes of God for Him to reveal truths which some men cannot discover, why is it not suitable to His attributes to reveal truths which no man with human reason alone can discover? We cannot possibly say God cannot, or will not do this.

Having then, no manner of proof that his is a perfect revelation, we cannot conclude it to be such, and consequently cannot conclude that God will not reveal to mankind truths not discoverable by human reason, but must wait to see whether He does or not. We cannot possibly say yet whether this revelation is perfect or whether it includes all the means to happiness having no evidence on either side *a priori*.[250]

God may eventually reveal things to man that human reason could not have learned on its own, from which may arise new duties, and even more happiness; and He also may, seeing our deviation from reason and the fatal consequences of it to us, find methods to engage us to our duty, which man could not have thought of; and He may give new motives to obey Him, or direct us to means which may help secure our virtue. Knowing our own failings and God's goodness, we are inclined to hope for assistance; but the method of His assisting us is impossible to discover.[251]

We have found that:

- Tindal's offered revelation, discoverable by the natural faculties of all men, is an imperfect revelation, in that it does not include all the means to happiness.

---

250 Newcome here is appealing to the Scientific Method – that we derive our knowledge from an observation of the facts, instead of asserting a view and declaring it perfect without evidence.

251 God's ways are not our ways. We cannot discern why He does certain things or allows certain things to happen in our lives. We could be delayed on the way to work by a malfunctioning traffic light and think, "Why me?" but it was really God's providence preventing us from being struck by a drunk driver in the next intersection. Isaiah 55:8-9 (ESV) states, "For my thoughts are not your thoughts, neither are your ways my ways, declares the Lord. For as the heavens are higher than the earth, so are my ways higher than your ways and my thoughts than your thoughts." Romans 11:33-34 (ESV) says, "Oh, the depth of the riches and wisdom and knowledge of God! How unsearchable are his judgments and how inscrutable his ways! 'For who has known the mind of the Lord, or who has been his counselor?'"

- No proof was offered why the revelation is a perfect revelation. So it follows, that what Tindal has offered, will not overthrow what I have advanced, which is: it does not appear disagreeable to the attributes of God for Him to reveal to mankind their natural duties; nor to assist them in the performance of them, or reveal to them truths not discoverable by human reason.

We then proceed to examine the Christian religion, and the evidence of it. Always remembering in our search to not to receive anything as God's Word, which is not agreeable to His nature or attributes, no matter what the asserted evidence is of it. Even our own senses are to be distrusted when the attributes of God are contradicted, for a temporary act or appearance of things are not as good evidence to us as God's goodness since our whole existence is evidence of it.[252]

---

252   Our senses are not to be trusted in their observations of things since we are finite and temporary, and only see the truth partially. Observations can be trusted when they line up with God's character, but when they contradict His character we must re-assess them. The fact that we can observe in the first place is evidence of God's goodness in that He allows us to exist by taking the time to create us so well in the first place. Our existence is evidence of His goodness.

Section IX

ENQUIRY 4:
Is Christianity from God?

A. What evidence do we have that the Christian religion is a divine revelation?

Is it worthy of God, and suitable to His nature, and agreeable to that revelation which we have already founded on the attributes of the deity? If it fails here, if it contradicts the attributes, we are not to receive it.

1. The Christian religion is worthy of God and suitable to His nature

In our examination of this point, we are to take in the whole Christian scheme, and as the Christian religion is founded upon one that came before it, namely Judaism, which it acknowledges to be divine, this also must be brought to the test.

Here we find, according to both the religion of the Jews and Christians, that man was formed happy, placed in a seat of perfect happiness, and was a free agent able to lose his happiness.[253] God did not leave him to himself, but as soon as He had formed him, kindly let him know the terms on which he stood, how he could forfeit his perfect standing, and how to preserve his happiness. Man had divine instruction, yet he abused his liberty, and suffered the consequence. He sinned, and was excluded from the seat of his perfect happiness, and consequently all mankind was excluded from it with him.

However, God did not force mankind to remain in this condition, to spend a few years on Earth in labor and sorrow, and then die in their sin; but having lost their happiness on Earth, He made them capable of happiness in the Heavens. To the end that mankind might not misunderstand their responsibilities and fall short of happiness, God Himself graciously instructed them, gave them divine precepts, sent to them preachers of righteousness, warned them by punishments on the wicked, and by deliverances of the good. He saved a few righteous persons when He destroyed the rest of the world, gave a Law from heaven written on tables of stone (wherein was expressed our duty to God and man), and He sent a divine Person, His Son, to assume our nature, and set us a perfect example.[254] God accepts His Son's perfect righteousness, for our imperfect, provided we sincerely

---

253   Many people wonder why God gave man free will if He knew there was a possibility of sin. C.S. Lewis writes that, "God created things which had free will. That means creatures that can go wrong or right. Some people think they can imagine a creature that was free but had no possibility of going wrong, but I can't. If a thing is free to be good it's also free to be bad. And free will is what has made evil possible. Why then did God give them free will? Because free will, though it makes evil possible, is also the only thing that makes possible any love or goodness or joy worth having. A world of automatons – of creatures that worked like machines – would hardly be worth creating...Of course, God knew what would happen if they used their freedom the wrong way: apparently, He thought that it was worth the risk... If God thinks this state of war in the universe is a price worth paying for free will – that is, for making a real world in which creatures can do real good or harm and something of real importance can happen, instead of a toy world which only moves when He pulls the strings – then we also may take it as being worth paying," (*The Case for Christianity*).

254   These are all evidences of God revealing Himself to man beyond "natural theology", or what is known as "special divine action."

endeavor to do our duty ,[255] and heartily repent of all our offenses against Him.[256]

Here is a method for our happiness, which human reason could not have contrived, but is worthy of the divine Being, and suitable to His attributes: God will forgive us our offenses against Him, for the sake of the perfect righteousness of Jesus Christ, provided we sincerely repent of them, and endeavor to do our duty. Before Christ, we hoped for pardon from the divine goodness, but reason could give us no assurances of it. He gave us a plumb-line for our conduct in the perfect example of our Savior, agreeable to the attributes, and to which if we faithfully attend, we cannot be mistaken in our duty:

With regard to ourselves, we are commanded to be temperate, sober, and chaste; everyone to possess his vessel in sanctification and honor,[257] and to flee youthful lusts which war against the soul.[258] With regard to others, we are commanded to invade the rights of no man; to render to all their dues;[259] are shown what are those dues; and have a straight rule given us, whereby to measure our actions to all mankind; and that is, to do to them as we would they should do to us.[260]

We are not only required to do no injury, and to render unto all their dues, but we are also commanded to do good; and told, that if we would be disciples of our Master, and inherit the blessing, we must be merciful, kind, tender-hearted, forbearing one another, forgiving one another, even as God for Christ's sake has forgiven us;[261] that, if we would be set at the right-hand of our Savior when He judges all men, we must feed the hungry,[262] clothe the naked, visit the sick,

---

255　No research indicated whether Newcome leaned one way or another on Calvinism or Arminianism. This "duty" she speaks of is listed out in Section VII, Enquiry 2, under A. What are Man's responsibilities? Given the emphasis she later places on Christ and His work alone, it seems as though she saw these duties as simply an indication that a person's heart was truly repentant and in a place of submission to God – and that included both inward and outward expressions of faith.

256　To ask for forgiveness for our sins.

257　1 Thessalonians 4:4

258　2 Timothy 2:22, 1 Peter 2:11

259　Romans 12:17

260　Matthew 7:12

261　Ephesians 4:22-23

262　Matthew 25:34-46

comfort the fatherless, the stranger, and the widow; that if we would have treasure in heaven, we must give to the poor; and if we would be children of the Most High, we must resemble Him who does good to all, and makes His sun rise on the evil, and the good, and sends the rain on the just and the unjust.[263] We are assured that unless the *motive* for all our charity is pure goodness and a sincere delight in the happiness of our fellow creatures, it will not profit us anything even if we gave our whole substance to feed the poor.[264]

In Judaism and Christianity, the attributes of the Deity are declared to us, and our duty to God is to be agreeable to these attributes. God is described as an eternal,[265] unchangeable,[266] almighty,[267] omnipresent,[268] omniscient,[269] wise,[270] holy,[271] just,[272] good[273] Being; we are commanded to worship, obey, fear, love, and at all times to trust Him. We are also instructed in the times and manner in which He will be worshipped. A Sabbath, or one day from seven, is appointed wherein we are to rest from our labor, and remember God's goodness in creating, and afterwards both His goodness in creating and redeeming us.

Sacrifices and ordinances are instituted under the Jewish covenant, by which they were to be reminded of their imperfections, their sins, and their dependency on the divine Being. Then baptism and the sacrament of the Lord's Supper under the Christian covenant, where in one we are solemnly initiated into our religion and made members of Christ's church, and in the other we commemorate the love of our Savior, testify ourselves to be His disciples, receive pardon of our sins, and repeat our professions of conforming to His laws.

Lastly, we are assured that the soul of man (his thinking part)

263 Matthew 5:45
264 1 Corinthians 13
265 Deuteronomy 33:27
266 Malachi 3:6, James 1:17
267 Genesis 17:1, 28:3, 35:11, etc.
268 Psalm 139, Prov. 5:21, 15:3, Hebrews 4:13, etc.
269 Job 42:2, Psalm 139, etc.
270 Ps. 147:5, Rom. 11:33
271 Is. 57:15, Ps. 99:3, 103:1, 111:9, 145:21, Rev. 4:8, etc.
272 Is. 45:21, Zeph. 3:5, Deut. 16:18, Prov. 16:11, Ps. 89:14
273 1 Chronicles 16:34, Ezra 3:11, Ps. 105, 106:1, 107:1

never dies, and that eternal misery will be the portion of vice,[274] and eternal happiness the portion of virtue;[275] that the unclean, those guilty of extortion, the unjust,[276] and those who shut their ears to the cries of the needy, shall go away into everlasting misery, but the righteous shall enter into life eternal.[277] From a consideration of the nature of the soul of man, and its powers and properties, we find it reasonable to conclude that the soul is not material, but of a substance distinct from, superior to, and more durable than, the physical body of man; and that it should be formed for eternal existence,[278] and (in sensible beings) acts according to reason. It follows then, that when it is conscious that it has abused its powers, acted unsuitably to its nature and beneath its station, it will feel guilt during its existence.

The Christian religion then, appearing worthy of God and suitable to His nature, the next question is, what is the evidence of it? For it will not follow that because it is worthy of God, it is His revelation, but it will follow that is rational for us to proceed in our Enquiry.

2. Examining the Evidence

We proceed then to an examination of the evidence of the Christian religion, and in order to judge it, it is first proper to consider what kind of evidence is to be expected; and supposing God would reveal Himself, what proof should we rationally expect Him to give us of such a revelation?[279]

This is certain, if the revelation is for the benefit of all mankind, and ought to be received as truth by all those to whom it is communicated, the evidence of it should be sufficient to determine the rational assent of all those who live after, as well as those who live at the time when the revelation is given.

The Christian religion, then, being of this sort, (for the benefit

---

274   Sin
275   Holiness
276   Galatians 5:19-21
277   Matthew 25:46
278   See footnotes on Substance Dualism.
279   See Section IV on rationally expected evidence (Proposition 2)

of all mankind and requiring belief from all those to whom it is communicated) ought to have evidence that is determined sufficient for the rational assent of all men.

Now then, we can think of no evidence so certain as to all mankind, as that which is given in the works of nature;[280] and it is reasonable to expect that the supreme Being should give mankind evidence of His will, after the same manner as He gave them evidence of His existence and attributes, that is, in His works. As He led us to a knowledge of His being, or gave us evidence of His being, by the works of nature, so we may justly expect He would give us evidence of His will in the same works, and by showing His power in nature. And how is it that the supreme Being can give us evidence of His will in the works of nature?

As the existence of things and constant, uniform laws by which bodies move or rest,[281] are a proof of an eternal, intelligent, Being; so a *change* in these laws would be an evidence of His will.

a. An Argument *for* Miracles

Premise 1:   No being can *change* His laws (He being sole Lord of nature) without His consent

Premise 2:   He cannot allow that they *change* to give evidence to falsehood (for that would be to act in opposition to His own character)

Conclusion: Therefore, a *change* in these laws is full evidence that what is delivered came from Him.[282]

We call a *change* in the laws of nature, a **miracle**.[283]

---

280   Psalm 19:1-6, Romans 1:18-20, also known as general revelation.
281   See Section VI footnotes on the unmoved Mover and the Law of Inertia
282   The laws of nature (thermodynamics, physics, etc.) give evidence of the existence of a God, while a change in those laws give evidence of His will.
283   Newcome is one of the earliest writers to have discussed the definition of a miracle as a change in the laws of nature, considering that those laws were discovered only a few decades before she wrote her book.

Now then, as it is rational to expect this evidence of a revelation, we also find that this is the evidence professed by those who believe in the Christian religion. We are then to examine, whether the Christian religion actually has this evidence or not.[284] In this search we ought to be very careful, that if this is the evidence to be expected, we can be certain this is also the evidence that counterfeits will claim to be in possession of.

In order then, to find whether the laws of nature were changed for the declaration of the Christian religion, we are to examine:

1. Whether the asserted facts are *changes* in the laws of nature.[285]
2. Whether there really ever were such facts.[286]

Now, to know whether the asserted facts are really *changes* in the laws of nature, we must explain what we mean by "the laws of nature": the constant, regular, uniform way, by which bodies are determined to motion or rest, and the constant, regular connections between certain causes and effects, are what we call laws of nature.[287] When certain bodies that are at rest move without any external force; or when certain bodies in motion move in a different manner from how they were ever known to move; or when certain known causes produce different effects from what they have been ever known to produce, different from what themselves can produce the next moment, or different from what all others of a like nature can ever produce; then we may justly and properly say that the laws of nature have been *changed*; that something is affected[288] which could not be affected naturally.

If a **miracle** is a *change* in the laws of nature, then in order to know that there is really a miracle, it is necessary first to know the laws of nature because it is impossible to prove the laws of nature are

284   If Christianity is from God, it will have the evidence of miracles. If miracles are a change in the laws of nature, and God is the only one who has the power to do so, then evidence in the form of a miracle is God's stamp of approval on Christianity.
285   Does the supposed event fit the criteria of a miracle, or was it simply an amazing human feat?
286   Is there evidence that the supposed event actually happened in history?
287   See Enquiry 1
288   Effected: brought about.

changed unless we first know what these laws are. Particularly, if we should see something new in the heavens, we could not say that the laws of nature were changed because we do not know all nature or all the laws or powers of bodies.[289] It might be a constant, regular effect of a certain cause, and we simply do not know any better. Time may yet bring us to a knowledge of the cause of this effect (as it has to a knowledge of the cause of eclipses, which have been, and perhaps yet may be in some primitive places ignorantly thought of as miracles).[290] It is evident then, that we must be fully acquainted with the laws of nature before we can say that they have been changed or that this is not a natural connection between cause and effect, that is, that it is a miracle.

Those who carry this matter further, and say we do not know all the laws of nature or the laws and powers of bodies, and that consequently, we cannot say that ever the laws of nature are changed, do not argue justly. It is not necessary that I know all the laws of nature, nor even all the laws and powers of any one body, nor all the effects of certain causes, to be able to say that the laws of nature are changed. There may be many powers in bodies, and even in those which we are most acquainted with, that are yet undiscovered. Also, there may be many effects not known by us, which may proceed from certain causes.

However, all bodies of the same nature will be moved by the same laws, and the same causes will regularly and constantly produce the same effects. But when bodies move contrary to those laws by which all bodies of the same nature move, and contrary to those by which themselves have up to this point moved, and when certain known causes produce new effects in single instances, and effects in which

---

289   We are not omniscient nor omnipresent. We did not create the laws, we only discovered them. Therefore, to us, the laws of nature are descriptive, not prescriptive. They describe *what we see usually* happens, but they do not prescribe *what has to* happen.

290   Before modern technological advances, there were a lot of natural phenomena that we could not explain, simply because we are finite in our experience. Again, we are not omnipresent (everywhere all at once) or omniscient (knowing all) so we have had to guess about things we could not explain. Before the invention of the telescope, we had no idea why phenomena like eclipses happened, so we assumed them to be "miraculous".

naturally there is no connection between the cause and effect,[291] then we may justly say that the laws of nature are changed.

Now having seen what is a change in the laws of nature, and that such a change is the evidence to be expected of a revelation, we proceed to examine the asserted facts, and to see whether there were changes in the laws of nature.

b. An Argument *from* Miracles

We find the claims given in evidence of the Christian religion are of this sort and (allowing the facts) are really changes in the laws of nature. For instance, the laws of nature were changed:

- When the sick, lame, withered, blind, deaf, dumb were cured of all those maladies by the speaking of a word, by the touching of clothes, or by an ointment made of spittle and clay. This is because there was no natural connection between the cause and the effect – as a word, a touch, or spittle and clay will not naturally, by any power of their own, restore health, limbs, or eyes.[292]
- When Peter walked upon the sea, as the sea cannot in its own power support walking persons, and in that instance, it acquired a new power.[293]
- When Jesus raised Lazarus from the dead by the speaking of a word, as a word will not naturally restore life, nor do we know any cause, except the divine power, equal to that effect.[294]
- When Jesus showed Himself alive after His crucifixion.[295]
- When people spoke languages they never learned.[296]

---

291   When a known cause produces a new effect in a special circumstance, or when there is no connection between a known cause and effect, we can identify it as the laws of nature being changed (i.e. a miracle).
292   John 9:6
293   Matthew 14:25-31
294   John 11:40-44
295   Acts 1:3
296   Acts 2:1-12

It is very evident that if there really ever were such facts as these above-mentioned, they were indeed changes in the laws of nature.[297]

We proceed then to the next thing to be enquired after, which is, what is our evidence of the facts?[298] In the first place, then, we are to consider, what is the evidence to be expected? Since a miracle is an interruption in the laws of nature, in order to give evidence it cannot be a frequent change in those laws. The reason being, we know nothing of the laws of nature *a priori*; and our whole knowledge of these laws came from long observation and experience – from seeing the constant, regular, uniform determinations of bodies, the powers of certain causes to produce certain effects, and the inability of such causes to produce certain other effects. Had we not years of experience observing the laws of nature, we could say nothing of a miracle.[299] If interruptions to the laws of nature were frequent, we could not determine what the laws of nature were, and consequently, could not say that these interruptions were miracles.

It is plain then, that it is of the very essence of a **miracle** not to be frequent in order to give evidence of a divine revelation. [300] If they are infrequent, then historical evidence is all the evidence that some persons can ever have that there really were any miracles. The question then is, whether we have this evidence? Whether we have reason to believe that the history of Jesus and His apostles is a true history; that the persons who relate and bear testimony to this history, had full knowledge of what they relate and bear testimony to. Also, that they were not deceived themselves, and were men of integrity, and did not deceive others.

---

297   If the events mentioned in the Bible did actually happen in history, they would be considered miracles because those events have no natural cause and effect connection and would require the assistance of a supernatural Being.

298   Did the miracles recorded in the Bible actually happen? What do the facts say?

299   If we did not know how the laws of nature worked, we could not say they had been changed. However, we do know how they work; therefore, we can determine when a change has taken place.

300   The characteristics of a true miracle include purpose (there had to be a reason for the miracle – to give evidence or a sign, or to confirm that something did indeed come from God) and it has to be special (they cannot be happening all the time, otherwise, they are not a change in the laws of nature, they would be part of the normal workings of the laws.

c. An Argument from Historical Evidence

In the first place, if persons relate and bear testimony to a history of events, and profess themselves present at, eyewitnesses of, and concerned in, those events, and if the professed events are of such a nature as to have lasting, visible effects; then it is demonstrated that those persons have full knowledge whether there ever were or were not such events, and consequently could not possibly be deceived themselves.

Secondly, if the same persons have been never known to falsify or deceive in other instances (if they have no blot in their characters), and to deceive us in this instance is entirely in opposition to their own interests, then we have good reason to think they do not deceive us in it, but are faithfully relating what they have knowledge of.[301]

1.) Eyewitness Accounts

We are then, in the first place, to examine whether the persons who relate and bear testimony to the history of Jesus and His apostles, actually claimed themselves to be present at, eyewitnesses of, and concerned in, the events which they relate and bear testimony to, and whether the professed events had such lasting visible effects that they could not possibly be mistaken concerning them, nor deceived themselves.

Here we find that these persons do actually claim to be themselves present at, concerned in, and eyewitnesses of, the events which they relate and bear testimony to; and the professed events had such lasting, visible effects that they could not possibly have been deceived themselves or mistaken concerning them.

Matthew and John give us a history of events, and claim to be themselves present at, concerned in, and eyewitnesses of, those events; and the professed events had lasting, visible effects; therefore,

---

301   If the disciples were not deceived themselves, and if they were men of character, then we can trust their testimony because they would not be the kind of men who would purposefully deceive others. See Section I footnote on Moral Testimony (Truth, Evidence, and Belief).

it is evident then that these persons must have full knowledge whether there ever were or were not, such events. Also, two other historians, called Mark and Luke, give us the same history. Luke published another history of events (the Book of Acts), in which Peter, James, John, Paul, and other disciples of Jesus, were the main persons present. This account he published while these persons were yet alive, and they could have denied the facts, if they had been false.[302]

Further, even though Matthew, Mark, Luke, and John were the only direct historians of the life and actions of Jesus and His apostles; Peter, James, John, and Jude were constant attenders of Jesus and they themselves refer to the related facts in their several Epistles to different churches. The whole of what they write is grounded upon a supposition of the facts. Therefore, Matthew, John, Peter, James, and Jude claim themselves to be present at, eyewitnesses of, and concerned in, the events which they relate and bear testimony to; and also those who attest to the history of the apostles - Luke, Mark, Peter, James, John, and Paul.

As one part of the Christian history depends on the other part of it (as Jesus' disciples, according to their own account of things, acted by His authority and commission), it is evident that if Jesus and the disciples did not do what the historical accounts said they did, the authors of those historical accounts would be grand deceivers.

As to the common objection of enthusiasm, it can have no weight here, as the things testified by these persons are of such a nature that they could not be possibly deceived concerning them. No person who can deliver to the world a consistent scheme of morality can be so far deceived as to imagine that they make the blind see, the lame walk, the dead come to life, or that they speak in languages

---

302   The gospel accounts were published while people who were eyewitnesses were still alive. Therefore, if the accounts were not true, they would have said something. William Lane Craig writes that, "The writings of the Greek historian Herodotus enable us to test the rate at which a legend accumulates; the tests show that even the span of two generations is too short to allow legendary tendencies to wipe out the hard core of historical fact," (W. Craig, *The Son Rises*, Wipf & Stock Pub: 2001, p.101).

which they never learned, if there were no such facts.[303]

It is evident then that the persons who relate and bear testimony to the history of Jesus and His apostles had full knowledge whether there ever were or were not such facts as they relate and bear testimony to, and consequently were not deceived themselves.

2.) Moral Testimony

The next thing then to be enquired after, is secondly, if they were ever known to falsify or deceive in any one instance; and if it was contrary to their interest to deceive.[304]

In the first place, they were never known to falsify or deceive in any instance, they had no blot in their characters, and their very worst enemies could not reproach them with immorality.

Secondly, it was against their interest to deceive. To deceive was contrary to their interest in this world because persecution and death were the consequences of the deception, if it was one.[305] Also, it was contrary to all future prospects because it is not possible for human nature to have such absurd notions of God, that his favor is to be gained by inventing a lie, and continuing in it.[306] Possibly, persons may have lied for God (that is, they may have supported a false cause

---

303   The sound, consistent reputations of the individual disciples/eyewitnesses do not lend themselves to the theory that the disciples would have been so passionate or enthused that they would have imagined the acts they perpetrated (ex. making the blind see, the lame walk, the dead come to life, or that they speak in languages which they never learned).

304   If they did not imagine the events, the second question to answer is whether or not the authors of the Gospel accounts were ever known to purposefully deceive someone, or if lying about the accounts would actually benefit them or not (i.e. did they have a reason to lie?)

305   There was no reason for the authors/disciples/eyewitnesses to lie. The consequence for preaching that Jesus was God, and that He and His followers performed miracles, was torture and death! Their lives would have been much easier if it had all been made up and they confirmed it to be so. They instead preached over and over that everything that was recorded was in fact true, and they paid the price for it.

306   It would be detrimental to their cause of spreading Christianity to lie about its origins. Who wants to follow a God that favors those who lie? No one would have trusted them and the church would never have grown. It was because of who the disciples/authors/eyewitnesses were that people trusted Jesus and caused the new religion of Christianity spread like wildfire.

which they thought to be His), but still in that case they genuinely thought it was His cause, because nobody has been so absurd as to imagine that the favor of God is to be gained by inventing a lie concerning Him, or by asserting it to be His cause if they certainly know it is not His cause because that is not lying for Him, but is against His character and is in opposition to Him.

Some say that though it is true the disciples acted against worldly interest, they believed that Jesus, the ringleader of this sect, planned to make Himself a King, and after His death, His disciples acted upon the same worldly motives. To this I answer, it nowhere appears that Jesus planned to make Himself a King, on the contrary, He constantly disclaimed whatever tended that way and declared His kingdom was not of this world. As for His disciples, whatever notion they at first might have of worldly advancement, the repeated declarations of their Master, His ignominious death and sufferings, and their own cruel treatment in the world, would have made them fully aware of what they were to expect on Earth, and that bonds, persecution, hatred of all men, and death, were to be the only rewards they were to expect in this world. [307]

Again, what view of worldly advancement had Paul – who was a learned and ingenious man, with a good reputation in his own nation, and who well knew what fate the spreaders of Christianity were to expect because of the part he himself had played in it?[308]

To put this matter out of question, whatever prospect of worldly interest persons may have living, they can have none of them when they are dying, and these persons sealed their testimony with their blood, and laid down their lives to confirm the truth of what they delivered.

3.) No One Dies for a Lie they know to be False

---

307   Mark 8:31-38, 10:45, Philippians 2:5-8, Luke 22:24-30, Matthew 17:22-23, John 15:18, 1 John 3:13.

308   One of the main problems with the argument that the disciples followed Jesus out of some idea of worldly gain is the issue of Paul the apostle. Paul had persecuted the Christians and was well-respected in his community. Converting to Christianity would be the opposite of worldly gain for him and he knew it. (See Philippians 1:21 and Galatians 2:20)

Now the question is, what could make them behave after this manner? Our understanding tells us that every effect must have a necessary cause, and a cause suited to the effect. Let them then tell us what is the necessary cause to this effect, and what could be the motive to so many persons to suffer not only persecution, but also death, for the sake of something they know to be false. In this case, they would be giving up life on Earth, and if they have a thought of Heaven, they would give it up too.[309] They would be choosing pain and renouncing pleasure, which is not fit for sensible beings.[310]

If they believed in God and an afterlife, then why would they deny His favor in exchange for nothing, or why they would knowingly and purposely choose to purchase misery in the next world, along with misery in this present one, by lying?

If it is said that they were Atheistic persons, and did not believe in God, and consequently had no future prospects; then I ask, what made them be willing to give up this world (if this is all they believe there is)?

If it is also objected, that after they had once published their story (whatever was their motive of doing it), that pride made them stick to it no matter what; I answer: when we argue that a certain behavior is the effect of pride, we need to be able to show that pride may have such an effect or give examples where there really has been such pride in the world (where someone would stick to lie in the face of death if they knew it to be false). But if we can do neither of these (as most certainly in the present case we cannot), then we cannot argue that the behavior of these persons was the effect of pride.

It is true that many persons have laid down their lives for erroneous opinions, but then it must be remembered, that they actually believed the error was the truth.[311] We find no instances where several persons have agreed to lay down their lives to maintain a known

---

309   If they die because they stick to the falsehood (if it is one) then they not only give up Earth, but Heaven too, because they are grand deceivers and God would not abide lying in His name.

310   No person of sound mind would lie, knowing pain would come, if they knew it was in fact a lie.

311   People have died for false causes before, but they sincerely thought that it was the truth. They were sincerely wrong and died because of it. However, no one dies for something they know to be false.

lie and falsehood, without any prospect of interest or gratification to themselves. There are criminals who will die with a lie in their mouth, but it is in the hopes of saving their lives, their reputations, or estates – they would not continue in a lie unless they had a motive for it.

What yet strengthens the evidence that the disciples were not deceivers is the great number of them. If it is irrational to think that one person would lay down his life to maintain a known falsehood, it is yet more irrational to think that many persons should agree to do it. Especially considering the nature of mankind – their desire for life, aversion to pain, and love of pleasure – it demonstrates that these persons did not die to maintain a known lie.[312]

To conclude, no higher evidence can be given that any persons are persons of integrity, and do not deceive us, then we have of those relate and bear testimony to the history of Jesus and His apostles. They are men of integrity and do not deceive us. Therefore, we cannot reasonably accept any other history, and yet reject the history which they delivered to us.[313]

As to the point whether those who relate and bear testimony to the history of Jesus and His apostles did give this evidence of their integrity, and lay down their lives for the sake of what they delivered – this is out of question with all. The sufferings and death of the founders of Christianity was so open and public, so well-attested, and suffered so many reproaches yet stands in so many records, that the greatest antagonists of this religion have not been fool-hardy enough to deny it. It can no more be doubted that the founders of Christianity suffered and died for Christianity than it can be doubted whether there were such emperors as Tiberius, Nero, Trajan, etc. in whose times they suffered and died.

We have then the highest evidence the nature of proposition will admit, that the persons who relate and bear testimony to the history

---

312   In the end, self-preservation would have won out and the deceivers would have recanted if it were all a great lie.

313   We cannot expect higher evidence than other written historical accounts to determine the truthfulness of the Gospels. If we reject the historicity of the Gospel accounts, and their evidence, we must reject everything else as well, because the evidence we have for them is the highest that can be expected.

of Jesus and His apostles, had full knowledge of what they relate and bear testimony to, and were not deceived themselves; and also that they were men of integrity, and did not deceive others. Then it follows that the history which they delivered ought to be received as a true one.

4.) The Growth of the Early Church

Further, we have not only the testimony of these persons for the truth of the facts, but we have likewise other collateral evidence and circumstances. Those who dispute the events, and claim that they were not true miracles, are called on to acknowledge the facts. Those who ascribe them to an evil power, also need to acknowledge the facts; and here then is the testimony of enemies.

Again, the professed facts were of such a nature, and had such lasting visible effects, that everybody who lived at the time when they were claimed to be done, had the opportunity to inform themselves concerning the truth of them. Thus the most common layperson, if he had not himself been present, might easily have informed himself whether Jesus had actually opened the eyes of the blind or raised Lazarus from the dead; and whether Peter and John had made a cripple walk. They had the testimony of a thousand people, if they had not had that of their own eyes, that one had been blind, another lame; and could themselves examine how far these cures had worked, or if Lazarus had been dead and was then alive.

If a **miracle** is to be an evidence to us that the laws of nature were changed in instances where we have a full knowledge of the laws of nature, lies regarding them will be discovered. Simply because the most illiterate person knows the laws and powers of nature, particularly, he knows that spittle and clay will not open the eyes of the blind, nor will the speaking of a word raise the dead to life, so he has it in his powers to examine whether it was a miracle or not.

Also, the great number of converts to Christianity in the time of the apostles is evidence of the facts. That there were a vast number of these early converts is disputed by none, and it is incredible that so many persons should embark in a religion contrary to all worldly interest, if they had not thoroughly examined the facts on which this religion was founded. True, vast numbers of converts have been made to false religions, but with this difference from the present case: these religions had the support of worldly power, and the embracing of them suited worldly interest. But there are no instances where a vast number of persons embarked in a religion contrary to both these – a religion which proposed no other worldly choice to its followers besides enslavement, whipping, and death and a religion that gave no relief from persecution, and which stood charged with this frightful motto, "Take up your cross and follow me."[314] It could be only the positive evidence of this religion being a revelation from God that made so many persons engage in it under such disadvantageous circumstances.

5.) No Deception Could Be Found

Again, there are no instances of lies or deception found with regard to the claimed events, and that is evidence on the side of the facts. We are not saying, however, that just because a lie went undiscovered, it is evidence that there wasn't one; but when many persons are invested in determining if there was a deception, and they don't find any, it is a probable argument that there is none to find.[315]

The Jews at the time were barely clinging to their Law and modes of worship (which everyday were losing ground by the increase of Christianity), and if the new converts had discovered a fraud in Christianity it would have restored the traditional Jewish religion to the world. Also, the pagans of the time were utter enemies to the setting up of what they called "new gods". All would have been endeavoring to detect deception as they were looking for ways to discredit Christianity. One argument for the facts then is that they stood the examination of a vast number of persons, whose interest it was in to detect them.

---

314   Matthew 16:24
315   Many, many people have not wanted Christianity to be true, and have tried to prove the authors of the Gospels were lying, yet none have succeeded. 2000 years later, there are over two billion people in the world that consider themselves Christian, which would not be the case if someone had definitively proved the NT Gospels false.

Lastly, considering the selfish and worldly views of all imposters, and the corrupted state of natural religion at the time when the Gospel was delivered, it seems utterly impossible that this Gospel should come from an imposter.[316]

This is certain: imposters have always worldly and selfish views when they attempt to impose them on mankind, and the particular motives for the deceptions of every imposter who has yet appeared in the world may be traced out *a posteriori* from his religion.[317] But from the religion given us by Jesus and His apostles, no worldly or selfish views are to be traced out in its founders. All are agreeable to the divine attributes and from the end of this religion (its doctrine and precepts), we come to the conclusion that it is divine wisdom and goodness, as only a Cause with the attributes of love, goodness, and justice could have produced or influenced an effect like Christianity.

Also, when we consider how illiterate the disciples were; how low their station in the world; and their lack of opportunities to deceive; this argument will receive further weight. Again, a consideration of the corrupted state of natural religion at the time when the Gospel was delivered, gives us further reason to believe that this Gospel came from God.[318] The teachers amongst the Jews had very much corrupted natural religion by their traditions. They laid a great stress on the ceremonials of the Law, and neglected that for which alone the ceremonials were instituted. They sacrificed to God instead of simply performing their natural duty to their parents, and made punctual payments of tithes in trifles, to excuse their neglect of the weightier matters of the Law like judgment, justice, and mercy. Consider the state of the Jews, when Jesus appeared and read the Sermon on the

---

316   The teachings of Jesus in the Gospels are the opposite of self-seeking. Jesus talked about denying oneself, and sacrifice. Men who had worldly ambition and were the self-seeking sort that tended to lie would not have produced such a doctrine.

317   We can figure out the motives a religion's founder has once it has been established. Their doctrines and teachings are usually a window into the thoughts and intents of their heart. Christianity's motives are the opposite of worldly and selfish.

318   At the time Christianity started, there was nothing like it. Judaism had imposed many rules and traditions on its adherents, proclaiming a religion of works-based faith, and the Pagan Roman gods were the opposite of the moral standard Jesus set for His followers. Christianity would not have naturally come out of that culture, therefore it had to come from somewhere outside of this environment.

Mount, and then judge whether this was the performance of a man who had all His teaching from the Scribes and Pharisees.[319]

6.) The Highest Quality of Historical Evidence

We have then, the highest historical evidence, which is all the evidence we possibly can have in the present case, of the truth of the professed facts; and we must, if we are consistent with ourselves, either receive this evidence, and acknowledge the facts, or receive no historical evidence, and acknowledge no facts, but what we ourselves are eyewitnesses of.

I now put the Christian historical evidence equal with other histories, which we everyday accept as true ones, but we may fairly carry the argument further and say, that we have no history like Christianity, which has such testimony, which was delivered and witnessed by so many persons, present at, and concerned in the events which they recorded and bear testimony to where the historians and witnesses gave such evidences of their integrity; and which is also confirmed by so many collateral evidences.[320]

---

319   With the state of the Jewish religion at the time, there is no way Jesus could have come up with the doctrine laid out in the Sermon on the Mount if all he knew was the influence and teaching of the local Scribes and Pharisees. They hated Him because what He taught was the opposite of what they taught in their synagogues.

320   Christianity has an embarrassment of riches when it comes to historical evidence. There is earlier and better quality and quantity manuscript evidence than any other religion in the world – almost 25,000 manuscripts catalogued at this point. Specifically, there are 5700+ Greek NT manuscripts, with only a gap of 30-300 years from the original events to the time they were recorded. The only other ancient manuscript that comes close is Homer's *Iliad* with 643 manuscripts with a 500-year gap, yet no one even questions that Homer wrote it when he is recorded to.

Section X

A.OBJECTION:
Jesus is an Imposter

So far then the Christian religion is correct as to the matter which it contains, and as to the manner in which its message is delivered; it at present stands worthy of God and is supported by the best historical evidence; but still we find objections against it, which will now be considered.

First, it is objected that Jesus claims to be prophesied of in the Jewish Books. He says the Scriptures testify of Him,[321] that Moses wrote of Him,[322] and if the Jews had believed Moses, they would have believed in Him, for he wrote of Him. However, since it does not appear that the Scriptures testify of Him, or that Moses wrote of Him, He is an imposter.

We agree with the objector that Jesus claims to be prophesied of in the Jewish Books and that if it appears that these Books do not foretell Him, He is not to be received as a teacher from God. We proceed then to examine this point: whether He is really foretold in the Jewish Books or not; and in order to, we must consider the nature and evidence of prophecy.

1. The Nature and Evidence of Prophecy

When the divine Being, by the mouth of a person, foretells future events, the foretold events are called **prophecies**, and the person who foretells them, a **Prophet**.

---

321   John 5:39
322   John 5:46

If the divine Being instructs a person to foretell future events (to prophesy), it is for some good end for either the generation at the time the prophecies are given, or for the one later when they are destined to be fulfilled.

If prophecies are designed for the generation at the time when they are given, then the evidence of them must be there as well, as God must give His people assurance that what is spoken shall surely come to pass. For example, if God plans to comfort a nation in distress or sorrow by foretelling future ease and deliverance to them or their descendants, then He will give that nation assurance that the things promised or foretold shall certainly come to pass.

If prophecies are designed for the generation later when they are destined to be fulfilled, then the evidence of them must be shown at their completion and the event must align with the previously recorded accounts of it. This would be evidence that those written accounts came from God, and that it was by Him that the event was foretold.

However, just because all future events can only be known or foretold by God, it does not mean that *all* events, which happen to align with a previously recorded account of them, mean those written accounts are automatically prophecies. Many persons who are good at discerning causes and effects could accurately guess future events (though they may not be completely certain, because there are future contingencies which no man can foresee) and what they foretell frequently comes to pass.

Also the previously recorded account of events, when it is in human power to fulfill them, could be a self-fulfilling prophecy. They may simply happen because people believe that they are prophecies. The actions of men can be greatly affected by their imagination and a belief that a thing will arrive, and often, they have the means to make it so.

Lastly, they may come to pass from a desire to convince people they are prophecies, and persons may fulfill them because people would think they are a prophet from God.[323] So, while there are instances in

---

323   There are instances where something foretold will come to pass, and it is not always evidence that a message has come from God. Sometimes, events will come to pass due to coincidence, people force it to come to pass because they believe it to be from God, or will cause it to come to pass simply due to self-fulfilling prophecy. The point is that the prophecies that are in the Scriptures, for the most part, required supernatural assistance.

which an event agreeing with a previously recorded account does *not* automatically mean that it came from God, in many others *it does,* particularly in the following cases:

b. An Argument for Prophecy from Miracles

Premise 1: The event foretold does not depend on natural causes to happen

Premise 2: The event comes to pass contrary to the normal course of nature

Premise 3: No being can change the laws of nature but the Lord of it

Premise 4: No being can foretell these changes but Him

Conclusion: Therefore, an event that requires a change in the laws of nature in order to come to pass has the highest evidence of prophecy.[324]

b. An Argument for Prophecy from Time

Premise 1: The event foretold depends on natural causes

Premise 2: It is foretold long before it arrives

Premise 3: It is not in human power with a knowledge of the previously recorded account to bring it to pass;

Premise 4: No Being but God can foresee a train of events to come and what will happen according to the course of nature.

Conclusion: Therefore, that previously recorded account is to be looked upon as a prophecy.[325]

---

324   The first criteria of a true prophecy is if it was fulfilled through a miracle (i.e. a change in the laws of nature), because then we know it came from God, since He is the only one who can perform miracles.

325   The second criteria of true prophecy is (if it can come to pass without a miracle) whether or not it was predicted long enough before the passing of the event that it was not humanly possible to predict apart from supernatural knowledge.

c. An Argument for Prophecy
from Crcumstance

Premise 1: The foretold events depend on natural causes.

Premise 2: It is in human power to fulfill them

Premise 3: The time for those events is limited

Premise 4: The persons who fulfill them are ignorant of them

Premise 5: Future times, seasons, and the order of events
to come, are only known to Him who appointed
successions of events and allotted to everything
that exists its own duration and particular
place in the succession of beings or things

Conclusion: The foretelling of such events is to be received
as prophecy.[326]

d. An Argument for Prophecy
from Concurring Events

Premise 1: Several events are foretold which concur and
suit with each other in order to some visible
end or design

Premise 2: Only God who framed and fitted beings and
things to each other, in order to the preservation
or happiness of the whole system of created
beings, can foretell concurring events

Conclusion: The foretelling of such events must be
acknowledged to be prophecy. [327]

Now, having a little considered the nature and evidence of
prophecy, and given some instances where the events give evidence

---

326   The third criteria of a miracle is if it could happen without a miracle, and it is
possible for a human to predict it, but has to happen within a specific time period that
is humanly impossible to control, or if the person fulfilling them does not know about
it ahead of time (ex. Isaiah prophesying that King Cyrus would let the Jews go back to
Israel).

327   The last criteria of a true prophecy that Newcome discusses is if the prophetic event
must occur in a specific succession or chain of events, in order for it to come to pass, it
must be the work of a Being who can order events in such a way as to guarantee their
occurrence in that specific manner.

that the previously recorded account of them came from God, we proceed to see whether Jesus validated His claim, and fulfilled prophecies.

2. Did Jesus Claim to Fulfill Prophecies?

We are to observe that, if prophecy may be delivered for the generation when it is given, as well as for that generation when it shall be fulfilled, it follows that if Jesus only fulfilled prophecies in the Jewish Books, there would be no evidence for Him from their completion, but because He makes claims to Gentiles as well as Jews, He ought to be received by both as that person He claimed to be.

Technically, He had the evidence of miracle and needed no other. However, He must fulfill the prophecies in the Jewish Books because He claimed such. If He fulfills such prophecies, and His evidence from His miracles is in full force, then He ought to be received as a teacher, from God, by all men.

If He fulfills the prophecies in the Jewish Books, He has the evidence of prophecy because the Jews acknowledge that these previously recorded accounts came from God. These prophecies must belong to the person who fulfills them, so if the Jews acknowledge they are prophecies from God, then they also must acknowledge that the person who fulfills them is the One foretold by God.

If He fulfilled the prophecies (and due to their completion showed that they came from God), then to all men He has the evidence of prophecy. Also, if the completing of that which was foretold concerning Him requires supernatural power, then has He the highest evidence of prophecy.[328]

Now, having given some instances in which Jesus must be allowed to validate His claim, we proceed to examine whether He does really validate it; that is, we proceed to an examination of the Jewish Books, and as He particularly claims to be foretold by Moses, it will be Moses we will examine in the first place.

---

328   If Jesus did indeed perform miracles (as only the Creator can do), if He fulfilled the prophecies that the Jews considered divine (meaning the fulfillment must come from God), and He fulfilled the prophecies in a supernatural way, then He has the highest evidence of prophecy to support His claim that He is the Messiah.

In *Deuteronomy 18:15*, Moses declares that a Prophet will arise with these characteristics:

> *The Lord your God will raise up for you a prophet like me*
> *from among you, from your brothers.*

Deuteronomy 18:18 - He should have this office, to be in the place of God, and speak the words of His mouth:

> *I will put my words in his mouth, and he shall speak*
> *to them all that I command him.*

Deuteronomy 18:19 - A punishment should accompany not listening to Him:

> *And whoever will not listen to my words that he shall speak*
> *in my name, I myself will require it of him.*

Deuteronomy 18:22 - The evidence given to Him whereby the people should know that what He spoke was really the Words of God, should be this – speaking in the name of the Lord, and having the thing which He speaks follow and come to pass:

> *When a prophet speaks in the name of the Lord, if the word*
> *does not come to pass or come true, that is a word that*
> *the Lord has not spoken.*

We are to observe concerning this Prophet described here by Moses:

    a. He was to deliver something of great importance called "the words of God's mouth", and there was a penalty for not listening to it.

    b. A particular evidence was to be given to Him.

    c. The particular evidence to be given to Him was to be given for a specific purpose – so that the people should know that what had been delivered to them by this Prophet was really the words of God.[329]

---

329   Deut. 18:21

d. Something new, something which had not been given before, was to be delivered by this Prophet. It follows then, that the Prophet described by Moses could not simply be some soothsayer, fortuneteller, or saint that you pray to that helps you find your lost items. If it were, God would not have given the warning that punishment would come for those who do not listen. God is not bothered by those who listen to the babblings of those who are false, however, He is bothered when people do not listen to the words of His Son.

Thus, when the people were frightened at the manner in which God had delivered the Law to Moses and said,

Let me not hear again the voice of the Lord my God, neither let me see this great fire anymore, lest I die.[330]

God answered,

"I approve their request.[331] *When I again deliver new commands unto the people, I will speak unto them in the Person of a man like you. Whoever does not listen to the words of this Prophet as if they are the words of God, I will punish his disbelief. Any imposter who shall presume to give laws in my Name without my commission, or one who shall draw my people into idolatry, shall be put to death..."* You will know an imposter if God does not bear him witness by some extraordinary sign.

Now then, the thing which was to follow or come to pass was some extraordinary sign, something **miraculous**; otherwise the Prophet, which was to be listened to, could not have been distinguished from an imposter, and if the thing which was to come to pass could be created by human power, an imposter could pass for

---

330   Deut. 18:16, Exodus 20:19
331   Deut. 18:17, etc.

the Prophet.[332]

It is evident then that the Prophet, who should be listened to in all that He should deliver, was to have the evidence of **miracles**, the same evidence which Moses had, whom it promised He would resemble.

Now then, we are to see, whether Moses' characteristics of a Prophet, and the promised evidence align in Jesus, and whether we have reason to think him to be the Prophet whom Moses describes:

He is raised up from among his brethren.

He resembles Moses in the working of miracles.

He delivered a doctrine worthy of God and suitable to His nature. And,

He spoke in the Name of the Lord, and the things which He spoke followed and came to pass;

He worked miracles.

What then keeps Jesus from being acknowledged as the Prophet foretold by Moses?[333] See His own claim and argument:

> *The works that I do bear witness of me that the Father has sent me.[334] The Father that sent me, bears witness of me.[335] The works that I do in my Father's name, they bear witness of me.[336] If I do not the works of my Father, believe me not.[337] But if I do, though you believe not me, believe the works, that you may know and that believe that the Father is in me, and*

---

332   There had to be something that proved the Prophet was who He says He was (miracles), otherwise the people would not know whether He was from God or an imposter. As mentioned before, miracles have purpose and in Jesus' case it was to show that He was indeed the Son of God.

333   Why do people not believe that Jesus is the Prophet spoken of by Moses?

334   John 5:36

335   John 8:18

336   John 10:25

337   John 10:37-38

I in him. Believe me for the very works sake.[338] *If I
had not done among them the works which no other
man did, they had not had sin.*[339] (If my miracles,
my evidence from God, had not been clearer, more
convincing than any other man's, who has ever yet
appeared in the world, their infidelity had not been
so unpardonable.) Again, *do not think that I will
accuse you; there is one that accuses you, even Moses
in whom you trust; for had you believed Moses, you
would have believed me, etc.*[340]

Here then, Jesus is the very Prophet Moses describes, and in His
miracles is the very evidence Moses promised. Both character and
attestation fulfilled in every point and circumstance, and He has a
right to be acknowledged as that Prophet which Moses foretold.

We see, not only did Jesus apply this prophecy to Himself, but
Peter[341] and Stephen[342] also applied it to Him, and argued with the
Jews that it was fulfilled.

If it should be said, false prophets can do signs and wonders or
work miracles (otherwise the Jews would not have been cautioned
not to be deceived by such means), and therefore, whatever can be a
possible character of a false prophet cannot be the evidence of a true
one.

I answer: false prophets can never work miracles and no being
can change the laws of nature without the consent of the Lord of it.
God cannot consent to the changing of His laws to give evidence to
falsehood, for that would be to act in opposition to Himself.[343]

---

338   John 14:11
339   John 15:22-24; If Jesus had never revealed Himself to them, they would not be held
accountable for not listening to him, but as verse 22 says, they now have no excuse.
340   John 5:45-46
341   Acts 3:22
342   Acts 7:37
343   God could not contradict His character of truth and utilize a miracle to give
evidence of a lie.

Imposters may, to some people, *appear* to work miracles, as they may, by a knowledge of certain powers of nature of which the common masses are ignorant, *seem* to them to do things that are supernatural; and on that account there is no need of caution against them.[344]

If it is argued that these words of Moses are not applicable to Jesus only, but to all other prophets who work miracles as well, I answer- they are in *all* parts only applicable to Jesus, as evidenced not only in the Jewish history, but also from the confession of one of their own prophets in the time of Ezra,[345] and since then no person has appeared like unto Moses.

However granting the thing, granting that these words could be applicable to other persons besides Jesus, it would still not lessen the evidence which they give Him. Suppose God Almighty should distinguish a succession of persons from the rest of mankind by particular characteristics, and foretell them by these characteristics, it would not lessen the evidence of any particular person amongst them that others were foretold also. When a person appears, and fulfills previously recorded accounts which only could be foretold by God, we are to receive him as witnessed by prophecy; and if another appears and fulfills the same prophecies, we are to receive him also as foretold by God, and our receiving him will not lessen the evidence of the first, unless God cannot give two persons equal powers. It will also not lessen the evidence which they give Jesus, and if He works miracles and teaches a doctrine worthy of God, He has a right to be received as foretold by Moses.

If it is said that those words of Moses are not prophecy at all, but are only the criteria to determine a Prophet from an imposter; I answer: they cannot be only such criteria, for they directly foretell the appearance of a specific Person:

---

344   This knowledge that the common masses are ignorant of may be a scientific or pseudo-scientific knowledge. It could even be some sort of magic trick or sleight of hand that makes what the imposter is doing appear supernatural. Newcome's original footnote referred to *Traité sur les Miracles* by Mr. Jacques Serces, 1729. This French book's full title in English is *A Treaty on Miracles in which we prove that the Devil can not do it to confirm Error*, which is self-explanatory.

345   Deut. 34:10

And the Lord said unto me, they have well spoken that which they have spoken. I will raise them up a Prophet like unto thee, and I will put my words into His mouth, and He shall speak unto them all that I command Him, etc.[346]

We find then upon an examination of Jewish Books that Jesus fulfills prophecy, and also that He has the highest evidence of it. He fulfills previously recorded accounts, which could only be given by the Lord of nature.

We could go on to show that Jesus not only fulfills this prophecy of Moses, but also many others in the Jewish Books, and that there are many descriptions in these Books of a person who was to appear and be a blessing to mankind, with several circumstances which were to attend His appearance, and also the time of it, which were fulfilled in Jesus, and at His appearance. These I will speak of afterwards, as it is evident from this prophecy alone that Jesus has made out His claim, and has a right to be received as a Prophet foretold by God.

B. OBJECTION:
Jesus is not the Messiah

Second, it is objected that Jesus also claims to be the Messiah of the Jews, but He is not this person and therefore an imposter.

I answer, if Jesus has a right to be received as the Prophet foretold by Moses, then has He the right to be received as the Messiah of the Jews, since that Prophet has a right to be listened to in whatever message He should deliver, and Jesus declares Himself to be the Messiah.[347]

However, the Jews say that the Messiah was to appear under different characteristics than those which Jesus appeared, so it would

---

346   Deut. 18:17-18
347   John 4:26. If Jesus is accepted as a true prophet by the Jews, and His message is that He is the Messiah, then it should be automatically accepted as being from God.

follow that Jesus is not the Messiah. Let the burden of proof be on him to give clear and express characteristics of a Messiah in the Jewish Books and then show that these do not belong to Jesus. Otherwise, we cannot accept the objection and measure doubtful interpretations and uncertain meanings against a testimony supported by both miracle and prophecy.[348] Upon an examination of the Jewish Scriptures, we find that the Jews can do no such thing; on the contrary, several acknowledged characteristics of the Messiah are found in Jesus.

1. Jesus Fulfilled Messianic Prophecies

Particularly, He is of the *tribe, family,* and *town,* of which the Jews confess that the Messiah was to be born; and He appeared at a *time* when they themselves expected Him; and during a *period* in which, unless their own Books are false, He must have appeared, and will be seen afterwards.

The Jews will object that, according to the Scriptures, the Messiah was to be a temporal Prince, and to reign visibly over the Jews. Let then the Jews produce their evidence for such an assertion. Let them produce plain and express testimony out of their own books that the Messiah was to be a temporal Prince, and at his first appearance on Earth He was to reign visibly over the Jews. The Jews cannot do this, nor is there any such testimony concerning the Messiah in the books which speak of Him. On the contrary, if we search the Jewish Books we shall find that those very texts (on which the Jews ground their expectation of a temporal Messiah) relate only to a spiritual Messiah, such a one as Jesus claimed to be. And if the Jews say, that the following texts (and others of the same nature), are not the grounds on which they expect a temporal Messiah, they must produce those that are and show that what they produce really do relate to the Messiah, and cannot possibly belong to any other person.

---

348   If someone can show what the written accounts say about the Messiah from the Jewish Scriptures and then show that Jesus did not fulfill them, then yes, it would be conceded that Jesus is not the Messiah. Otherwise, we should trust the evidence of miracles (a sign of God's approval) and fulfilled prophecy (a sign that His words are God's).

In that Day shall the Branch of the Lord be beautiful and glorious.[349]

For unto us a Child is born, unto us a Son is given; and the government will be upon His shoulder. His name will be called Wonderful, Counselor, Mighty God, Everlasting Father, Prince of Peace. Of the increase of His government and peace there will be no end, upon the throne of David and over His kingdom, to order it and establish it with judgment and justice from that time forward, even forever. The zeal of the Lord of hosts will perform this.[350]

"But you, Bethlehem Ephrathah, though you are little among the thousands of Judah, yet out of you shall come forth to Me the One to be Ruler in Israel, whose goings forth are from old, from everlasting."[351]

There shall come forth a Rod from the stem of Jesse, and a Branch shall grow out of his roots. The Spirit of the Lord shall rest upon Him, The Spirit of wisdom and understanding, The Spirit of counsel and might, The Spirit of knowledge and of the fear of the Lord. His delight is in the fear of the Lord, and He shall not judge by the sight of His eyes, nor decide by the hearing of His ears; But with righteousness He shall judge the poor, and decide with equity for the meek of the earth; He shall strike the earth with the rod of His mouth, and with the breath of His lips He shall slay the wicked. Righteousness shall be the belt of His loins, and faithfulness the belt of His waist.[352]

In mercy the throne will be established; and One will sit on it in truth, in the tabernacle of David, judging

---

349   Isaiah 4:2
350   Is. 9:6-7
351   Micah 5:2
352   Isaiah 11:1-5

and seeking justice and hastening righteousness.[353]

Behold, a king will reign in righteousness, etc.[354]

'Behold, the days are coming,' says the Lord, 'That I will raise to David a Branch of righteousness; a King shall reign and prosper, and execute judgment and righteousness in the earth. In His days Judah will be saved, and Israel will dwell safely; now this is His name by which He will be called: THE LORD OUR RIGHTEOUSNESS.[355]

'Behold! My Servant whom I uphold, My Elect One in whom My soul delights! I have put My Spirit upon Him; He will bring forth justice to the Gentiles. He will not cry out, nor raise His voice, nor cause His voice to be heard in the street. A bruised reed He will not break, and smoking flax He will not quench; He will bring forth justice for truth. He will not fail nor be discouraged, Till He has established justice in the earth; and the coastlands shall wait for His law.' Thus says God the Lord, Who created the heavens and stretched them out, Who spread forth the earth and that which comes from it, Who gives breath to the people on it, And spirit to those who walk on it: 'I, the Lord, have called You in righteousness, And will hold Your hand; I will keep You and give You as a covenant to the people, As a light to the Gentiles, To open blind eyes, To bring out prisoners from the prison, Those who sit in darkness from the prison house. I am the Lord, that is My name; And My glory I will not give to another, Nor My praise to carved images.'[356]

353   Is. 16:5
354   Is. 32:1
355   Jeremiah 23:5-6
356   Isaiah 42:1-8

Behold, My Servant shall deal prudently; He shall be exalted and extolled and be very high. Just as many were astonished at you, So His visage was marred more than any man, and His form more than the sons of men; so shall He sprinkle many nations. Kings shall shut their mouths at Him; for what had not been told them they shall see, and what they had not heard they shall consider.[357]

'I was watching in the night visions, and behold, One like the Son of Man, coming with the clouds of heaven! He came to the Ancient of Days, and they brought Him near before Him. Then to Him was given dominion and glory and a kingdom, that all peoples, nations, and languages should serve Him. His dominion is an everlasting dominion, which shall not pass away, and His kingdom the one which shall not be destroyed.'[358]

'Rejoice greatly, O daughter of Zion! Shout, O daughter of Jerusalem! Behold, your King is coming to you; He is just and having salvation, lowly and riding on a donkey – a colt, the foal of a donkey.'[359]

'Sing and rejoice, O daughter of Zion! For behold, I am coming and I will dwell in your midst,' says the Lord. 'Many nations shall be joined to the Lord in that day, and they shall become My people. And I will dwell in your midst. Then you will know that the Lord of hosts has sent Me to you. And the Lord will take possession of Judah as His inheritance in the Holy Land, and will again choose Jerusalem.'[360]

357   Is. 52:13-15
358   Daniel 7:13-14
359   Zechariah 9:9
360   Zech. 2:10-12

And the Lord shall be King over all the earth. In that day it shall be – 'The Lord is one,' and His name one.[361]

'And in that day there shall be a Root of Jesse, Who shall stand as a banner to the people; For the Gentiles shall seek Him, And His resting place shall be glorious.' [362]

And He will destroy on this mountain the surface of the covering cast over all people, and the veil that is spread over all nations. He will swallow up death forever in victory...[363]

Say to those who are fearful-hearted, 'Be strong, do not fear! Behold, your God will come with vengeance, with the recompense of God; He will come and save you.' Then the eyes of the blind shall be opened, and the ears of the deaf shall be unstopped. Then the lame shall leap like a deer, and the tongue of the dumb, sing. For waters shall burst forth in the wilderness, and streams in the desert.[364]

'The glory of the Lord shall be revealed, and all flesh shall see it together; for the mouth of the Lord has spoken.' [365]

The Gentiles shall come to your light, and kings to the brightness of your rising.[366]

I will also give You as a light to the Gentiles, that You should be My salvation to the ends of the earth.[367]

361   Zech. 14:9
362   Isaiah 11:10
363   Is. 25:7-8
364   Isaiah 35:4-6
365   Is. 40:5
366   Is. 60:3
367   Is. 49:6

'The Spirit of the Lord God is upon Me, because the Lord has anointed Me to preach good tidings to the poor; He has sent Me to heal the brokenhearted, to proclaim liberty to the captives, and the opening of the prison to those who are bound...' [368]

'Seventy weeks are determined for your people and for your holy city, to finish the transgression, to make an end of sins, to make reconciliation for iniquity, to bring in everlasting righteousness, to seal up vision and prophecy, and to anoint the Most Holy.' [369]

And in the days of these kings the God of heaven will set up a kingdom, which shall never be destroyed; and the kingdom shall not be left to other people; it shall break in pieces and consume all these kingdoms, and it shall stand forever. [370]

So the Lord will reign over them in Mount Zion from now on, even forever. [371]

All your children shall be taught by the Lord, and great shall be the peace of your children. [372]

Now we say that either these characteristics and circumstances of a King and Kingdom (along with others of a like nature) are the grounds on which the Jews found their expectation of a temporal Messiah, or they are not. If they are, then we can prove (and it is evident to every impartial inquirer who considers these texts) that they can only relate to a Spiritual King and Kingdom, such a King as Jesus claimed to be, and such a Kingdom as He claimed His was; and that it is impossible to apply them to a temporal one. If these are not the texts on which the Jews found their expectation of a

368   Is. 61:1-2
369   Daniel 9:24
370   Dan. 2:44
371   Micah 4:7b
372   Isaiah 54:13

temporal Messiah, they must produce those that are; and before we acknowledge that the Messiah was to be a temporal Prince – contrary to the evidence of miracle and prophecy – we must see clear and express testimony that He was to be such. It must be proved from words that can have no other possible meaning. However, as has been observed, the Jew has no such clear and express testimony that the Messiah was to be a temporal Prince, nor any expressions concerning His being such. Therefore, Jesus is the Messiah for no thing has yet to be found in the Jewish Books against it.

C. OBJECTION:
Jesus Abolished the Law

Third, it is objected: the Jews were commanded to observe their Law forever, but Jesus and His apostles abolished this Law; therefore Jesus and His apostles are imposters.

The question then is, whether God required of the Jews a never-ending observation of their whole Law, and whether the expressions concerning the duration of this Law can have but one possible meaning – which is that it was God's will that it should be observed forever, and never give way to another covenant.

In order to resolve this point, we must remember that in a divine revelation no one part can contradict another, and particular texts must first be reconciled between themselves, before anything can be advanced from any of them.

1. The Creator of the Law can Change the Law

Now Moses and other prophets commanded the Jews to observe forever the Law given to them by God. Moses likewise assures them that a Prophet should arise *like unto himself,* who should *speak to them the Words of God,* and to whom if they *did not listen,* it would be *required of them.* However, the calling of the Gentiles is also foretold by many of the prophets.

Those texts then which require a never-ending observation of the Jewish Law (specifically, *a Person who speaks in the Name of the Lord, and the thing which he speaks, follows and comes to pass, should be listened to*, and also those which foretell the calling of the Gentiles) must have all meanings that are consistent with each other.

When a Person then appears with the promised evidence, the Jews were to listen to him and to receive him as the promised Prophet. But if this Person *seems to* abolish the Law of Moses, then the Jews were to examine the wording of their Law and see if it can possibly be understood in a different sense (whether this Law may be "abolished" i.e. give way to another covenant).

This is the true point to be considered here: for if the expressions concerning the duration of this Law can be understood in a limited sense, and do not strictly mean a never-ending duration, then we ought to understand them as they are interpreted by Those who have the evidence of **miracle** and **prophecy**.

Upon examination of these texts, we immediately find that they are not only capable of being understood in a limited sense, but that really, they can have no other interpretation, as the calling of the would Gentiles be inconsistent with a never-ending observation of the Law of Moses, since some part of this Law consists in a separation of the Jews from other nations.

Upon the whole then, the true state of the matter seems to be this: the Law was to be observed as long as it was a Law, until the Power who made it should abrogate it (introduce a new Law to cancel it out) – until the Prophet should arise Who should be as a God to the people and give them a new covenant (a time when the Gentiles should be called and all nations serve the Lord).

2. The Law can (and should) be Interpreted in a Limited Sense

The "forever" does not relate to the Law itself but to *the people's duty to it* – they were to observe it forever, that is, as long as it was a Law. It is also in this sense that the expression "forever" is understood when it relates to laws ratified by human legislators. The people are required to observe them "forever", that is, *as long as they are laws*. However, it is understood that the legislator can later annul these laws, if he thinks it is fit to do so.

Suppose that God, when He gave these laws, planned they should be "abolished" and eventually give way to another covenant. Would He not have still commanded the Jews to observe them forever? Doubtless He would have done this, it being their indispensable duty to do so – to observe them as long as they were laws and until He pleased to abrogate them. We cannot suppose He would tell them that there is a possibility He may change the Law later, as this would have been a potential means to lessen their regard for the current Law which it was their duty to observe.

Yet again, we may and ought to conclude that several of the expressions concerning the duration of the Jewish Law related only to the moral part of it;[373] and as to this, it is very evident that Jesus, according to His own Words, might properly be said to *come not to destroy the Law, but to fulfill*.[374] We may yet further observe that the expression "forever" is often used in a limited sense in the

---

373   The only part of the Law that was intended to be perpetual (eternal) was the moral statutes, not the ceremonial or civil ones. Dr. R.C. Sproul writes, "We make a distinction between moral laws, civil laws, and ceremonial laws such as the dietary laws and physical circumcision. That's helpful because there's a certain sense in which practicing some of the laws from the Old Testament as Christians would actually be blasphemy. Paul stresses in Galatians, for example, that if we were to require circumcision, we would be sinning. Now, the distinction between moral, civil, and ceremonial laws is helpful, but for the old covenant Jew, it was somewhat artificial. That's because it was a matter of the utmost moral consequences whether they kept the ceremonial laws. It was a moral issue for Daniel and his friends not to eat as the Babylonians did (Dan. 1). But the distinction between the moral, civil, and ceremonial laws means that there's a bedrock body of righteous laws that God gives to His covenant people that have abiding significance and relevance before and after the coming of Christ. During the period of Reformed scholasticism in the seventeenth and eighteenth centuries, Reformed theologians said that God legislates to Israel and to the new covenant church on two distinct bases: on the basis of divine natural law and on the basis of divine purpose. In this case, the theologians did not mean the *lex naturalis*, the law that is revealed in nature and in the conscience. By 'natural law,' they meant those laws that are rooted and grounded in God's own character. For God to abrogate these laws would be to do violence to His own person. For example, if God in the old covenant said, 'You shall have no other gods before Me,' but now He says, 'It is okay for you to have other gods and to be involved in idolatry,' God would be doing violence to His own holy character. Statutes legislated on the basis of this natural law will be enforced at all times. On the other hand, there is legislation made on the basis of the divine purpose in redemption, such as the dietary laws, that when their purpose is fulfilled, God can abrogate without doing violence to His own character. I think that's a helpful distinction," (https://www.ligonier.org/learn/articles/which-laws-apply/).
374   Matthew 5:17

Jewish Scriptures. An instance would be the everlasting priesthood promised to Aaron and his sons[375] that was given over to the Messiah once He came. Again, from God's own words concerning this Law we have reason to think it was only occasional, and given for a time. For example, it says He temporarily *gave them over to statutes which were not good*, etc.[376]

Again, from the nature and office of the Person foretold by Moses, and the particular evidence that was to be given Him, it is evident that this Messiah was to be Author of a new covenant.

In order to make the expressions in his own books concerning the duration of the Jewish Law be any objection against Jesus' being the Prophet foretold by Moses or the Messiah of the Jews, the Jew must show that these expressions can have only one possible sense – which is, that this law was to be observed as long as the world should last and never give way to another covenant; but, as has been seen, the Jew cannot possibly do this, therefore the wording in the Jewish Books, concerning the eternality of the Jewish Law, cannot be used as an objection against Jesus' being the Person He claimed to be.

D. OBJECTION:
Jesus and His Apostles Misapplied Scripture to Themselves

Fourth, it is objected that Jesus and His apostles applied many places of Scripture to themselves, which did not belong to them and are therefore imposters.

Before we examine the truth of this charge, we may remark that it would be very strange that the persons who were in possession of the very best evidence which could be given them, **miracle** and **prophecy**, and who were crafty enough to deceive us this far, should

---

375   Exodus 40:15, Numbers 25:13
376   Ezekiel 20:25

yet be so weak as to invalidate their own evidence by misapplications. Instead, we might expect they would have let their cause rest upon a good footing once they had gotten it there, and not have taken the most probable step to the ruin of it.

However, we will answer the charge as it stands. The question then is whether the texts applied by Jesus and His apostles are in fact misapplications. Now if Jesus, or His apostles, gave an interpretation to words which they could not possibly give, if they applied characteristics to themselves which could not belong to them, or if they pretend to be spoken of when they are not spoken of, then they are guilty of misapplications and are imposters.

But we must observe that nothing but their interpreting impossible meanings can be called misapplications, and as they were in possession of **miracle** and **prophecy**, they have a right before all other persons to interpret difficult passages. A possible interpretation supported by **miracle** and **prophecy** ought to be received before that which is only the product of human judgment.

1. Understanding the Jewish Covenant

We are then to proceed to an examination of the objected places, and in order to do this, think it proper to have a general understanding of the Jewish Covenant.[377] The Jewish Covenant consisted of many rites, ceremonies, and sacrifices; which seem in their own nature to have no worth or excellency in them and to have nothing to approve of them but the commands of the Legislator. Again, the Legislator Himself places no worth or excellency in them, tells the Jews that He gave them *statutes which were not good*,[378] and assures them that most proper observation of these statutes would be to no purpose, nor make them acceptable to Him, if they were deficient in their other duties. This is the Jewish Law as we find it.

Now let us have a general understanding of the view of the Law in light of the Gospel: These rites, ceremonies, sacrifices, and whole Law, were preparation for and symbolic of the covenant by Jesus.

---

377 The Old Covenant, or those laws that applied to the Jews in the Old Testament.
378 Ezekiel 20:25

They were given only for a time because of transgression,[379] and until Jesus appeared to bless us, in turning every one of us from our iniquities.[380] Thus wrote the author to the Hebrews, *'Being made perfect, He became the Author of eternal salvation unto all them that obey Him.'*[381] *'By His own blood He entered the most holy place once for all, having obtained eternal salvation for us'*[382], and *'now, once at the end of the ages, He has appeared to put away sin by the sacrifice of Himself.'*[383]

Now in what manner the first covenant was symbolic and representative of the second, the author of Hebrews in several chapters sets it before us. He says,

> *The priests under the law serve as an example and shadow of heavenly things,*[384] *that the high priest went alone, once every year, into the Holy of Holies, the Holy Ghost this signifying, that the way into the holiest of all, was not yet made manifest while as the first tabernacle was yet standing,*[385] *which was a figure for the time then present, in which were offered both gifts and sacrifices, etc.*

And speaking of the rites, sacrifices, and sprinklings under the Law by the blood of calves and goats, he says,

> *It was therefore necessary that the copies of the things in the heavens should be purified with these, but the heavenly things themselves* (represented by those copies) *with better sacrifices than these. For Christ has not entered into the holy places made with hands, which are the copies of the true, but into heaven itself, now to appear in the presence of God for us.*[386]

---

379   Galatians 3:8,17
380   Acts 3:26
381   Hebrews 5:9
382   Heb. 9:12b
383   Heb. 9:26b
384   Heb. 8:5, 9:24
385   Heb. 9:7-8
386   Heb. 9:23-24

He plainly tells us that the priests, high priests, tabernacles, sacrifices, and Law were shadows, patterns, copies, and examples of the covenant by Jesus. And Jesus Himself says that, *the Law and Prophets prophesied until John the Baptist.*[387] *That He came to fulfill the Law and Prophets; and that until Heaven and Earth pass, one jot or tittle shall in no way pass from the Law till all is fulfilled;*[388] that is, the Law should in no part be abolished till that covenant should arrive, of which the Law was only a resemblance. Again Jesus says, *He will not eat any more of the Passover till it is fulfilled in the Kingdom of Heaven,*[389] that is, till the Lamb is sacrificed, which this Passover lamb was to represent.

Now then, this being the account which Jesus and His apostles give us of the Jewish Covenant, the question is, whether it is a possible one? If it is, it will follow that it ought to be received as a true one, being supported by **miracle** and **prophecy**.

Upon the first view, we find that this is not only a possible account of the Jewish Covenant, but probably the most rational and consistent one that can be given of it. If it was suitable to the Divine Wisdom to give Jesus to live and die for the sake of mankind, it is reasonable to expect that a mode of worship, which He Himself would institute, should bear resemblance to this great propitiatory sacrifice – that the whole Jewish Covenant should foreshadow His death before He came – and we can confirm it did foreshadow His death since He has come.

The Jews cannot object to the reasonableness of such an institution, they who were commanded to express being delivered from their sin by symbols of it, who yearly offered up the Passover lamb, the firstlings of their flocks, and who observed the Feast of Tabernacles.[390] Other nations also cannot object to it, it being a common practice with them (as may be shown from many instances taken from different countries) to celebrate great rescues with symbols of those deliverances.

If the account given of the Jewish Covenant by Jesus and His

---

387   Matthew 11:13
388   Matthew 5:17-18
389   Luke 22:16
390   Exodus 7-8, Leviticus 23:34

apostles is a possible one, it ought to be received as a true one being supported by **miracle** and **prophecy**. If it ought to be received as a true one, many of those difficulties, which arise from certain applications made by these persons, will vanish, as will appear from a consideration of them. Further, as God might make the Law symbolic of the Gospel, so might He, if He pleased, purposely make some events under the first covenant resemble others under the second. The reason why He would do this can be considered later; all we at present want it, that it be allowed for Him to do it, there being nothing in it disagreeable to His attributes. Again, it is likewise possible for God, that is, it is not unsuitable to His nature, to give the Jewish nation signs of temporal deliverance which should bear resemblance to a greater deliverance – the appearance of the Messiah. As He often pointed out temporal deliverances by signs of them, as may be shown from many instances, it could be no contradiction to His attributes to make these signs, if He pleased, symbols of that great deliverance.

Yet once more, if the first covenant was given for the sake of the second, and only given for a limited time because of transgressions, then we may expect that the prophets under the first should be full of descriptions of the second and that what message they give should be directed at something beyond the present state of things, in order to draw the people's attention to the great deliverance planned for them.[391]

2. Did Jesus and His Apostles Misapply Scripture to Themselves?

We now proceed to examine some applications made by Jesus and His apostles, in order to see whether they are inappropriate ones. We will divide the applied texts into two sorts; and first speak of those prophecies which seem to be indeterminate - meaning neither applicable to the present circumstance of affairs at the time of delivery

---

391   If the first covenant was given to introduce (or prepare the people for) the second, it makes sense that the prophecies given by the prophets in the Old Testament would be shadows or symbols of things to come, to get the people to focus on the future, to give the people hope that something or Someone better was coming to deliver them from their transgressions.

or to the prophet who delivered them.[392] Second, of those prophecies which seem determinate - that is, those which at first view appear to relate to that particular prophet, time, or state of things.

a. Prophecies Intended to be Fulfilled Later

Of the first sort are the following ones:

> *All ye shall be offended because of me this night, for it is written, I will smite the Shepherd, and the sheep of the flock shall be scattered abroad.*[393] *And he was numbered with the transgressors, etc.*[394]

These places are applied to Jesus by Himself; now the question is, what is the evidence that they related to Him?

1.) They exactly *in all parts* and circumstances correspond with the character of Jesus.
2.) There is the evidence of **miracle** and **prophecy** that they do relate to Him.

All we need in the present argument is this: if it cannot be proved that these texts could not possibly relate to Jesus, it cannot be proved that He has misapplied them. Since it cannot be disproven that they relate to Jesus, then it cannot be proven that He has misapplied them. Also, the following texts at first view seem to relate to the particular prophet at the time of delivery:

> *Behold a virgin shall conceive, and bear a Son, and shall call His name Emmanuel.*[395]

> *When Israel was a Child, then I loved Him, and called my Son out of Egypt.*[396]

---

392 Prophecies that don't apply to the time in which they are first given because they are intended to be fulfilled at a later time.
393 Matthew 26:31, Zech. 13:7
394 Mark 15:28, Is 53:12
395 Matt. 1:23, Is. 7:14
396 Matt. 2:15, Hosea 11:1

They gave me gall for my meat and in my thirst, they gave me vinegar to drink.[397]

They part my garments among them, and cast lots for my clothing.[398]

They weighed for my price thirty pieces of silver. And the Lord said unto me, cast it unto the potter: a goodly price that I was prized at of them. And I took the thirty pieces of silver, and cast them to the potter in the House of the Lord.[399]

"I will declare the decree: The Lord has said to Me, 'You are My Son, Today I have begotten You. Ask of Me, and I will give You The nations for Your inheritance, and the ends of the earth for Your possession.[400]

I have set the Lord always before me; because He is at my right hand I shall not be moved. Therefore my heart is glad, and my glory rejoices; My flesh also will rest in hope. For You will not leave my soul in Hell, nor will You allow Your Holy One to see corruption. You will show me the path of life; In Your presence is the fullness of joy; at Your right hand are pleasures forevermore.[401]

These, and many other places, which at first view seem to relate to the times in which they were spoken, are differently interpreted by Jesus and His apostles to apply to themselves.

The point we are next to examine then is, whether the applications made by these persons are possible ones. No sooner is this point examined, but we find that though some of these texts do at first view seem to relate to the times in which they were spoken,

397   Ps. 69:21, Matt. 27:34
398   Matt. 27:35, Ps. 22:18
399   Matt. 27:9, Zech. 11:12
400   Psalm 2:7-8
401   Ps. 16:8-11

they really do not, and must relate to other persons, or times. For example, *"Thou art my Son, this day have I begotten thee. I will give thee the heathen for thine inheritance, and the uttermost parts of the Earth for thy possession."* These were circumstances never applicable to David, therefore, he could not in these places be speaking of himself. The words cited out of the sixteenth Psalm could not relate to David, as he could not call himself the Holy One – this term being unsuitable to his character and to his humble nature which often appears in his writings.

Also, those particular expressions, *They gave me gall for my meat and in my thirst they gave me vinegar to drink,* [402] *they part my garments among them, and cast lots for my clothing,*[403] which were applied to Jesus by one of His apostles, we also have reason to think from a study of David's history that these were circumstances that never happened in his own life.

Now then, if these characteristics and circumstances delivered by David could not relate to himself, they must relate to some other Person, and if they do this, He who has the most right to them is He who can give the evidence of **miracle** and **prophecy** that they really relate to Him.

b. Prophecies with a Double Fulfillment

But secondly, as for those texts that directly suit the circumstances of affairs when delivered, that particular prophet, or the then state of things, the answer is direct: If it was not unsuitable to the wisdom of God to let some events under the first covenant resemble the great events under the second and if it was no contradiction to His attributes sometimes to give His people a sign of temporal deliverance which should bear resemblance to the greatest deliverance they were capable of receiving, then could it be no misapplication to apply the words of the first event to the second, of the sign to the thing signified – they being fulfilled according to the will of God in both cases.

For instance, supposing God when he gave Ahaz a sign from

402   Ps. 69:21, Matt. 27:34
403   Matt. 27:35, Ps. 22:18

Pekah and Remaliah,[404] He likewise intended that this should be a sign of that great future deliverance of mankind, by a Child born of a virgin. Then, when Jesus was born of a virgin, might Matthew properly say, *Now all this was done that it might be fulfilled, which was spoken of the Lord by the Prophet* (that it might be fulfilled which was spoken of the Lord by the Prophet, when he gave a sign which prefigured the birth of the Messiah), *Behold a virgin shall be with child*, etc.

Or, supposing God when He sent His people into Egypt, planned to send His own Son there as well, and intended that one event should symbolize the other, then, when Jesus came out of Egypt, might Matthew again justly say, *That it might be fulfilled, which was spoken of the Lord by the Prophet, saying, out of Egypt I have called my Son.*

However, in the present argument it is not necessary that the sign given to Ahaz should be a sign of the birth of the Messiah; or the event of Israel's being called out of Egypt must symbolize the calling of the Messiah from there, in order to justify Matthew's application. For, if a Messiah was intended, the whole manner and circumstances of His life and death must be also predetermined by God. Well then might Matthew - when Jesus was born of virgin, or when he came out of Egypt, upon a consideration of God's determinate counsel and knowledge - say *Now, all this was done, that it might be fulfilled which was spoken of the Lord by the Prophet*, (that this event which God has long ago determined should come to pass, may now do so, according to the expression of the prophet,) *Behold a virgin shall be with Child, etc. out of Egypt I have called my Son.* We need not seek many solutions of the above proposed difficulty, as one possible one is sufficient, as has been before observed.

The whole mistake concerning these applications seems to be taking them in a wrong view, and imagining that Matthew brings them as proof that Jesus is the Messiah. He offers no such thing, nor is it his business in this place. He is only telling a plain narrative, the history of Jesus, and by the way remarks upon several events in which the will of God was fulfilled according to the expressions of the prophets.

---

404   Is. 7:14

In short, unless it can be proved, that the texts applied by Matthew could not possibly relate to Jesus – that God could not, if He pleased, make events under the first covenant resemble others under the second, or give signs of temporal deliverance which should be signs also of deliverance by Messiah, or that the manner and circumstance of the appearance of the Messiah was not predetermined by God – then it cannot be proved that he has been guilty of misapplication. Since neither of the above-mentioned instances (much less all of them) can be proved, then it cannot be proved that Matthew has been guilty of misapplication.

c. Matthew's Supposed "Nazarene" Slip-Up

Secondly, another mark of falsehood is objected against the Christian religion and that is that Matthew makes a false quotation, and says, *He [Jesus] came and dwelt in a city called Nazareth: that it might be fulfilled which was spoken by the prophets, he shall be called a Nazarene.*[405]

This objection is almost too slight to answer: suppose the Jews had a tradition, which arose from the mouth of some of their prophets, that the Messiah was to be a Nazarene – this is a much more easy supposition than that Matthew made a false quotation, which would be a detriment to his purpose and could not possibly have been any way an advantage to his cause.[406] If Matthew was not an imposter, he would have no reason to make a false quotation, so we ought not to look upon it as such.

---

405   Matthew 2:23; The reason this verse in Matthew is a point of contention is due to the fact that nowhere in the Old Testament or written records of the prophets does a prophecy exist that the Messiah would come from Nazareth.

406   Newcome answers that it's possible the Jews had an oral tradition that was not written down that the Messiah would be a Nazarene. The Jewish traditions were often passed down orally, and not all were written down. It is much more likely that Matthew made a supposition based on an old oral tradition, rather than he falsely quoted a prophecy to make it fit Jesus of Nazareth. Matthew lying about prophecies would have done more harm to his cause of proving Jesus as the true Messiah than helping it. It simply does not fit with the integrity of Matthew's character or help in the accomplishment of that task he had set out to do. There are many possible answers to this challenge, and many can be found in Wayne Jackson's helpful article here: "Was Matthew Mistaken in the "Nazarene" Prophecy?" *ChristianCourier.com.* https://www.christiancourier.com/articles/573-was-matthew-mistaken-in-the-nazarene-prophecy

d. The Elijah Challenge

Another objection remains and that is, Elijah was to come before the coming of the Messiah, but Elijah has not come, therefore, Jesus is not the Messiah. The argument is that the followers of Jesus do not claim that Elijah has come, and since John the Baptist was not Elijah (as he stated himself),[407] Elijah has not come.

Now the account given by Jesus about this matter is that *John the Baptist was the Elijah which was to come;*[408] that he was the person promised by the prophets *under the name of* Elijah. The question is whether this assertion of Jesus concerning John the Baptist is consistent with Jewish prophecy – that is, whether the calling of one person by the name of another whom he resembles, whose character he takes, and by whose spirit and power he acts (which is the account given of John the Baptist by the angel Gabriel[409]) is agreeable to Jewish Scriptures.

This way of speaking is certainly agreeable to Jewish Scriptures, where we often find the characters and offices of persons given to us in their names, and the same person called by different names. Instances of the first kind are frequent. Of the second, the following one is sufficient: It is said that "David", "the Son of David", and "the Lord" shall reign over the House of Jacob forever.[410]

It follows then that:

1.) Provided John the Baptist acted by the spirit and power of Elijah – that is he acted as Elijah would have himself acted if he had been upon Earth – it was not unsuitable to Jewish prophecy to foretell him under the name of Elijah.

2.) John the Baptist did indeed act in the spirit and power of Elijah – that is, he acted as Elijah would himself have acted if he had been upon Earth, for which we have the evidence of **miracle** and **prophecy**.

---

407   John 1:21
408   Matthew 11:14
409   Luke 1:17
410   Ezekiel 37:25; Jer. 33:17-21; Micah 4:7

3.) Then it was not unsuitable to Jewish prophecy to foretell him under the name of Elijah.

4.) If it was not unsuitable to Jewish prophecy to foretell John the Baptist under the name of Elijah, then Jesus' assertion that John the Baptist was the promised "Elijah" was not unsuitable to Jewish prophecy.

5.) If Jesus' assertion concerning John the Baptist is neither unsuitable to Jewish prophecy, nor is an impossible one, then it ought to be received before any other assertion, having the evidence of **miracle** and **prophecy**, and John the Baptist ought to be received as the promised "Elijah".

6.) Also, the fact that the speaking of persons under the names of others whom they resemble is common to other nations besides the Jews, is too well known to need further instances.

Section XI

The Implications for the Jewish Scriptures if Jesus is not the Messiah

Having shown that the Christian religion has the **evidence** of **miracle** and **prophecy** - that the Jews cannot consistently (with a belief of Moses) reject Jesus as not being the Messiah (the Person He claims to be) and having seen the insignificance of the objections commonly urged against Him, I proceed to show that the Jews so far are unable to prove that Jesus is not the Messiah, and that on the contrary, their own books are full of fraud if He is not this Person.

A. God's Promise to Abraham is Unfulfilled

First, God in a particular manner calls Abraham from his kindred and his country, and three times solemnly assures him that, *in him and his Seed all the nations of the Earth should be blessed.*[411] Now there is no attempt to make it appear that all the nations of the Earth have been really blessed in Abraham or in any person descended from him, unless it is in Jesus. Even if we were to understand the words according to the interpretation which some put on them (though it is not the obvious and literal one), that Abraham should be simply a *standard* of blessedness to mankind, and people should say when they bless, "God make you as Abraham", they are *even in*

---

411   Genesis 12:3, 18:18, 22:18

this sense unfulfilled. Abraham was never a standard of blessedness to any nation (unless perhaps a short time to the Jewish), much less to all; and his descendants even fell into bondage and slavery, recovered and had short-lived prosperity, came again into distress, and have continued many ages in a condition that is the opposite of blessedness.

This promise is then either yet unfulfilled, or fulfilled in Jesus; and if it is unfulfilled, then there is a mark of falsehood in the Jewish religion, it being impossible for God in His character to promise and not to perform in due time.[412]

If it be replied that this promise is yet to be fulfilled, and that *a thousand years with the Lord are as one day;*[413] I answer, that though *a thousand years with the Lord are as one day*, yet they are not so with man; and that when the Supreme Being condescends to communicate Himself to man, He must deal with him according to his nature, as well as His own. He cannot then give so solemn a promise of such importance to Abraham, and not fulfill it within three thousand years, and besides let the Seed of Abraham continue for many generations in such a distressed and dispersed condition, so that all hopes and human prospect of its ever being fulfilled ceases.[414]

The Jews might counter by saying that if you accept that God waited about two thousand years between Abraham and Jesus, for whatever reason according to His wisdom, then there might be a reason God in His wisdom would wait even longer. However, in the past when God deferred His actions, usually it was communicated to His people through a prophet, to continue to show the people He had a perfect plan and to not lose hope. Considering there has not been a true prophet since the time of Jesus, it confirms that God had to have executed His plan at that time, otherwise at this time in history,

---

412   If the Jews hold to the belief that the promise God made to Abraham (that through him and his descendants all the earth will be blessed) was not fulfilled spiritually in Jesus, it is still unfulfilled and that means that God did not fulfill His promise to them, since they are still in earthly distress. This would not correctly reflect God's character of goodness and love, and would be a contradiction in His nature, which is impossible. God cannot be good and not good, loving and not loving, at the same time.

413   2 Peter 3:8

414   God would not wait so long that His people would completely and thoroughly lose all hope.

there would still be prophets communicating messages from God to not lose hope. But now as all prophecy has ceased for above two thousand years, there is no prospect of its ever being fulfilled, and it stands as a mark of falsehood in the Jewish religion, if Jesus is not the Messiah.

This is the plain and direct view in which this text is to be considered; and people strangely mistake things who consider it too simply and only give it in evidence of the *Christian* religion. Jesus must be first proven to be the Messiah before we can apply the blessedness, and those who deny His being the Messiah deny the blessedness. Yet this text affords a strong argument to the *Jew* that Jesus is the Messiah and as he cannot claim that it is fulfilled in any person if not in Jesus, he is driven to acknowledge that either that God promised and did not perform, or that Jesus is the Messiah.

B. Jacob is a False Prophet

Secondly, Jacob blessing his sons, declares that the *scepter shall not depart from Judah, nor a lawgiver, from between his feet, until Shiloh comes.*[415] Here then is a remarkable Person foretold to come into the world before a certain period. The question then is, whether the Person foretold is the Messiah, or some other person. However, the Jews cannot possibly apply this prophecy to any other person, therefore, it is yet unfulfilled, or fulfilled in Jesus. If it is yet unfulfilled, then there is a mark of falsehood in the Jewish religion, the time having been significantly passed since Jacob declared that this person should appear.

C. Moses is a False Prophet

Thirdly, Moses' promise to the people – that God would send them a Prophet like unto himself, who should be in the place of God, and speak the words of his mouth, etc. – is fulfilled, or not fulfilled. If it is not fulfilled, there is another mark of falsehood in the Jewish religion; if it is fulfilled, that it can be fulfilled in no other Person than

---

415   Genesis 49:10

Jesus is evident from the Jewish accounts of their own prophets, none of whom were like unto Moses, and from the direct confession of one of them, *and there arose not a prophet since in Israel like unto Moses.*[416]

D. God's Promise to David is Unfulfilled

Fourth, all those promises to David of *establishing his throne forever and ever, letting his Seed remain as long as the Sun and Moon endure,* etc.[417] must be fulfilled in Jesus, or are delusion and fraud. Ten tribes were taken from David in the second generation after him, and all government has been taken from his family for more than 1700 years. Shall we then assert that God promised and did not perform, or that these promises may yet be fulfilled, in spite of the fact that there has been such a long interruption to power for the House of David? The point is evident: either these promises are Jewish forgeries or they are fulfilled in Jesus.

Indeed, it seems as if God, by taking ten tribes from Rehoboam, purposely designed to show the people that it was not a temporal Kingdom, which was to be established in the House of David, and these promises had another significance. If we consider the last words of David, we have reason to think that he himself understood as much.

> *The Rock of Israel spoke to me: 'He who rules over men must be just, Ruling in the fear of God. And he shall be like the light of the morning when the sun rises, A morning without clouds, Like the tender grass springing out of the earth, By clear shining after rain.' Although my house is not so with God, Yet He has made with me an everlasting covenant, Ordered in all things and secure. For this is all my salvation and all my desire, will He not make it increase?* [418]

---

416   Deut. 34:10-11
417   Psalm 89
418   2 Samuel 23: 2-5

E. Isaiah, Daniel, and Zechariah are False Prophets

Fifth, the fifty-third chapter of Isaiah relates to the Messiah, or it does not relate to him; and if it does not relate to the Messiah, then the Jew must show to whom it does relate, and who that person is that is so great, *that kings shut their mouths at him,* yet *is led like a lamb to the slaughter wounded for our transgressions; bears the sins of many; makes intercession for his transgressors; see his Seed, and prolongs his days, after his soul is make an offering for sin;* let them show who this person is, if it be not the Messiah. If they cannot do this, then there is another mark of falsehood in the Jewish religion, as the time for the appearance of this person is limited by the prophet Daniel (see below) that he must have already come if Daniel is not an imposter. For that Isaiah and Daniel describe the same person, is evident from comparing the characteristics given by each of them.

The following remarkable prophecy is fulfilled in Jesus, or the person who delivered it is an imposter:

> *Seventy weeks are determined for your people and for your holy city, to finish the transgression, to make an end of sins, to make reconciliation for iniquity, to bring in everlasting righteousness, to seal up vision and prophecy, and to anoint the Most Holy, etc. And after the sixty-two weeks Messiah shall be cut off, but not for Himself; and the people of the prince who is to come shall destroy the city and the sanctuary. The end of it shall be with a flood, and till the end of the war desolations are determined.*[419]

Now this prophecy cannot possibly be applied to any person who has yet appeared in the world unless it be Jesus: and though the Jews and some persons for them, would gladly apply it to one of their own high priests, yet it is so impossible they should do this, given the characteristics of the Person described, and the work He

---

419   Daniel 9:24, 26

was to perform: *finishing transgression, making an end of sins, bringing in everlasting righteousness, sealing up vision and prophecy, etc.* being no way applicable to any such person besides Jesus.

If then this prophecy cannot possibly be applied to any person who has yet appeared in the world except to Jesus, then it is fulfilled in Him, or is unfulfilled; and since it cannot possibly be unfulfilled unless Daniel who delivered it is an imposter; because according to him this person was to appear before the destruction of the city and sanctuary, and both these have been destroyed for over 1700 years.[420]

That this prophecy is applicable to Jesus in all its parts is even admitted to by the adversaries of Christianity when they take pains to show that it is a *Christian* (and not a Jewish) forgery.

If we consider this prophecy rightly, we shall not need to be critical in a calculation of Daniel's Seventy Weeks; it is enough that it was to be fulfilled before the destruction of the city and sanctuary: so that these being destroyed, it must be fulfilled or Daniel who delivered it is an imposter.

The true end of this remarkable prophecy (like the fifty-third chapter of Isaiah) seems to be to answer objections which might arise on account of a suffering Messiah, and to confirm and establish the weak in future ages.[421]

In conclusion,

1. Abraham had been assured that in his Seed all the families of the Earth should be blessed,

2. Moses had told the people that God would raise them up a Prophet from amidst their brethren, who would speak to them the words of God, and to whom they should listen to, and

3. Nathan, Isaiah, Jeremiah, and other prophets, promised that the throne of David should be established forever, that a King should rule in righteousness, etc. and were full of descriptions of this King and Kingdom;

---

420   Remember that Susanna is writing this in the early 1700's.
421   To confirm the gospel and give hope to the hopeless.

4. Lest the Jews might from hence conceive hopes of a temporal prince and worldly prosperity and grandeur, God kindly guarded them against so dangerous a mistake, and let them know by His prophet Isaiah that the Prince who was to be their Deliverer was to have no outward from or comeliness, but to be a man of sorrows and acquainted with grief, and that the evil He was to deliver them from was their sins; and that the manner in which He was to do it was by wounds, sufferings, stripes, and death.

5. Daniel confirms this, and while perhaps unacceptable to the Jews, is the truth, and fixes a period, (namely the destruction of their city and sanctuary) before which, He assures them their Prince should be treated with wounds, sufferings, stripes, death, and be cut off.

F. Malachi and Haggai are False Prophets

The time is so limited for the fulfilling of another remarkable prophecy, that it must already be fulfilled, or the person who delivered it is an imposter.

> *And the Lord, whom you seek, will suddenly come to His temple, even the Messenger of the covenant, in whom you delight. Behold, He is coming," says the Lord of hosts.*[422]

Now there is no pretense, nor can be any, that this text is fulfilled if not in Jesus (in His being the Messiah and in person the temple) and if it is not fulfilled, then neither can it ever be – the temple having been destroyed. If it neither is, nor can be fulfilled, unless Jesus is the Messiah, then it is either fulfilled in Him or is delusion and falsehood.

So again, those other texts like the following…

---

422   Malachi 3:1

'I will shake all nations, and they shall come to the desire of all nations, and I will fill this temple with glory,' says the Lord of hosts... 'The glory of this latter temple shall be greater than the former,' says the Lord of hosts.[423]

...can in no sense be true, according to the best historical accounts of both temples, if Jesus is not the Messiah.

Again, lastly, there are several prophecies concerning the calling of the Gentiles, which are yet unfulfilled, or are fulfilled by the calling of them to the Christian religion. If they are yet unfulfilled, then we cannot reconcile the wisdom and justice of God with His allowing so remarkable and amazing a conversion of Gentiles to a false religion, which could also be a way to draw the Jews into error by an application of this event to their prophecies. If they are fulfilled, that they can only be fulfilled in the conversion of the Gentiles to Christianity, is evident.

Now if one remarkable text standing for many ages is unfulfilled, it raises suspicion of falsehood, several texts doing so, and some of them such as now never can be fulfilled, are evident proofs of it.

We can have no greater certainty of a revelation than we have: that God cannot deceive, that He will not require our assent to His will without giving us sufficient evidence that it is such, that He will deal with us according to our nature, etc.

He cannot then promise:

1. To Abraham, that *in his Seed all the families of the Earth should be blessed*, and yet defer this blessedness longer than 3000 years;

2. To Moses, that He *would raise up a Prophet like unto himself, who should speak the Words of God*, yet never send any such person;

3. To David, *to establish his throne forever*, yet immediately take ten tribes from him, and let his seed be scattered all over the face of the Earth for more than 1700 years;

423   Haggai 2:7,9

4. *To come suddenly to His temple, and fill it with glory*, yet let the temple be destroyed so that it is impossible He should do this;

5. *To make an end of sins, to make reconciliation for iniquity, and to bring in everlasting righteousness, and to seal up the vision and prophecy*, yet never send any Person on such an errand.

These are direct impossibilities according to the nature of God, and I must conclude, according to my proposition, that the Jewish religion is fraudulent if Jesus is not the Messiah. It is remarkable and worth observing that the evidence of Jesus' being the Messiah increased with each of the difficulties that rose against it. Every circumstance was guarded which might have been a stumbling block for the Jew. This seems to be the wisdom of God. Thus, when Jesus appeared and preached the true God, gave the most perfect system of morality, and worked miracles; He ought to have been received in the least as a teacher from God on account of His miracles and also as the Prophet foretold by Moses.

Accordingly, He expects their conviction upon this evidence: *Believe me for the very works sake, etc. If I had not done among you the works which no other man did, etc.* And again, when John sent two of his disciples to ask Him, *Are you the coming One, or do we look for another?* He only answers by recounting His works: *'Go and tell John the things which you hear and see: The blind see and the lame walk; the lepers are cleansed and the deaf hear; the dead are raised up and the poor have the gospel preached to them. And blessed is he who is not offended because of Me.'* (The number and nature of My works, My miracles, are full evidence that I am the promised Prophet, and blessed is he who, not prejudiced by worldly views, can receive this evidence and be My disciple).

Here then, the works of Jesus (His miracles) were full evidence that He was the Prophet Moses foretold and the promised Messiah. However, when He came to suffer the Jews had a stumbling block owing to their own prejudices and worldly attachments. Now was the hour come, when blessed was he who was not offended at a suffering Messiah. Now was it time for the Jews again to look into their books to which Jesus over and over kindly refers them. Here Isaiah, Daniel, and Zechariah, set them right by telling them, that *the*

Messiah was to be a Man of sorrows, and acquainted with grief; that He was to pour out His soul to death; that after threescore and two weeks He should be cut off, but not for Himself; and that the sword should awake against a Man that was Fellow to the Lord of Hosts.

Again, when persecution arose, then were those remarkable prophecies concerning the calling of the Gentiles that were fulfilled, and fulfilled under this extraordinary unfavorable circumstance – that the conversion was to a persecuted Church.

When the city and temple were destroyed, then had the Jews demonstration that the Messiah was to come within a specific time period; or they must admit that Daniel (who told them that the Messiah should be cut off before this period), and Malachi and Haggai (who had promised that the Lord should come suddenly to His temple, and that the glory of the second Temple shall be greater than that of the former) – were imposters. To this day, the dispersed and distressed condition of the Jews, as well as their unfulfilled prophecies, is evidence against their unbelief.

Though it is not necessary that God, after He has once revealed Himself, should give fresh evidence to His revelation in different ages, *it is necessary* that He does not mislead and give grounds for hope of deliverance but not let this deliverance ever arrive. Or further, let an imposter (Jesus) arise to whom the characteristics of the promised and expected Person are so suitable, that by that means He draws multitudes into error. In this case, the people favored with a revelation are in a worse condition than all others, as one part of them is deceived by an imposter, and the other is left to languish in fruitless hopes and expectations.

The Jewish religion advances inconsistencies and impossibilities, if Jesus is not the Messiah; and if He is this Person, the whole of it is rational and consistent.

In the first place, it is rational to expect that the Messiah, a Person who was to speak the words of God, to be listened to in all things, and be the Author of a new covenant, should be foretold by Jewish prophets, particularly by Moses, this being a connecting evidence. That the Author of the first covenant was the Author of the second covenant – that the very God who brought the people out of Egypt and gave them their Law, also sent them that Person who fulfilled it. As it is rational to expect that the Messiah should be foretold in the Jewish Scriptures, so in Jesus we find a concurrence of all the prophesied characteristics of the Messiah.

He is truly:

1. The blessing promised to Abraham, and in the Savior of the world all the families of the Earth are blessed;

2. The Prophet Moses describes, He delivered a doctrine worthy of God, and *spoke in His Name, and the thing which He spoke followed and came to pass*; He had the divine attestation that (according to His own declaration) *He did not speak of Himself, but whatever the Father commanded, that He spoke;* [424]

3. The King promised to David, Isaiah, and Daniel; in His divine nature truly reigns over the House of Israel forever; *does not judge after the sight of His eyes, neither reprove after the hearing of His ears, but with righteousness judges the poor, and reprove with equity; and His Kingdom is such as shall not pass away, nor be left to other Hands, but shall stand forever;*

4. He is the Man of sufferings that Isaiah, Daniel, and Zechariah describe;

5. He is born of the tribe, family, and in the town foretold;

6. He appeared at the promised, and what's more, at the expected time.

When therefore all these things concur, when miracle, prophecy, and prophesied characteristics all meet in Jesus, where is the ground for disbelief? Why is Jesus not acknowledged as the Messiah of the Jews?

One thing we must observe, and that is, that in a dispute between a Jew and a Christian who both acknowledge the divinity of the Old Testament, the Christian evidence (the evidence that Jesus is the Messiah), increases with time, and consequently the Jewish cause grows everyday worse and worse. Their prophecies are unfulfilled if not fulfilled in Jesus and they have everyday more reason to believe their prophecies are fulfilled in Him, or are fraudulent.

---

424   John 12:49

G. The Implications for the Deist if Jesus is the Messiah

On the other hand, every independent argument for the divinity of the Jewish religion is a proof of Christianity to the Deist as well. The evidence to him that Jesus is the Messiah, the Person He claimed to be, in short, is this: Jesus appeared, taught a doctrine worthy of God, and worked miracles to confirm His divine mission. While Jesus' miracles remain validated, He has a right to be received as a Person sent by God. He also claimed to fulfill prophecies, and to be spoken of in a certain Book, and therefore He must have fulfilled prophecies and be spoken of in that Book. By this Book then, which He appealed to, He must be tried; and if it appears that He made an impossible claim, He is to be rejected. But no sooner is this examined, that we find that He does not make an impossible claim; on the contrary, such a Person, as He appears to be, is exactly described and foretold in this Book. And further we find that He has the highest evidence of prophecy.

If any doubt yet remains concerning the meaning of certain texts, it must be remembered that a possible sense supported by **miracle** and **prophecy**, ought to be received before any other whatsoever.

Conclusion

To this point, we have considered several applications of prophecy made by Jesus and his apostles to themselves, supported by the evidence of **miracle** and **prophecy**. We now proceed to look at them in another view, and to examine how far they may be reckoned to give evidence, and be judged rational parts of a great design.

First, though these characteristics and circumstances might not alone be sufficient to prove a revelation, yet joined with **miracle** and **prophecy**, they give additional evidence, and form a threefold cord not to be broken.

Miracle alone was sufficient evidence that Jesus was sent by God, His fulfilling prophecies proved Him to be the Messiah of the Jews, and the prophesied characteristics and circumstances are extra insurance to guard against those prejudices and unreasonable doubts of mankind, which might possibly emerge in one's mind because of His common appearance and sufferings. Surely, it is not only probable that the Christian religion is a divine revelation, which would be sufficient to determine every rational inquirer to embrace it, but it has been demonstrated that miracles, clear and express prophecies, and a number of prophesied characteristics and circumstances, cannot meet in an imposter.

Second, while some of the prophesied characteristics and descriptions of the Messiah might be given to remove disapproval which might arise from His common appearance and sufferings; so might other prophecies which describe His grandeur, offices, and Kingdom, be delivered wholly for the sake of that generation to which they were given – to keep up the hopes and expectations of the people, and make them be on constant watch for a great Deliverer.

Third, if Jesus is the Person He claims to be, the Deliverer of us from our sins, then the dignity of His Person, and importance of His errand, make it reasonable to expect that the prophets who lived before Him should be full of characteristics and descriptions of Him; and these characteristics and descriptions may teach us in what manner we should receive and honor Him.

Fourth, as the making of ceremonies and sacrifices under the Jewish Law to resemble the sacrifice by Jesus was a proper mode of worship for God to institute (because in these was the death of Jesus the great sacrifice constantly shown forth), so was it reasonable God should make the first covenant a pattern of the second, that the Jews might be more inclined to part with the first – to give up the shadow for the substance, when the perfect covenant should arrive.

This is the purpose of the author of Hebrews – to show a resemblance between the Law and Gospel. They strangely mistake things who say that this author is proving Christianity by typical arguments. He is far from attempting to prove Christianity at that time, so much so that he declares he will not do it, that *leaving the elementary principles of the doctrine of Christ, he will go on to perfection.*[425] He gives a reason why he will not do it, namely because he looked on it as an impossible work to *renew again by repentance, those who had once been enlightened* and were fallen off;[426] he could not hope to offer new arguments which might convince such apostates. Writing then as to believers, he goes on to set before them the difference between the Law and the Gospel – the *imperfection of the one, and the perfection of the other*. He shows them how the Law was unable to do what they wanted from it, *take away sins*,[427] but that in the covenant by Jesus, *their sins and iniquities would be remembered no more. That the Law could make nothing perfect, but the bringing in of a better hope did*; that under the first covenant, *the High Priest, who offered for the sins of others, himself wanted a sacrifice*; that under the second, we had *a High Priest who was holy, harmless, undefiled, separate from sinners, who after He had once offered one sacrifice for sins, forever sat down on the right-hand of God;*[428] *that* the covenant by Moses was only a pattern, example, shadow, figure, of the covenant by Jesus. From the imperfection then of that old covenant, this first covenant (as he calls it) – from its being

---

425 Hebrews 6:1
426 Heb. 6:4-6
427 Heb. 10:4
428 Heb. 10:12,17; 7:19, 27, 26.

unable *to take away sins*; its being only a shadow, pattern, figure of the second; as well as from God's promise to the *Jews to give them a new covenant* – this author proves that God never intended that the first should remain always, but that *as it grew old, it should vanish away, that there should be a disannulling of the commandment going before, for the weakness and unprofitableness thereof;* and that as the *Priesthood being changed, there was of necessity of change also of the Law.*[429]

Fifth, if some events under the first covenant were made to resemble others under the second, it was of great use to the Jews to reconcile them to difficulties under this last, and was a training of them up to believe the mysteries of the Gospel. Thus, if they should make a difficulty of believing that Jesus bore their sins on the cross, this difficulty would rationally be removed when they remembered that the scapegoat bore their sins into the wilderness. If they should object to the possibility of Jesus' Resurrection after lying in the grave three days, they might remember that Jonah was delivered from the belly of the whale after lying there an equal time. If they doubted salvation by looking to a crucified Savior, Moses would put them in mind that the Israelites were healed of bodily disease by looking on the serpent. Therefore, the Jews could not rationally object to the second covenant on account of any difficulties it contained when they were used to believing in equal difficulties in the first.

To conclude, if God was pleased to give signs of deliverances and blessings under the first covenant which resembled others under the second, which pointed to the great Deliverer Jesus, it was because He wanted us to see the ineffectiveness of temporal atonement and that there is but one deliverance of importance to mankind, the eternal deliverance by Jesus the Redeemer.

---

429   Heb. 8:6-13; 7:12, 18

Part Three

The Signature Apologetic Work
of Susanna Newcome:

AN

ENQUIRY

INTO THE

EVIDENCE

OF THE

Christian Religion

First Edition published in 1728, 1729
By Cambridge and William and John Innys in London.

Second Edition published in 1732
By William Innys in London.

Table of Contents

Editor's Introduction 164

Susanna's Preface 165

Section I   *Definitions:* Truth, Evidence, and Belief   169

Section II   *Definitions:* Pleasure and Pain   171

Section III   *Propositions:* The Fit-ness and Unfit-ness of Things   173

Section IV   *Propositions:* Reasonable Expectations of the Evidence   175

Section V   *Propositions:* To Examine Christianity is a Rational Pursuit   177

Section VI   *Enquiry 1:* What is the Evidence for God?   179

Section VII   *Enquiry 2:* After Happiness   197

Section VIII   *Enquiry 3:* Is it Rational that God would Reveal Himself?   209

Section IX   *Enquiry 4:* Is Christianity from God?   219

Section X   Answering Objections to Christianity   235

     Objection 1: Jesus is an Imposter

     Objection 2: Jesus is not the Messiah

     Objection 3: Jesus abolished the Law

     Objection 4: Jesus and His apostles misapplied Scripture to themselves

Section XI   The Implications for the Jewish Scriptures if Jesus is not the Messiah   265

Conclusion of Enquiry   275

Editor's Introduction

As I transcribed *Enquiry,* I made only the following adjustments, simply for ease of reading and clarity of thought:

- The long "s" (*Chriſtian*) of the time is replaced with a modern short "s" (*Christian*).

- The British English spelling is replaced with American English spelling (realise > realize).

- I only kept the capitalization of proper nouns, and changed all the other nouns that were capitalized (which was a common practice in the 18th century) to the lower case. I also capitalized the pronouns Him, Himself, He, Author, Cause, Deity, Being, etc. when it refers to God to differentiate between when she is describing God as Him and man as "him".

- I adjusted the punctuation, spacing, formatting, and grammar for clarification.

- I matched the original italics for emphasis.

- The page numbers do not correlate with the original manuscript due to formatting differences.

- The only footnotes are Susanna's original ones.

- All of the Scripture references are from the original *King James Version*, 1611 Edition, that Susanna used.

Susanna's Preface to Enquiry
(1732)

I t being intended that a Second Edition of *An Enquiry into the Evidence of the Christian Religion* should be published, I thought it proper just to mention to the reader that I have made some few additions to it.

Particularly, I have added to, and strengthened my arguments, that the system of the universe did not always exist, but must have had a Cause of its existence external and antecedent to it. And I have been more full and clear in my proof of the attributes of that Being who exists without Cause, and is the Author of the existence of this system.

And as I have been fuller and clearer in the proof of the attributes of the Deity, so have I in that natural religion, or means to happiness, which is founded on them; and I will presume to say, that the natural religion which I advance, demonstratively follows from the attributes.

I have in one point gone higher than I did before; and as I had proved that if the Author of man's existence was a wise, good, and powerful Being, man must be made capable of obtaining happiness; so I now prove from the attributes of wisdom, goodness, and power, that his happiness shall be everlasting, and that he who by a right use of his powers shall obtain happiness, will enjoy it to all eternity.

I have been more particular in an enquiry whether it was suitable to the attributes of God for Him to reveal Himself, because it has been lately advanced by a very considerable writer, that the law, rule, or religion, given to all men, is a perfect law, rule, or religion, and can have nothing added to it; from whence it will follow, (though this Gentlemen does not expressly say so much) that God cannot at all reveal Himself; and upon searching this point, I still find that it is very suitable to the attributes of God for Him to reveal Himself; and that the law, rule, or religion given to all men, is a very imperfect law, rule, or religion, and may have something added to it.

I have not yet found reason to retract any thing which I before advanced; still continue to assert there is no proof of a God *a priori*; and am ready to make good that assertion.

I have only to add, my sincere wishes, that, if I have delivered any thing contrary to the Truth, it may not be received.

From Susanna's First Edition Preface

I have observed that what often confuses arguments, and makes them unsatisfactory, is using terms without determining meanings, and building on propositions not proven but simply taken for granted. I have therefore in the following pages taken a different approach; and given definitions of all those terms whose precise meaning is necessary for the reader to understand in order to fully comprehend my arguments; and endeavored to go as in depth as one can go on my subject — built only on a claim allowed by everybody, which is that: pleasure is preferable to pain.

This method has been found to be most satisfactory to myself, so I hope it will prove to be the same for the reader as well, and that the setting of the evidence for the Christian religion before them in a short, plain, and easy light, will be a way to lead them to truth.

Some of my readers will, perhaps, be surprised to see me assert that there is no proof of God a priori; but I am persuaded, that if they think closely on the subject, they will find that I am not mistaken, and that we can only come to a knowledge of the existence of a Being who exists without a cause, from a consideration of the existence of things.

I have but one more thing to say by way of Preface, and that is, on behalf of Christianity, which upon the strictest examination, appears to me the true one. Let us hope that those who oppose Christianity, do it by reasoning and argument; by going to the bottom of the subject, and keeping close to the point in hand: and not let the arguing of church leaders, biblical scholars, and theologians, concerning the meaning of certain texts, be received as evidence that those texts are false to the reader; or that they add to the case of those who oppose Christianity. In short, let us not reject the Christian religion, until it is proven to be unworthy of God; or until it needs more evidence of being His revelation.

Section I

DEFINITIONS

I. A proposition which expresses the existence, nature, relations, powers, &c. of beings, or things, or facts; that is, which expresses things as they are, is called truth.

II. Evidence is the ground of the mind's assent to truth, or the means or medium by which truth is conveyed to the mind. There is,

    1. Evidence of sense; our own senses are evidence to us of certain facts.

    2. There is demonstration; or we can by our own powers find connections betwixt truths, and from things known, discover others unknown.

    3. There is moral proof; or the testimony of persons concerning the evidence of their senses, and an appearance of circumstances and things.

III. The highest degree of this last kind of evidence is called moral certainty.

IV. A lower degree of it is called probability.

V. An assent to propositions, of which we have not evidence of sense, nor can demonstrate, is called belief, or opinion.

VI. When our belief or opinion concerning the existence, nature, or relations of beings, or things, or facts, agrees with the existence, nature, relations of beings or things, or facts, and the mind takes things to be what they really are, then we are said to have a true, or right opinion or belief concerning those things.

VII. When our belief or opinion concerning the existence, nature, relations of beings, or things, or facts, does not agree with the existence, nature, relations of beings or things, or facts, but the mind takes things to be what they really are not, then the mind has a false opinion or belief concerning those things.

Section II

DEFINITIONS

Pleasure and pain need not, nor can properly be defined.

I.   Happiness, is a term for collected pleasure, or a sum total of pleasure.

II.   Misery, is a term for collected pain, or a sum total of pain.

III.   That being may be called a happy being, who enjoys pleasure without interruption of pain.

IV.   That being a miserable being, who suffers pain without enjoyment of pleasure.

V.   Every being is in some degree happy, the sum total of whose pleasure exceeds his pains.

VI.   Every being is in some degree miserable, the sum total of whose pains exceeds his pleasures

VII.   Any degree of pleasure to a being, which procures to that being a greater degree of pain, is not to be reckoned as part of his happiness, but misery.

VIII.   Any degree of pain to a being, which procures to that being a greater degree of pleasure, is not to be reckoned as part of his misery, but happiness.

IX.   Perfect happiness is the enjoying the highest degree of pleasure that sensible beings are capable of, without any interruption of pain.

Section III

PROPOSITIONS

I.   To all sensible beings pleasure is preferable to pain.

II.   If to all sensible beings pleasure is preferable to pain, then all such beings must will and desire pleasure, and will an avoidance of pain.

III. What sensible beings must always prefer, will, and desire, is most fit for them.

IV.   What sensible beings must always will contrary to, shun and avoid, is most unfit for them.

V.   Happiness is then in its own nature most fit for sensible beings.

VI.   Misery is in its own nature most unfit for them.

VII. If happiness is in its own nature most fit for sensible beings, and misery in its own nature most unfit for them, then there are fitnesses and unfitnesses of things arising from the nature of sensible beings antecedent to all law and appointment; and the happiness of sensible beings is a fitness of things, and the misery of sensible beings, an unfitness of things.

VIII. And it farther follows, that if the happiness of sensible beings is a fitness of things, and the misery of sensible beings an unfitness of things, that whatever is a means to the happiness of sensible beings, is likewise fitting, or fit, and that whatever is a means to the misery of sensible beings, is unfitting, or unfit.

IX.   That all those actions of sensible beings which tend to the happiness of sensible beings, are most fit.

X.   That all those actions of sensible beings which tend to the misery of sensible beings, are most unfit.

XI.   That right or true opinions concerning the existence, nature, relations, powers of beings, and things, and facts, and concerning the tendency of our actions, are fit.

And,

XII.   That all false opinions concerning the existence, nature, relations, powers of beings and things, and facts, and the tendency of our actions, are unfit.

XIII.   That an examination into the evidence of the existence, nature, relations, powers of beings and things, and facts, and the tendency of our actions, is fit.

That

XIV.   An assent to evidence is fit.

XV.   And a dissent from evidence unfit.

Section IV

PROPOSITIONS

That power of the mind by which it discovers the existence, nature, relations, powers, &c. of beings, and things, and the fitness, and unfitness of things from antecedent knowledge; that is, which finds truth from its connection with truth antecedently known, or believed, is called reason.

As reason is that power of the mind by which it finds truth, and the fitness and unfitness of things, it follows, that whatever is true or fit, is also rational, reasonable, or according to Reason.

And that,

1. It is reasonable that sensible beings should be happy.

2. That it is unreasonable they should be miserable.

3. That whatever is a means to the happiness of sensible beings is rational, or according to Reason.

4. That whatever is a means to the misery of such beings is irrational, or contrary to reason.

5. That all those actions of beings which are means to their happiness, are rational.

6. That all those actions of beings which are means to their misery, are irrational.

7. That whoever does not, as far as he has ability, search out the means to his happiness, is irrational.

8. That whoever does not make use of those means, when found, is irrational.

9.   That an enquiry after truth is rational.

10.   That an assent to it is rational.

11.   That when a proposition is proposed, which if true will affect our happiness in the highest degree, it is highly irrational not to examine whether it be true or not.

12.   That in order to a rational assent, it is rational to consider what kind of evidence propositions of that nature are capable of. That is, in order to an end, it is rational to consider by what means it is to be obtained, and as some truths can be supported with evidence of sense; or demonstration; others only by testimony of persons, and an appearance of circumstances and things; it must be proper to consider what kind of proof propositions of this nature are capable of.

13.   That it is highly irrational to expect that evidence of propositions, which the nature of such propositions will not admit. As thus, suppose the question was concerning historical facts, pretended to be before our own times; of these there can be no higher evidence than testimony of persons, and a concurrence of circumstances, and things, and events. It must be then highly irrational to expect other kind of evidence of such propositions.

14.   That when moral proof or probability is the only evidence propositions are capable of, this ought to determine the assent to such propositions as truly as demonstration ought to determine the assent to propositions which can be demonstrated.

An assent to evidence, is an assent according to reason; and a dissent from evidence a dissent contrary to reason: and the irrationality of the dissent consists in dissenting from evidence, as such, be that evidence what it will.

Section V

PROPOSITIONS

That the Christian religion is a divine revelation, is a proposition, which if true will affect our happiness in the highest degree; it is then highly irrational not to consider whether it be true or not.

That if the Christian religion be true, the happiness of all those to whom it is promulgated, must consist in believing this religion and obeying its precepts, is evident from the nature of this religion and its repeated declarations; it must be then highly irrational not to examine whether it be true or not.

In order then to find whether the Christian religion be a divine revelation, we will go to the very bottom of things; and first see what is our evidence of a God: and before we examine whether a certain supposed Being has revealed Himself, we will consider whether we have reason to believe, that there is really such a Being.

Section VI

ENQUIRIES

Enquiry the first: What is our Evidence of a God?

I. In the first place then we find the mind empty and void, without any innate ideas of such a Being, or any notion of a God, till it ascends to it by that which is the basis of all knowledge, ideas of sensation.

And as there are no innate ideas of a God, so likewise we can have no proof of such a Being *a priori*; and if there is really such a Being, we can only come to a knowledge of His existence, from a consideration of the existence of things.

We then perceive and feel that certain things do exist, which things we find must exist either with, or without, a cause. If they exist without a cause, then it follows that they must have existed eternally, it being certain that nothing can have a beginning without a cause. If they exist with a cause, then we must consider, what can be the cause of their existence?

1. The question then is, whether we have reason to think, that the things which we see and perceive do exist, existed eternally without a cause, or whether there is a cause of their existence? The most likely method to obtain satisfaction in this point, is to consider the things which do exist, and what we know of the manner of their existence.

And here we find certain chains of causes and effects, and many parts of this system owing their existence to an antecedent cause, consequently, we cannot with reason assert that the whole system exists without cause.

[From 1728 Edition] *Thus, if the body* X *produces the body* Y, *and the body* Y, *the body* Z, *yet still there must be a cause of the production of* X, *otherwise there would be a beginning without a cause, which is impossible: and if there must be a cause of the production of the body* X, *that is, if there must be a cause of every link in a certain chain or series of causes and effects, then the whole chain or series of causes and effects cannot exist without a cause.*

Nay, from seeing and considering the manner of the existence of this system, and that many of the parts of it in every period of time are caused, we find it no less than a contradiction to assert that the whole system exists without a cause: and to assert that certain parts of a system do not exist without cause, yet that the whole system exists without cause is the same to assert that the parts do not belong to the whole; that A *is not a letter,* B *not a letter,* C *not a letter, and yet all three letters.*

Again, those who assert, that this system exists without cause, assert that this system always existed in the same manner, that it does now exist; then those who assert that this system exists without cause, must either assert that every part of this system this moment exists without cause, which they know to be a direct falsity; (they being able themselves to tell the cause of the existence of many things in this system;) or that the parts do not belong to the whole, which is an express contradiction.

Now then, when we see that many of the parts of this system do not exist without cause; when the contrary opinion (the opinion that this system exists without cause,) involves us in direct falsities or contradictions, and is supported by no one show of one reason whatsoever; we must, if we determine according to evidence and the reason of things, determine, that this system does not exist without cause, and consequently has not existed eternally.

As thus, if we take any species of beings, we say justly, that no one individual of that species ever existed without a cause, then we cannot say, that the whole species composed of those individuals, existed without a cause. If every link in a certain chain has a cause, then must the whole chain have a cause.

If it is replied, that though every link in a chain, every individual of a species must have a cause; yet that the cause is only in the chain itself, in the species, and that a succession of such individuals is infinite, and consequently, without cause. I answer, a succession which depends on something external to the succession for its continuance, which is the case of all the successions in this system, must have a cause external and antecedent to it.

For, whatever has been always, and without cause, must be always; and there cannot be a cause of the ceasing to be, of that, which had no beginning, nor cause. And, if a succession of beings, suppose men, has been always, and without cause, there can be no cause of the ceasing to be of a succession of men.

But a succession of men is liable to cease from several causes. It may cease by outward accidents; and it is possible that those things which have often been partially destructive to mankind, may become universally so, and the whole species destroyed by them.

It may cease from a want of the support and assistance of other beings and things; and mankind be extinct from a want of sustenance.

A succession of beings then, which is dependent on something external to the succession for its continuance, may quite cease; and if it may quite cease, then it could not exist without cause; there being no cause of the ceasing to be of that, which has no cause of its existence.

[From 1728 edition] *A material system, which is composed of parts that are changeable, cannot exist without a cause, distinct from, as well as prior to, such a system. Whenever there is a change, there must be a cause of that change; otherwise there would be a beginning without a cause. Now the cause of this change must be in the materials of the system, or in something which is not the materials of the system. But the cause of this change cannot be in the materials of the system; for then there would be a beginning without a cause: and as every change in a material system is made in a certain period of time, and owes its production to a preceding cause; could the materials of a system of themselves produce this change, there would be a beginning without a cause, which is impossible.*

And if the cause of change in a material system cannot be in itself, then it follows, that if there is a change in a material system, it must be caused by something distinct from, as well as prior to, all the changes in this system.

The same will be the case as to motion in a material system. There is no motion but what is the effect of a former motion; consequently there is no motion in such a system which has been from eternity, or that has not been caused; now the cause of motion in a material system cannot be in the material system itself, it being impossible for matter to begin motion; and to suppose matter to begin motion is to suppose a beginning without a cause. Consequently there must be a cause of motion in a material system prior to and distinct from such a system [...].

Man is not only a being dependent for happiness, but likewise for his very existence, on which account it is demonstration, that he could not exist without a cause.

Thus we find man cannot live at all without the support and assistance of other beings and things, and that there is something out of himself, which is necessary to his very existence.

2. A succession of beings, each of which cannot exist but in pain, without the support and assistance of something external to the succession, (which is the case of all the successions in this system) must have a cause external, and antecedent to it.

   If there is pain in an individual of a succession, there is cause of that pain; otherwise, there would be a beginning, without a cause. The cause of pain in such an individual, must be in the succession, or not in it. But there cannot be a cause of pain in that which exists without cause. Consequently, a succession of beings, each of which cannot exist but in pain without the support and assistance of something external to the succession, could not exist without cause; which cause must be external, and antecedent it.

3. If beings cannot exist but in pain, without the support and assistance of other beings or things; then there is a fitness in the parts of such beings, to suffer pain without such support and assistance, and a fitness to receive pleasure from it; and a fitness in these other beings, and things, to give pleasure. But such a fitness of parts to certain ends, and fitness of different beings, and successions of beings to each other; and all these fitnesses concurring to one grand use, or end, which is the preservation

of the whole, must have a cause external, and antecedent to them.

4. There is through all inanimate nature a fitness of certain things to others, and a dependency of some parts of this system on other parts of it. Particularly, all vegetables depend on something external to themselves, and even species, for being what they are, and for their continuing to exist. And there is a fitness in the inanimate part of nature to give pleasure, or preserve existence in the animate, for which it seems alone to exist. And the whole system of beings, and things, is as one grand machine composed of a vast variety of parts, each part depending on other parts, and all concurring to certain uses, or ends, which is the preservation or happiness of the whole. Such a variety of fitnesses then in order to the preservation, or happiness of a whole system of beings, must have a Cause external, and antecedent to them.

5. If a material system is composed of parts that are changeable, there must be a Cause external, and antecedent, to all the changes in such a system.

Whenever there is a change, there is a cause of that change; otherwise, there would be a beginning, without a cause.
Now the cause of change in a material system, must be in the materials of the system, or not in the materials of the system. If it is in the materials of the system, then the materials must exist antecedently to all the changes in the system, and likewise, they must exist without Cause; (for, if the materials had a cause of their existence, then that cause, would be the original cause of all the changes in the system; and then, our proposition would be proved) but, if the materials of the system exist without a cause, they cannot possibly have a cause of change in them; for then there would be a cause of change in that which exists without cause; there would be in that which has no cause of its existence, a cause of its not being, what it is, which is a contradiction.

And, if the cause of change in a material system cannot be in the system, then it follows, that it must be distinct from, and antecedent to, all the changes in such a system.

6. There is no motion in a material system, which is not the effect of something antecedent to it, or that has not been caused. Now the cause of motion in a material system, cannot be in the system, it being impossible for matter to begin motion. Consequently, there must be a cause of motion in a material system, distinct from, and antecedent to the system.

If it should be said, that matter may begin motion, (though I suppose very few will venture to say this) then I prove, that motion in a material system must have a cause external, and antecedent to it, the same way that I prove all the changes in a material system, must have a Cause external, and antecedent to them.

7. From the frame and constitution of this system, it is evident, that it did not exist without Cause.

A system that never had a beginning, never can have an end, and if it has always existed, it must always exist; otherwise (as has been observed) there would be a cause of the destruction of that which exists without cause, and has always existed, which is impossible. But from the nature and constitution of things, the decrease[430] of fluids in the planets; and of light and bulk in the Sun, and fixed stars; and from the resistance that is made to the motions of the heavenly bodies, it is evident that this system cannot always exist; and if it cannot always exist, then neither has it always existed; that is, it did not exist without Cause.

As for the argument, "that had the world lasted from all eternity, as it now is; it is altogether impossible, but that Arts and Sciences must have been brought to a far greater perfection, than they have as yet attained"; I take it to be inconclusive, and so shall let it pass; only

430   See Dr. Cheyne's *Philosophical Principles of Religion*

put those who make use of it in mind, that supposing this system had lasted from all eternity, no one reason can be assigned, why Arts and Sciences should not be invented in this age, or any other particular one, as well as a 1000, or 10000 ages ago; and consequently, no argument can be drawn from their being invented in this age, or any other age, to prove the world not eternal.

But if we can show, as we certainly can, that the whole appearance of nature, agrees with this system's beginning to exist at a certain time, we have from hence evidence that it is not eternal. And if we have a history that informs us, that this system did actually begin to exist at that time; then our argument against the eternity of this system is strengthened.

We have then from the whole appearance of nature, and the history of the creation, evidence, that this system did not exist eternally, and consequently, did not exist without cause.

If it is said, that though the existence of this system may be the effect of a cause; yet that nothing which I have offered gives us reason to believe, that the matter of which it is compounded, is not eternal: I answer, that this is a point, which at present does not at all concern my enquiry; if there is a Being, who framed, and fitted up this system, and made man in particular, a sensible, intelligent being, capable of pleasure and pain, I have all that I want under the present Argument. And the other enquiry, may more properly be left to some future opportunity.

II.　　We have then full evidence, and have proved under several particulars, that this system did not exist eternally, and consequently did not exist without Cause. Come we then to consider, secondly, what is the cause of its existence.

Now, as this system, which began to exist, must owe its existence to an antecedent cause; so likewise must that antecedent cause, if it began to exist, owe its existence to another antecedent cause; and so must all beings, and things, until we ascend to a Being, who never began to exist; which Being, who never began to exist, can have nothing antecedent to it, and consequently, can have no cause of its existence.

As we are sure then that the material world does exist, and that it does not exist without cause; but owes its existence to something antecedent to it; we are sure likewise, that if that to which it owes its existence, does not exist without cause; yet that it derives its existence from something which does, and that the Being to whom this system owes its existence, is a Being who exists absolutely without cause, and is eternal.

And having said thus much, and that the Being, who is the fountain of existence to other beings and things, is a Being who exists absolutely without cause, and is eternal, we have said all that is proper upon this head, having no ideas which can lead us to a knowledge of the manner of His existence. And as our knowledge of such a Being, wholly arises from a consideration of the existence of things, we can have no knowledge of Him farther than the existence of things will lead us. But things which exist with a cause, will not lead us to a knowledge of the manner of existence of a Being, who exists absolutely without cause, and is eternal.

Neither will they lead us to a knowledge of the substance of this Being; there being no connection between the substance of a Being; and His works. In these particulars then is our enquiry to stop.

But though the things which do exist, will not lead us to a knowledge of the manner of existence, nor to the substance of a Being, who exists absolutely without cause, and is eternal; yet they will lead us to several of His attributes, and from an effect we can justly argue to its cause; and we may find certain attributes connected with others. Thus, secondly, we can prove that the Being who framed, and fitted up this system, is an intelligent Being.

When we see a machine composed of a vast variety of parts, which regularly, and constantly do distinct offices, and all concur to one grand use, or end, we pronounce it to be the

effect of intelligence; having observed like effects to be owing to intelligence, and not knowing any other Cause that is capable of producing them. When we see the grand machine of the universe composed of a vast variety of parts, all suited, and fitted to each other, and each part regularly, and constantly doing distinct offices, in order to the preservation of the whole, if we pronounce not this to be the effect of intelligence, we are inconsistent with ourselves, and with constant experience; we judge differently in this case, from what we would do in all others of a like nature.

We have then reason to believe the universe the effect of intelligence, or have no reason to believe any machine, that we did not see the forming of, the effect of intelligence.

Again, not only the nature of things which do exist, and the manner of their existence, lead us to an intelligent Cause; but likewise, intelligence being in this system, it is from thence evident, that the Cause of this system is an intelligent Being.

It is impossible for a Being to give a perfection which He possesses not Himself; for then there would be an effect without a cause, or a beginning without a cause, which is impossible. And to assert that an unintelligent being can give intelligence, is to assert that there may be an effect without a cause.

III.   We find that the Being, who framed and fitted up this system, and gave it its present form and appearance, must be a Being of great power.

We are sure that the power of this Being must be equal to the effects of it; that is, that He must be capable of making and sustaining a world, because in fact He has done it: we are sure likewise, that His power must be unlimited by any Being which derives its existence from Him; that none of His own creatures can successfully resist His power; for then He would give a perfection which He possessed not Himself; there would be an effect without a cause, or a beginning without a cause, which is impossible. And this is full enough for us at present, under a general consideration of His power.

IV.   The Being who framed, and fitted up this system, must be a wise Being.

Wisdom lays down the best end, and pursues it by the best means; that is, by means most effectual to the proposed end.

The best end that any Being can propose is the happiness of beings.

If then sensible beings are capable of happiness, if existence is better than non-existence to them, (and our desire after a continuance of existence, is conviction to us, that it is) then the supreme Being, when He determined to make such beings, laid down the best end.

That He makes use of means most effectual to this end, and to the preservation of all kinds of beings, not only their continuing to exist is evidence; but likewise these means are everywhere visible.

Thus we find instincts, or desires in all beings, which push them on to preserve existence. Different beings are wonderfully framed, and constituted, and fitted to each other, as has been observed in order to the continuance of existence, and all things concur to the preservation of the system.

If any then should doubt the wisdom of the end; that is, whether existence is better than non-existence to sensible beings; they must wait for farther evidence, which will appear in due time. But the wisdom of the means, in order to the continuance of existence, cannot be questioned, they being, through all nature most conspicuous.

V.   The Being who exists without cause, must be an independent Being.

Independency is included in existing without cause, and as a Being who exists without cause, derives nothing from another; so can nothing be taken from Him by any other. There can be no cause of the destruction of that, which has no cause of its existence. And a Being who derives nothing from another, and can have nothing taken from Him by any other, is an independent Being.

VI.   The independent Being, who exists without cause, must be unchangeable; that is, He must always exist with the same powers, attributes, and qualities, and consequently must always act by the same motives and reasons.

If a Being with certain powers, attributes, and qualities, has no cause of its existence, then these powers, attributes, and qualities have no cause.

If powers, attributes, and qualities in a Being have no cause, they can never cease to be in that Being; for then there would be a cause of the ceasing to be of that which never had a beginning, which is impossible.

Again, wherever there is a change, there is a cause of that change; otherwise, there would be a beginning without a cause.

The cause of change in a Being, must be either external, or internal.

But there can be no external cause of change in an independent Being, who exists without cause; for then He would be a dependent being, dependent on other beings or things for powers, attributes, and qualities, which had no cause; which is a contradiction.

And for a Being, who exists without cause, to have in Himself a cause of change; that is, a cause of not being what He is, is likewise a contradiction.

It follows then, that a Being who exists without cause, must always exist with the same powers, attributes, and qualities. And if a Being must always exist with the same powers, attributes, and qualities, then must He always act by the same motives and reasons, and be an unchangeable Being.

VII. The intelligent, independent Being, who exists without cause, and is Author of this system, must be perfectly happy.

There is no pain without cause. The cause of pain in a being, must be either external, or internal. It cannot be external to an independent Being; for then He would be a dependent being, dependent on other beings, or things, for His happiness. A Being who exists without cause, cannot have a cause of pain in Himself. Then it follows, that

1. An intelligent, independent Being, cannot suffer pain.
2. An intelligent, independent Being, is not only incapable of suffering pain, but likewise He must enjoy pleasure, or, be a happy Being.

A Being who communicates pleasure to other beings, must enjoy pleasure Himself; otherwise, He would give a perfection, which he possessed not; there would be an effect without a cause, or a beginning without a cause, which is impossible.

Again, a consciousness of possessing powers, capable of being exerted to certain ends, and a real exerting of them to those ends, must give great pleasure to the Being who possesses, and exerts these powers. And the greater the powers, and the more certain their effects, the greater is the pleasure to the Possessor of them.

A power then of making, and sustaining of a world; of forming beings, and things, and suiting of them to each other, in order to the preservation or happiness of the whole; and the real exercise of this power, must give great pleasure to the Being who possesses it.

Further, the intelligent, independent Being, who exists without cause, must not only be a happy Being; that is, enjoy pleasure without any interruption of pain; but He must likewise be perfectly happy; that is, He must enjoy the highest degree of pleasure, that any being is capable of.

As He is the fountain of pleasure to other beings; that is, of all that rational pleasure which does not produce pain, He must Himself enjoy the highest degree of it; otherwise He would give more than He possessed, there would be an effect without a cause.

Again, as the powers of a Creator vastly exceed the powers of His creatures, so must His pleasure from a consciousness of such powers, and from the real exercise of them, vastly exceed any pleasure which they can have from a consciousness, or exercise of their powers.

Further, there is great pleasure in communicating pleasure, in a consciousness of bestowing that on beings, which they always must prefer, and choose; a Being then who communicates to other beings all that true pleasure, or happiness which they possess, must have pleasure from a communication of happiness, which no created being can be capable of.

Lastly, as the Supreme Being is an independent Being, He has pleasure which no dependent being is, or can be capable of.

He must have great pleasure from reflecting, that whatever He has, it is underived, held of none, nor can possibly be taken from Him; that He is self-sufficient, and His felicity everlasting.

VIII. The perfectly happy, independent Being, who exists without cause, must be a good Being.

A good Being is one who always wills the happiness of beings, and promotes it as far as He has power. Now a happy, independent Being, must will happiness to other beings.

First, because pleasure is in itself a motive to the will. All beings must prefer pleasure to pain. They must prefer it as such, wherever it is, and in other beings, as well as in themselves.

What they must prefer, they must will, when there is not a motive to the contrary.

But a perfectly happy, independent Being, can have no motive to will the contrary; that is, to will pain, as such. Motives to will pain, arise in weak, dependent beings, liable to injuries and want, from a sense or dread of pain; but a happy, independent Being, can neither fear, nor suffer, consequently, can have no motives to will pain as such. And if a Being can have no motive to will pain as such, and has always motives to will pleasure; that is, happiness, then He must always will happiness.

Again, the perfect happiness which a Being Himself enjoys, is a motive to Him to will happiness to other beings; and a Being always pleased and happy, always wills happiness.

Further, as the Supreme Being is a Creator, He must always will happiness to His creatures, He must will them that which they must always prefer; otherwise He would will in opposition to Himself, He would will the imperfection of His own works, which is impossible.

It is abundantly evident then, that the Supreme Being must always will happiness to other beings.

And, as He must always will the happiness of beings, so must He always act agreeably to His will, and to promote their happiness as far as He has power.

Dependent beings subject to pain, may often be turned aside from executing that which they will, by a dread of danger, or consequences, but a happy, independent Being has nothing to suffer or fear; consequently, can be by nothing turned aside from executing that which He wills, when He has power to do it.

It is evident then, that the happy, independent Being who is the Author of this system, is a good Being; one who always wills happiness to other beings, and promotes it as far as He has power.

It follows, that His end in creation was to communicate happiness; and that whatever pleasure He might Himself take in the performance, He could have none in opposition to the happiness of His creatures; for then (as He always must will their happiness) He would will in opposition to Himself, which is impossible.

We find then, the attribute of goodness, in the Author of this system, connected with His happiness; and particularly we find, that His end in making sensible beings, was to communicate happiness to them.

But *secondly*, we not only find the attribute of goodness in the Author of this system connected with His happiness, but we likewise find in fact that He is a good Being, and can prove it directly *a posteriori*, from His works.

Whatever tends to our preservation, is framed, constituted, and fitted to give us pleasure. Whatever tends to our destruction, is framed, constituted, and fitted to give us pain.

As things good for us grow hurtful when used immoderately, pain is annexed to the immoderate use of them in order to stop us from the evil; here is wisdom and goodness.

Again, as He has made us capable of contributing to the happiness or misery of those of our own species, so has He annexed pleasure to a consciousness of designing, or promoting of their happiness; pain, to a consciousness of designing, or promoting of their misery; and from hence we have demonstration, that He is a good Being.

No man makes happy, but he secretly applauds the action; no man makes miserable, but he secretly condemns himself. No man designs ill, and stands unreproached by himself; no man designs good, that has not pleasure, even from that intention. No man voluntarily inflicts misery, but to gratify some passion or desire, which seemed to stand in opposition to the happiness of others; and no man but suffers remorse and anguish, when the gratification, which excited the evil action, ceases. Nay, no man so much as sees the miserable without feeling pain, unless some particular displeasure has been conceived against the sufferer, on account of supposed injury to ourselves, or others.

From hence alone then, from God's annexing happiness to a consciousness of designing and promoting the happiness of others, and pain to a consciousness of designing or promoting their misery; and from that pity, which is naturally in all men, we have demonstration that God is a good Being.

And now we have proved, that God is a good Being, our Argument is complete, that He is a wise Being, and that when He made sensible beings, He laid down the best end, which was, their happiness.

IX.   As God is a good Being; that is, as He wills and promotes the happiness of all Beings, so far as He has power, so is He a Being, who in all His actings with sensible beings, acts according to reason and a fitness of things; that is, He really promotes their happiness.

Beings may will happiness to other beings, and promote it as far as they have power, and yet fall very short of their end; of which we ourselves are sad instances. They may want ability to discern, or power to execute that which is best, and most for the happiness of beings. But in neither of these cases can the Supreme Being be defective, He always must know the fitness and unfitness of things; what tends to the happiness, and what to the misery of His creatures, and cannot possibly want power to act agreeably to His will.

And first, a Being who is Creator, who has wisdom sufficient to form a world and suit and fit all beings and things to each other in order to the preservation of the whole, and who has fitted a variety of things to give pleasure to His creatures, must know whether beings could be made capable of happiness; that is, whether existence would be better than non-existence to them. And He also must know the best possible state of existence for all ranks and orders of beings; that is, that state which would produce the most happiness to the whole creation.

And as He must know whether existence would be better than non-existence to sensible beings; and also the best possible state of existence for all ranks and orders of beings; so must He always know what is best for His creatures in all stages of their existence, and what will tend to the happiness or misery of the creatures whom He has formed.

And as the Supreme Being, who is the Author of this system, must at all times know the fitnesses and unfitnesses of things; what will contribute to the happiness or misery of His creatures; so must He always have power to act agreeably to these fitnesses; that is, to do that which will most contribute to their happiness.

As He is an independent Being, His powers are independent, consequently, cannot be limited or restrained by any being whatsoever.

As He is Creator, His power cannot be limited by His creatures; those whom He has formed cannot successfully resist Him.

And if His power cannot be restrained or limited by any being whatsoever, He has power to act agreeably to the fitness of things; that is, to do that which will most contribute to the happiness of beings.

It is evident then, that as the Supreme Being always wills happiness to other beings, knows the fitnesses and unfitnesses of things, what will contribute to the happiness or misery of His creatures; and has power to act agreeably to these fitnesses, that is, to really promote their happiness; He must in all His actings with such beings, act according to reason, and a fitness of things; that is, He must do that which is most for the happiness such beings.

And now having proved that the Being who exists without cause, and who is the Author of the universe, is an intelligent, powerful, wise, good Being; and a Being, who in all His actings with sensible beings, acts according to reason, and a fitness of things; that is, really promotes their happiness; all the other moral attributes, which are generally ascribed to the Deity, as justice, holiness, faithfulness, etc. are included.

A Creator can only be said to be unjust to His creatures one of these ways; either,

By making them incapable of happiness,

By defeating them of any happiness He has made them capable of,

Or by not making them happy in proportion to their deserving to be.

But a Being who knows the fitnesses and unfitnesses of things, what will contribute to the happiness or misery of His creatures; who always wills their happiness; and in all His actings with them acts according to reason, and a fitness of things, could not make them incapable of obtaining happiness, nor defeat them of that happiness they were made capable of; nor so order things that they should not be happy in proportion to their desert.

And as justice is included in the attribute of goodness, and in acting according to reason and a fitness of things, so is holiness and faithfulness. And as a Being who never swerves from reason is holy, so neither can He deceive, promise, and not perform; that is, He is faithful and true.

X. He is Omnipresent.

That is, as He always governs His creatures in the best manner, He is at all times so far present with them, as to be able to do this.

[From 1728 Edition] *By omnipresent, I mean that He is at all times so present with His works, as to have a perfect view and knowledge of them; and as a wise being could not make a system, which He could not at all times supervise, govern, and direct...*

XI. He is Omniscient.

That is, He must know the nature and powers of His creatures, and all their actions; a Creator must have perfect knowledge of that which He has formed.

XII. He is a free Agent, and does not act by necessity, but choice.

Now that God is a free Agent, I prove by one single argument.

Every man naturally thinks himself a free agent, and blames or applauds himself after certain actions; which blaming, or applauding of himself, is an effect of a consciousness, it was in his power to have done otherwise.

Now then, if man is not a free agent, but is obliged in the circumstances he is at any time in, and causes he is under, to do that one thing he does, and cannot possibly do otherwise, he has faculties given him upon the exercise of which he is necessarily deceived, and the Author of his existence, by giving him such faculties has necessitated him into error; and consequently acted contrary to reason, and a fitness of things in His creation.

But the Author of his existence, is a Being, who always acts according to reason, and a fitness of things, consequently, cannot necessitate Him into error, or deceive Him; then it follows that man is a free agent.

But if man is a free agent, God must be one; otherwise, there would be an effect without a cause, or a beginning without a cause; or a perfection in a creature, which is not in the Creator, which is an impossibility.

There are many other arguments which prove man a free agent, and all these prove that God is a free Agent.

And there are many arguments taken from the nature of God, and His works, which prove Him a free Agent; but these having been fully urged by other hands, I omit them, imagining that what I have said, is sufficient to prove my point.

And now having proved that the Author of this system is an eternal, intelligent, wise, powerful, independent, unchangeable, good, just, holy, omnipresent, omniscient Being; and a Being who always acts according to reason, and a fitness of things: we include all these attributes in one general word, and call Him a perfect Being.

Perfect is a relative word, and signifies the agreement of something to a certain measure, or standard in our minds. Thus, a Being, who always lays down the best end, and pursues it by the best means, is perfectly wise, wise without any default or abatement.

Beings may be counted more or less perfect, as they possess powers, which are capable of being means to happiness, and as they really exert them to that end.

And that Being who possesses all those powers, attributes, and qualities, which are capable of being means to the happiness of Himself, and other beings, in the highest, and most perfect degree they can be possessed, and who really does employ them to the end, is the best of all beings, and a perfect Being.

We have then full evidence, that the Being, who framed and fitted up this system, is an eternal, intelligent, powerful, wise, independent, unchangeable, good, holy, just, faithful, omnipresent, free Being, and a Being who in all His actings with sensible beings, acts according to reason, and a fitness of things; or, that He is a perfect Being. And whoever believes that there is no such Being, must likewise believe there may be a beginning without a cause, or an effect without a cause; that is, he must believe impossibilities, or contradictions. And whoever does not act agreeably to the belief of such a Being, acts directly contrary to reason, and a fitness of things.

Section VII

ENQUIRIES

Enquiry the second: After Happiness

I.   What are those actions of man, that are agreeable to the belief of an eternal, intelligent, wise, good, etc.... Being? Or, supposing there is really such a Being who is the Author of man's existence, how must man act, to act according to reason, and a fitness of things? How must he act in order to obtain happiness?

And this enquiry is highly proper, previous to our enquiry into the evidence of a pretended revelation; for if the pretended revelation should require any practice of us inconsistent with the attributes of the Deity, we are to reject it.

1. In the first place, then, we find, that man is formed with certain powers and faculties, which powers and faculties must be given him by his Maker, in order to the happiness of himself, or other beings. It is necessary, then, that he keep all these powers and faculties unimpaired, that so he may be able at any time to do that which he is able to do naturally.

If he impairs his powers, and faculties, he loses the means to his happiness; he likewise loses a pleasure which would naturally arise from the exerting of unimpaired powers and faculties: and add to this, he must displease that Being who gave them to him.

Whatever, then, tends to weaken the powers of either the mind, or body of man, that lessens his ability to perceive, apprehend, reason, judge, will, or act; directly tends to make man miserable.

Under this head it may be shown, that all degrees of eating and drinking, beyond what tends to health, and refreshment; an indulgence in sensual gratifications; and all those vices which may be ranged under the general word intemperance, are contrary to man's happiness.

2. As it is man's duty to keep his powers unimpaired, so also is it, to endeavor to preserve his existence.

If God has made man, and given him means to preserve his existence, He wills that they be made use of to that end.

Whoever, then, neglects the means to self-preservation, or abuses them, to the injuring of his health, acts directly contrary to the will of God, and consequently to his own happiness.

And if he who neglects the means of self-preservation, or abuses them to the injuring of his health, acts contrary to the will of God, and his own happiness; in a much greater degree does he do so, who willfully deprives himself of existence. This is direct opposition to God, is throwing Him back His favors, and is the highest degree of rebellion against Him.

II. With regard to his own species, it is evident, that happiness must arise to man,

First, from his being a just, or righteous being, that is, one who violates the rights of no man, and renders to all their dues.

Second, from his being a good being, that is, one who wills and promotes the happiness of all mankind, as much as is in his power.

Every man is by the frame and constitution of things, possessed of some right or property, which cannot be violated without pain and injury to him; then God wills that this right or property be not violated, and that every man be left uninterruptedly to possess that which by the constitution of things belongs to him.

1. Under this head it may be shown, that murder, adultery, theft, oppression, tyranny, slander, backbiting, deceit, lying, treachery, insolence, flattery, etc. are so many instances of injustice, and consequently opposite to the will of God.

Again, all mankind, by the frame and constitution of things, stand in certain relations to each other, from which the relations there arise dues and rights which cannot be withheld from those to whom they are due, without pain, and injury to them; then God wills that they be not withheld, but that every man have that which by the constitution of things belongs to him.

Here it might particularly be shown, that all undutifulness of children to parents, parent's neglect of children, whether in point of instruction, or maintenance; all disturbances of the peace of society, and of that of families; all breach of contracts (particularly all breach of marriage contracts), breach of promises, etc. are withholding of dues, and consequently opposite to the will of God.

And as God wills that the rights of no man be violated, and that all have their dues, so must He constitute things that happiness must be the effect of righteousness, and misery of unrighteousness.

And could just and righteous actions produce misery to man; unjust, cruel, and tyrannical ones, happiness; God must have constituted things contrary to reason, and a fitness of things, and be not a good Being; or He must act in opposition to Himself.

2. As happiness must be the effect of righteousness, yet much more must it of goodness; and every man must be happy in proportion as he is a good being, and miserable in proportion as he is an evil one.

God always wills happiness to the whole creation, and has made man capable of willing and promoting the happiness of his species; then God wills that man always will happiness, and promote it as far as he is able.

Man may not always be able to do that which tends to the happiness of others; he may want ability to discern what is best for them, or power to execute it; and so far as he falls short in either of these particulars, he is an imperfect being. But he may always will happiness, and God always wills that he do this; that he be a benevolent being.

Here it may be shown, that envy, hatred, malice, pride, are so many instances of malevolence, and consequently directly opposite to the will of God.

And as God always wills that man will happiness, and be a benevolent being; so does He, that He promote it as far as He has power. Man may will happiness, yet for the sake of what he possesses, falls short in promoting it. He may say, *he fed, he clothed*; but when that which should feed and clothe, is to be parted with by himself, in that thing desire to be pardoned: But God not only wills, but in all actings with sensible beings, promotes their happiness: consequently man must, if he would be acceptable to God, promote happiness whenever he has opportunity.

He must save from evil, or deliver out of it; feed the hungry; clothe the naked; visit the sick; deliver the oppressed; protect the fatherless, the stranger, and the widow: these are actions which God wills that man perform as often as he has opportunity, in consequence of benevolence or willing good. That is, God always wills that man be a good being.

And if happiness shall be the effect of righteousness, yet much more, and in a far greater degree, shall it of goodness. If doing no ill, withholding not that which is due, is pleasing unto God, yet much more pleasing shall doing good be to Him. This is joining with our Maker in the great work in which He Himself is employed; and is resembling of the Deity.

III.   Man is placed amidst creatures of much lower powers than himself, who are fitted to serve him with their labor, or to be sustenance for him. And they are not free agents, but determined by instincts to preserve themselves, and their species; which is certain evidence that they were formed for the use of some other beings.

Some of these creatures, however useful in the creation, and to man in particular instances, yet would be destructive to him if their species were numerous; these, then, he has a right, from his duty of self-preservation, to destroy. Others of them which can assist him with their labor, or serve him for food, and which seem formed for no other end but the use of man, we presume that God wills that he should make use of. But then he is to remember, when he makes the creatures labor, to do it with mercy; to lay no grievous burden on them, and what is not proportioned to their strength; to use them with no unnecessary severity, but to be as compassionate towards them, as is consistent with their being serviceable to him. And further, when he takes away their lives, he is to remember to do it in that manner which is least painful to them.

This is behaving towards the creatures acceptably to the Creator, who wills the good of the whole creation.

IV.   With regard to the Supreme Being, who is the Creator, the Preserver, and the Bestower of happiness on man, it is evident, that certain duties arise from man to this Being, in the performance of which, he must find happiness. And as man has ability to discover the relation which he stands in to God, God must will that he discover this relation, and that he perform towards Him those duties which arise from it

It is true, God is not like man, to receive damage if we pay Him not that which belongs to Him; but still it is man's duty to render to God that which is due to Him, whether the withholding it be injury, or not. And, it is man's duty to God:

1. To acknowledge with all humility, the power, wisdom, and goodness, by which he was formed.

2. To render thanks to the divine Majesty for his existence, his preservation, and his capacity for happiness; for all that he possesses that is desirable and good.

3. As the Supreme Being is the most powerful of all beings, it is man's duty to fear Him more than all other beings; that is, to more fear to offend Him.

4. As all things are under the disposal of providence, it is man's duty to God to be patient under whatever befalls him, and never to repine at the dispensations of the most High.

5. To trust in God. As God always knows what is best for us, as He constantly wills our happiness, and has power to execute what He wills, we are to trust that He will deliver us, when a deliverance is best for us.

6. To endeavor to know His will. As the divine will is that rule by which we must act, if we would obtain happiness, we ought to endeavor after a knowledge of it, which is to be obtained by a consideration of His attributes.

7. To perform His will. Better is it not to know the divine will, than to know it, and not conform to it. To know the divine will, and not to conform to it, is setting up to be wiser than God, and is rebellion against Him.

8. As man is an offender before God, as he is conscious of not always conforming to His will, it is his duty to acknowledge himself to be such, and to beg of God to pardon him.

9. To love God. When we have pleasure in the happiness of a Being, we are said to love Him.

   If we have pleasure in the happiness of a Being, or if we love a Being, His pleasure is a motive of action to us.

   A great motive to us to love a Being, or have pleasure in His happiness, is kindness received; and the love generally arises in proportion to the apprehended kindnesses.

   When then we consider the Supreme Being as the Author and Fountain of our existence, and of all that we possess that is desirable and good, we are justly excited to love Him, that is, to have pleasure when His will is conformed to.

   This I apprehend is loving of God, the consequence of which love is, that His will is a motive of action to us separate from the consideration of our own interest.

   And surely if any kindnesses can excite love, excite us to take pleasure when the will of a Being is conformed to; those which we have received from the divine Being will excite it.

10. It is our duty to God to worship Him.

    As we are to acknowledge God's attributes, and our dependency on Him; to thank Him for what we possess, and to implore His pardon for our offenses against Him; and as our bodies, as well as souls, are His; it is proper that these duties be accompanied with such bodily postures, as nature, or custom, have made expressive of the dispositions of our minds. Thus kneeling is the posture of a supplicant; we ought then to fall on our knees when we approach the great God of Heaven.

11. To worship Him in public. When we have discovered the Being and attributes of God, and the relation which we stand in to Him, we ought publicly to testify to others that we acknowledge Him as our God. This is duty to men as well as God, that they may be excited also to worship Him.

12. To set apart some particular time for His service. As all our time, that is, our whole lives, are given us by Him, it is our duty to set apart some portion of them for His worship.

Lastly, it is man's duty to God:

13. To resemble Him in His attribute of goodness, and to be a good being. In what better state could a being be formed, than to have powers given him by which he is capable of resembling his Maker? How undutiful, then, is man to God, how ungrateful, how unworthy of what he possesses, if he does not employ them to this end?

All these are immediate duties from man to God; which arise from that relation which he stands in to Him. And as God gives man powers to discover the relation which he stands in to Himself, so must He will that he acts agreeable to it; and make happiness the consequence.

Thus I have traced out the heads of that conduct of man by which he is to obtain happiness; that is, I have showed what actions of man are agreeable to the belief of an eternal, intelligent, powerful, wise, good, just, etc. Being. And if there really is such a Being, who is the Author of man's existence, it is demonstration that the practice which I have been describing, is his way to happiness.

I call this practice natural religion, or virtue.

And a contrary behavior, vice.

And though that part of our duty which relates to ourselves, and other created beings, is called morality,

And that part of it which immediately relates to God, is piety, or is natural religion properly so called; yet when we consider all our duties as the will of God, and that every breach of morality is opposition to Him, this also is a part of natural religion.

And now having, from the attributes of God, traced out man's way to happiness; having shown what must be the means to it, if God is just, and good, I proceed farther, and would examine how far happiness is the effect of the practice which I have been describing, by the order and constitution of things.

First, we find that keeping our powers unimpaired, is a means to health and cheerfulness, and the great pleasures of thinking and reasoning. And that on the contrary, all intemperance produces pain.

Second, we find that there is a great natural pleasure in the esteem of men; and this pleasure virtue secures to us; it is not being in the power of man to disesteem virtue, however he may be tempted to forsake it. On the other side, vice is sure to meet with contempt; a thing terrible to man.

Third, doing no injury to any, rendering to all their dues, and doing good, is a natural means to the good offices and friendship of men; and self-love makes the just, the benevolent, the good, be beloved.

Fourth, a consciousness of virtue fills us with pleasant reflections, a consciousness of vice with painful ones. It is not in the power of man, as has been observed, to prefer vice to virtue, however he may be tempted to embrace the former, and abandon the latter. When, then, the pleasure which invited to vice ceases, and man looks back on his past conduct, a consciousness that he has abused his powers, acted unworthy of his nature, and below other beings, must fill him with shame, remorse, and anguish. On the other side, a remembrance of virtue, a consciousness of having acted right, worthily, and according to the dignity of his nature, must give him pleasure inexpressible.

Fifth, we find ourselves capable of great pleasure or pain from expectation; we hope, and fear, and apprehend good or evil before it arrives; and this hope or fear of good and evil, is very much in proportion to a consciousness of deserving it. When, then, we are conscious that we have acted a righteous and a good part; that we have done ill to no man; and extended our goodness to many; that we have joined with our Maker in His great work of doing good, and that we resemble Him, we are full of just confidence and expectation of good from God and man; we have a joyful hope and expectation of happiness.

On the other side, when we have injured and oppressed; been malevolent, tyrannical, and unjust, and shut our ears to the cries of the needy, we are full of fear and dread of evil; have shame and anguish at looking backward, and horror at looking forward.

We find then that the practice which I have been describing, the practice of virtue, is naturally productive of happiness.

But though thus it is according to the constitution of things, yet many are the facts on the other side; and frequently do we see the good and the evil, just and unjust, involved in the same calamity; and no man knows the one from the other, but that which befalls them here.

Evil men raise themselves to prosperity, by injustice, cruelty, and oppression. They rise even upon the miseries of the good, and the good perish by the evil.

These are frequent facts, and they put us upon searching farther into the dispensations of God; for this we are never to depart from, that by righteousness and goodness shall man obtain happiness. This is as certain as the attributes of God.

And we find, that if virtue does not procure us happiness in this world; if righteous and good men are not happy; nor so in proportion to their desert; that this life is not, cannot be man's best and final state; but that he shall exist after the dissolution of his body, in order to future happiness.

The question then is, whether happiness is always the effect of virtue in this world? Whether happiness is constantly in proportion to righteousness and goodness? If it is, then the point, which I have been laboring, is yielded; virtue is the way to happiness. If it is not, if misery is sometimes the portion of the righteous and good, a fact few will dispute, then we are sure that happiness is [ahead]; that man shall exist in a future state, when his present sufferings shall be followed with great felicity.

If virtue has not its effect in this world, we are sure that it shall have it; sure as we are that God is just and good, and always acts according to reason, and a fitness of things.

And if existence is only prolonged to man, and the righteous and good cease from suffering, and the evil from oppressing, the former will be happy in their own reflections, and the latter miserable in theirs, without any positive rewards or punishments from God; though that there shall be rewards and punishments from Him, is rational to expect.

As then God always wills happiness to His creatures, and acts according to reason, and a fitness of things; has made man capable of obtaining happiness; as virtue is the way to happiness; as the virtuous are not always happy in this world, nor so in proportion to their virtue; it follows, that their existence shall be prolonged after the dissolution of their bodies, in order to their future happiness.

We prove then man's future existence, from the attributes of God, and the miseries which often attend righteous and good men in this world. And as we prove man's future existence from the before-mentioned particulars, so from a consideration of the nature and powers of man, we find it reasonable to expect it.

We cannot apprehend that reasoning and thinking are properties of matter, but of a different and superior substance, having great experience of the properties of matter, and never finding that it had any of this sort; nay, as far as we know any thing of matter, it is utterly incapable of such powers and properties.

And if reasoning and thinking are not properties of matter, but of a different and superior substance, then the dissolution of a certain composition of matter, the ceasing to exist of the body of man, is no reason why a different and superior substance should cease to exist.

If two substances have the same nature, powers, and properties, the dissolution of the one gives us reason to expect the dissolution of the other; but if they have different natures, powers, and properties, we have no reason to apprehend that that which happens to the one, will also to the other. Nay, we have reason to expect the contrary.

Lastly, it seems absurd to suppose that such powers as man is possessed of, his powers of reasoning, thinking, judging, etc. should be given for so short a time as the life of man, and to so little purpose as only to procure a transient pleasure.

It is rational then to expect man's future existence, from a consideration of his nature and powers: but from the goodness and justice of God we depend on it; we depend that God will proportion happiness to virtue, and that the Judge of all the earth will do right.

And now having from the attributes of God proven that man must be capable of obtaining happiness, and that virtue is the means by which this happiness is to be obtained; I proceed a step farther, and prove that it shall be everlasting.

And I prove it from God's goodness and power.

- God always wills happiness to his creatures.
- Has power to continue in existence the beings whom He has formed.
- Then He will always continue existence to the happy; and those who by a right use of their powers have obtained happiness, shall enjoy it to all eternity.

Whether then the virtuous obtain happiness on this, or the other side of the grave, the difference is but of small importance to them; this is certain, they shall obtain it; and when it is obtained, they shall enjoy it to all eternity.

Everlasting happiness to the righteous and good is a consequence of God's justice, goodness, and power. If it is asked, Who is equal to the task which I have set? Where is the man who lives and falls not short of his duty?

I answer, God is no hard Taskmaster; He knew what we should be capable of before He formed us; saw our necessary failings and imperfections, and would not have formed us if we had not been capable of obtaining happiness, notwithstanding these failings and imperfections. These then are not a bar to our happiness.

But so far as man willfully shuts his eyes against his duty; so far as he yields to present pleasure in opposition to reason; so far as he is unjust, cruel, and tyrannical, a spreader of unhappiness; so far as he is malevolent, a disposition hateful to God, and detested by Him; that is, so far as he is an evil being; so far, for any thing that I can find to the contrary, he must take the consequence, and fall short of happiness.

The most rational method, after such behavior, most certainly is to be very sorry, and to ask God pardon for the offense against him; and to be very diligent for the future; and we hope God will forgive it; but still we cannot say that this man is in the same condition with him who has always walked uprightly. God may forgive him, but he hardly will approve of himself.

Section VIII

ENQUIRIES

Enquiry the third: After a Revelation

Is it rational to expect that God will reveal Himself?

And this enquiry is highly proper, previous to an enquiry into the evidence of a pretended revelation; for, if it is not agreeable to the attributes of God for Him to reveal Himself, a farther search will be to no purpose.

I.   Now if we consider the attributes of God abstractedly, there arises no argument against a revelation; and if it was not unworthy the divine Being to create, it appears not to be unworthy of Him to direct, take care of, and govern.

Is there any objection against a revelation from a consideration of the nature of man? Surely there appears none; we find mankind, not withstanding their reason, often falling short of happiness, ignorant of natural duties and of the means to happiness, or which is worse, and of much more fatal consequence to them, not practicing what they know.

First, we find great part of mankind ignorant of several natural duties and of the means to happiness.

If we consider mankind in the beginning just come out of the hands of their Maker, we shall find them (unless divinely instructed) entirely ignorant of almost all natural duties, and of the means to happiness; without reason to guide them, (there being no reasoning before experience) nor any motives to act by but present pain and pleasure.

They must indifferently take either good or evil, having no ideas or notions of either, nor instincts to direct them to what alone was good for them, nor to the quantities, which would conduce to health and life.

They must learn temperance by excess; truth by error; and to search after the greatest good, by experiencing that certain degrees, or kinds of present pleasure produce pain.

Such must be the condition of mankind at first, if left to themselves without a revelation; their first guides would be pain and pleasure, and these very insufficient ones; they could not lead them all the way to happiness which they were naturally capable of, nor so much as secure them from taking things immediately destructive to them.

Second, after mankind has had the experience of their forefathers to build their conduct on, after some knowledge has been transmitted to them from others, yet we find great numbers not able by their own powers to find out all natural duties, and very few the great motive (eternal happiness) to the performance of them.

1. Some want natural abilities to discover all natural duties. It is true, after mankind has subsisted some time, the duties of morality must lie obvious to very mean capacities, if they will faithfully inquire after them; but so will not our immediate duties to God; fear may cause us to mistake the deity, and consequently not to worship Him in a manner suitable to His nature and attributes.

2. Many that have ability, yet want opportunity to trace out all their natural duties, and the obligations to them. Great part of mankind are necessitated to get their bread by the sweat of their brows, and have not leisure to search after all that knowledge which may be beneficial to them.

3. Multitudes are kept from truth by the craft of interested deceivers. Such is the misfortune of mankind, that they have not been left to follow the dictates of their own reason, but have been led backward from truth.

Religion in many ages and nations has been calculated to serve some private views, and then imposed on mankind as divine. Morality has been corrupted, and the grossest absurdities placed in its room. This has been a most pernicious blow to natural religion, and to our discovery of truth by reason.

It is evident then that if all mankind have entirely been left to themselves without a revelation, particularly if God did not reveal Himself to mankind as soon as He had formed them, some part of them must have been ignorant of several natural duties, and consequently must have fallen short of happiness which they are naturally capable of.

It follows then, as there is no objection against a revelation from the attributes of God considered abstractedly, so there is none from a consideration of the nature of man; on the contrary, instruction in our natural duties seems highly beneficial to man, and on that account from the divine goodness we hope for it.

Particularly we hope, and trust, that God, when he formed mankind, did not leave them to grope in the dark, in a worse condition than the brutes, who have instincts to guide them to what alone is good for them, and never to excess in it; we hope that divine wisdom supplied man's want of experience, and them their way to happiness.

And we will farther hope, that God who sees the many constant impediments on mankind to the discovery of all their natural duties, the weaknesses of their natures; the necessities upon them to get their bread by labor; and the prejudices which they lie under from the impositions of deceivers; either has interposed, or will interpose to guide them to truth.

II.   As mankind often fail in another particular, a particular where a failure is of much more fatal consequence to them than a want of knowledge of their duty, that is, in the practice of it, we also in this case hope for divine assistance.

If man falls short in the knowledge of his duty, he loses a happiness which he is naturally capable of, if, in the practice of what he knows, he exposes himself to the divine displeasure, and to his own severe reflections lasting as his existence. In the first case he loses happiness, in the second he procures to himself misery.

As then it does not appear disagreeable to the attributes of God for him to instruct mankind in their natural duties, neither does it to assist them in the performance of them; to help them in a case where a failure is of most fatal consequence to them.

Possibly God may make farther manifestations of Himself to faster bind mankind to their duty; He may give new motives to our obedience, find means which may help to be a security of our virtue; or contrive methods for our happiness, which human reason cannot invent.

We cannot say God cannot, or will not do this or more; and as it does not appear unsuitable to His nature for Him to assist us, we from His goodness hope that He will do it.

And now having found that a revelation does not appear unsuitable to the attributes of God, or nature of man, we should next proceed to examine into the evidences of a pretended one, namely the Christian religion, but first think it proper to consider what has been lately delivered by a considerable writer [Tindal], which if true, will overthrow what I have been advancing under the two last particulars, which was:

1. That if mankind are entirely left to themselves without a revelation, great part of them must be ignorant of several duties, and consequently fall sort of happiness which they are naturally capable of; and that it appears agreeable to the attributes of God for Him to instruct them in their natural duties. And,

2. If there is no argument from the attributes of God, or the nature of man, why God should not reveal to mankind truths not discoverable by human reason.

The sum of what this gentleman has advanced, that seems to affect my argument, follows.

- That God has from[431] the beginning given mankind some *rule, law, or religion*, in the observation of which they must obtain happiness, or be acceptable to Him.

- That He has given all men, at all times, sufficient means to know this *law, rule, or religion*.

431 *Christianity as Old as the Creation*, Ch. I, page 3, 4, 5.

- That the *law, rule, or religion* cannot be more extensive than the means of knowing it.
- That the only means of knowing this *rule, law, or religion* which has been given to all men, is the use of those faculties by which they are distinguished from brutes; and that the using these after the best manner they can, must answer the end for which God gave them, and justify their conduct.
- That this *law, rule, or religion,* is perfect.
- That nothing can be added to it.

Now then as that only is a perfect *law, rule, or religion* which includes all the means to happiness, (for a *law, rule, or religion,* which does not includes all the means to happiness is manifestly imperfect, and may have something added to it by God, namely means to more or greater happiness, it being suitable to his attributes to afford us means to all possible happiness) according to this gentleman (since the law cannot be more extensive than the means of knowing it) every man can by the use of those faculties by which he is distinguished from the brutes, obtain all the happiness which he is naturally capable of, or which any man is naturally capable of and the perfect *law, rule, or religion,* includes nothing which every man cannot perform.

And as the *law, rule, or religion,* measured by the natural faculties of all men, includes all the means to happiness, it follows that God will not reveal to mankind[432] any natural duties which all men by their reason cannot discover to be such; not truths undiscoverable by human reason.

In answer to then to this gentleman, I say, that the *law, rule, or religion* measured by the use which every man is capable of making of those faculties by which he is distinguished from brutes, cannot be a perfect *law, rule, or religion,* or secure to every man all the happiness

---

432   This first conclusion, *that God will not reveal to mankind any natural duties which all men by their reason cannot discover to be such,* is not this gentleman's: he supposes God may reveal to mankind all natural duties; but such a supposal is inconsistent with the perfection of the *law, rule,* or *religion,* given to all mankind; and if the *law, etc.* given to all mankind is perfect, and can have nothing added to it, then God cannot *reveal to mankind any natural duties not discoverable by the reason of all men.*

he is naturally capable of, or which some men are naturally capable of, unless we give up the attributes of God.

For if the Creator of man is a just, good, and powerful Being, and a Being who, in all His actings with His creatures, acts according to reason, and a fitness of things, it demonstratively follows, that every man has several duties to himself, to God, and to mankind, from the performance of each of which must arise happiness; that every act of temperance, righteousness, goodness, piety, produces happiness; that it recommends to God's favor, and secures to us pleasant reflections lasting as our existence.

It follows then, that the more our duties are known and practiced, the greater is our happiness; and that where there is ignorance of the relation which we stand in to God, and man, and of the duties arising from thence; where there is not knowledge to lead to all actions of temperance, righteousness, goodness, piety, there must be a falling short of happiness; at least of that happiness which proceeds from a reflection on our actions.

And, as it is undoubted fact that some men cannot by the use of their natural faculties obtain equal knowledge of natural duties, of temperance, righteousness, goodness, piety, with others, nor what themselves are capable of obtaining with instruction, it follows, that they cannot, by the use of their faculties, obtain equal happiness with others, nor what themselves are naturally capable of obtaining.

If it is said, that what is the duty of some men, is not the duty of others, it being impossible that can be any man's duty which he has not opportunity of knowing to be such; but that *all have knowledge sufficient for the circumstances they are in.* [433]

I answer, one of the points I insist on is, that some men, on account of greater knowledge than others, have more duties; but then I also insist, that if they have more duties, they have a greater capacity for happiness, since [there] can be no duty which does not produce happiness.

All, in the circumstances they are in, shall be capable of some degree of happiness; and no man shall ever suffer, that is, receive

---

433 *Christianity as Old as Creation*, Ch. I, p. 5.

punishment, for not doing that which he had not power to do: but all men cannot by the use of their faculties obtain equal happiness with others, it being impossible for those who never had it in their thoughts to do certain actions, to have all that pleasure which naturally and necessarily attends the performance of them.

It is evident then, that if the Creator of man is a just, good, and powerful Being, and a Being who in all His actings with his creatures, acts according to reason, and a fitness of things, that the *law, rule, or religion* measured by the use which all men are capable of making of those faculties, by which they are distinguished from the brutes, and which includes nothing which every man with the meanest capacity, and fewest opportunities, cannot discover to be a duty, (since the law cannot be more extensive than the means of knowing it) is a very imperfect *law, rule, or religion*.

If yet the justice of God should this way be impeached for not letting all men have equal opportunities or capacities for happiness; for so constituting things that some men by the use if their natural powers cannot obtain that happiness, which others are capable of obtaining by the use of theirs, nor what themselves are capable of obtaining by instruction: I return, it is undoubtedly certain, and a consequence of God's attributes, that He has constituted things in the best possible manner for the good of the whole; but where generations of beings exist who are free agents, there must be different opportunities or capacities for happiness, since vice naturally impairs the powers and faculties of beings. And where there is not free agency, there can be but a small capacity for happiness. And all that happiness which arises to man from God's favor, and his own reflection on his actions, proceeds from his being a free agent.

We find then, upon a review of our argument, that,

- All mankind cannot by the use of those faculties which distinguish them from brutes, obtain all that happiness which they are naturally capable of, and that all have not equal opportunities or capacities for happiness, and consequently, that the *law, rule, or religion*, measured by the use which every man is capable of making of his faculties, is an imperfect *law, rule, or religion*; and that,

- As it is imperfect, it is suitable to the attributes of God for Him to add to it, and to reveal to mankind all those natural duties from the practice of which they may obtain happiness.

This gentleman's argument then, not overthrowing what I advanced in the first place; proceed we to see how far it affects what I delivered in the second, which is,

[First,] that it does not appear disagreeable to the attributes of God, for Him to reveal to mankind truths not discoverable by human reason.

[Second,] the reason given by him why God will not reveal to man any such truths is because the *rule, law, or religion*, which God has at all times given to all men, and is discoverable by the use of those faculties by which they are distinguished from brutes, is perfect.

But we have proved that this *rule, law, or religion*, is very imperfect; and that it does not include all the means to happiness.

There is, then, from [Tindal's book], no manner of proof that God will not reveal to mankind truths not discoverable by human reason.

But perhaps it will be said, that the *law, rule, or religion*, discoverable by human reason, though not by the reason of every man, is perfect; that this includes all the means to happiness, and can have nothing added to it.

But then I would ask the proof of such an assertion, and what reason we have to think that this is a perfect *law, rule, or religion*.

The reason why the *law, rule, or religion* given to all men, is *perfect*, will not prove that which is only given to a few, is *perfect*.

And if it is suitable to attributes of God for Him to reveal truths which some men by their reason cannot discover, (as we have proved it is, and it will follow if we allow that God can at all reveal Himself) why is it not suitable to His attributes to reveal truths which no men by their reason can discover? We cannot possibly say God cannot, or will not do this.

Having then, no manner of proof that this is a perfect *law, rule, or religion*, we cannot conclude it to be such, and consequently cannot conclude that God will not reveal to mankind truths not discoverable by human reason, but must wait to see whether He does or not.

That an observation of this law will give us a high degree of happiness, is certain; but whether it is perfect, or imperfect, whether it does, or does not, include all the means to happiness, we cannot possibly say, having no evidence on either side *a priori*.

God may, for any thing appears to the contrary, make discoveries to man that human reason could not have attained to, from whence may arise new duties, and an increase of happiness; as also He may, seeing our deviation from reason, and the fatal consequences of it to us, find methods to engage us to our duty, which man could not have thought of; and He may give new motives to our obedience, or direct us to means which may help to be a security of our virtue.

From a remembrance then of our own failings, and God's goodness, we are inclined to hope for assistance; but the method of His assisting us it is impossible to discover.

Finding then, that,

- The *law, rule, or religion*, discoverable by the natural faculties of all men, is an imperfect *law, rule, or religion*, that it does not include all the means to happiness; and,

- No proof being offered why the *law, rule, or religion*, discoverable by human reason, though not by the reason of every man, is a perfect *law, rule, or religion*, it follows, that what this ingenious gentleman has offered, will not overthrow what I have advanced, which was,

That it does not appear disagreeable to the attributes of God for Him to reveal to mankind their natural duties; nor to assist them in the performance of them, or reveal to them truths not discoverable by human reason.

Proceed we then, as we were going, to examine into the Christian religion, and the evidence of it.

Always remembering in our search, a caution which we set out with, and that is, not to receive any thing as God's Word, which is not agreeable to His nature or attributes, whatever be the pretended evidences of it.

Particularly, even our own senses are to be distrusted when the attributes of God are contradicted: for not these are so good evidences to us of a transient act, or appearance of things, as they are of God's goodness, they being constant evidences of this during our whole existence.

Section IX

ENQUIRIES

Enquiry the fourth:
Into the Christian Religion

What evidence have we that the Christian religion is a divine revelation?

And in the first place, is it worthy of God, and suitable to His nature, and agreeable to that scheme of natural religion, which we have already founded on the attributes of the Deity? If it fails here, if it contradicts the attributes, we are not to receive it.

And in our examination of this point, we are to take in the whole Christian scheme. And as the Christian religion is founded upon one antecedent to it, namely the religion of the Jews, which it acknowledges to be divine, this also must be brought to the test.

And here we find, according to this whole religion, (considering both as making one) that man was formed happy, placed in a seat of felicity, yet being a free agent liable to lose his happiness.

And that God did not leave him to himself, but soon as He had formed him, kindly let him know the terms on which he stood, how he would forfeit, and how preserve his happiness.

That, notwithstanding man had divine instruction, yet he abused his liberty, and suffered the consequence. He sinned, and was excluded from the seat of his felicity, and consequently all mankind was excluded from it with him.

That God did not suffer mankind to remain in this condition, to spend a few years here in labor and sorrow, and then to return to the Earth from whence they were taken, but having lost their happiness on Earth, He made them capable of happiness in the Heavens.

And to the end they might not mistake their duty and fall short of happiness, God Himself vouchsafed to instruct them; He gave them divine precepts; He sent to them preachers of righteousness; He warned them by punishments on the wicked, and by deliverances of the good; He saved a few righteous persons when He destroyed the rest of the world; He gave a Law from heaven written on tables of stone; wherein was expressed our duty to God and man; and He sent a divine Person, His Son, to assume our nature, and set us a perfect example. And He accepts His perfect, for our imperfect righteousness, provided we sincerely endeavor to do our duty, and heartily repent of all our offenses against Him.

Here is a method for our happiness, which human reason could not have contrived, but worthy of the divine Being, and suitable to His attributes. God will forgive us our offenses against Him, for the sake of the perfect righteousness of *Jesus Christ*, provided we sincerely repent of them, and endeavor to do our duty.

We before, from the divine goodness, hoped for pardon, but reason could give us no assurances of it.

And to enable us to imitate the perfect example of this our Savior, He gave us a rule for our conduct, agreeable to what we had before discovered from the attributes, and to which if we faithfully attend, we cannot be mistaken in our duty.

1. With regard to ourselves, we are commanded to be temperate, sober, and chaste; *every one to possess*[434] *his vessel in sanctification and honor*, and *to flee youthful lusts which war against the soul*.

2. With regard to others, we are commanded to invade the rights of no man; to *render*[435] *to all their dues*; are shown what are those dues; and have a straight rule given us, whereby to measure our actions to all mankind; and that is, to do *to them*[436] *as we would they should do to us*.

---

434   1 Thessalonians 4:4
435   Romans 13:17
436   Matthew 7:12

And we are not only required to do no injury, and to render unto all their dues, but we are also commanded to do good; told, that if we would be disciples of our Master, and inherit the blessing, we must be *merciful, kind, tender-hearted, forbearing one another, forgiving*[437] *one another, even as God for Christ's sake has forgiven us*; that, if we would be set at the right-hand of our Savior when He judges all men, we must *feed the hungry*[438], *clothe the naked, visit the sick, comfort the fatherless, the stranger, and the widow*; that if *we would have treasure in heaven, we must give to the poor*; and if we would be *children of the Most High, we must resemble Him who does good to all, and maketh His*[439] *sun rise on the evil, and the good, and sendeth rain on the just and the unjust.*

And we are assured that unless the motive to all our charity be pure benevolence, a sincere delight in the happiness of our fellow creatures, *not even our*[440] *whole substance given to feed the poor, will profit us any thing.*

3. In this religion the attributes of the Deity which we had discovered by reason, are declared to us, and our duty to God is delivered agreeable to these attributes.

Here God is described as an *eternal,*[441] *unchangeable,*[442] *almighty,*[443] *omnipresent,*[444] *omniscient,*[445] *wise,*[446] *holy,*[447] *just,*[448] *good*[449] Being; we are commanded to *worship,* to *obey,* to *fear,* and to *love* Him, and at all times to trust in Him. And we are instructed in the times and manner in which He will be worshipped.

---

437 Ephesians 4:22-23
438 Matthew 25:34-46
439 Matthew 5:45
440 1 Corinthians 13
441 Deuteronomy 33:27
442 Malachi 3:6, James 1:17
443 Genesis 17:1, 28:3, 35:11, etc.
444 Psalm 139, Prov. 5:21, 15:3, Hebrews 4:13, etc.
445 Job 42:2, Psalm 139, etc.
446 Ps. 147:5, Rom. 11:33
447 Is. 57:15, Ps. 99:3, 103:1, 111:9, 145:21, Rev. 4:8, etc.
448 Is. 45:21, Zeph. 3:5, Deut. 16:18, Prov. 16:11, Ps. 89:14
449 1 Chronicles 16:34, Ezra 3:11, Ps. 100:5, 106:1, 107:1

Further, we have in this religion means for the security of our virtue.

A Sabbath, or one day in seven, is appointed wherein we are to rest from our labor, and remember God's goodness in creating, and afterwards His goodness in both creating and redeeming us.

Sacrifices and ordinances are instituted under the *Jewish* dispensation, by which that People were to be reminded of their imperfections, their sins, and their dependency on the divine Being; and baptism, and the sacrament of the Lord's Supper under the *Christian*, in the one of which we are solemnly initiated into our religion, made members of *Christ's* church; and in the other we commemorate the love of our Savior, testify ourselves to be His disciples, receive pardon of our sins, and repeat our professions of conforming to His laws.

Lastly, we are assured that the soul of man, his thinking part, never dies, and that eternal misery will be the portion of vice, as well as eternal happiness of virtue; that the *unclean*, the *extortioners*, and *unjust*,[450] those who *shut their ears to the cries of the needy, shall go away into everlasting misery, but the righteous into life eternal.*[451]

From a consideration of the nature of the soul of man, its powers, and properties, we found it reasonable to conclude it not material, but of a substance distinct from, superior to, and more durable than the body of man; and that it should be formed for perpetual existence, is agreeable to reason; and if so, then it follows, that when it is conscious that it has abused its powers, acted unsuitably to its nature, and below other beings, it will have painful reflections during its existence.

This religion, then, appearing worthy of God, and suitable to His nature, the next question is, what is the evidence of it? For it will not follow that because it is worthy of God, it is His revelation, but it will follow, that is rational for us to proceed in our Enquiry.

We proceed then, to an examination of the evidence of the Christian religion, and in order to judge of it, think it first proper to consider what kind of evidence is to be expected; and supporting

---

450   Galatians 5:19-21
451   Matthew 25:46

God would reveal Himself, what proof may we rationally expect Him to give us of such a revelation?

This is certain, if the revelation is for the benefit of all mankind, and ought to be received as truth by all those to whom it is communicated, the evidence of it should be sufficient to determine the rational assent of all those to whom it is communicated, as well those who live after, as at the time when such a revelation is given.

The Christian religion, then, being of this sort, (for the benefit of all mankind, and requiring belief from all those to whom it is communicated) it ought to have such an evidence, as is sufficient to determine the rational assent of all men.

Now then, we can think of no evidence so certain to all mankind, as that which is given in the works of nature; and it is reasonable to expect that the Supreme Being should give mankind evidence of His will, after the same manner as He gave them evidence of His existence and attributes, that is, in His works. And as He led us to a knowledge of His being, or gave us evidence of His being, by the works of nature; so we may justly expect He would give us evidence of His will in the same works, and by showing His power in nature. And how is it that the Supreme Being can give us evidence of His will in the works of nature? Why, as the existence of things, and constant, regular, uniform laws by which bodies move or rest, are a proof of an *eternal, intelligent,* etc. Being; so a change in these laws would be an evidence of His will; and as no being can change His laws, He being sole Lord of nature, without His consent, and as He cannot consent they should be changed to give evidence to falsehood, (for that would be to act in opposition to His own will) it follows, that a change in these laws is full evidence that what is delivered, came from Him.

We call a change in the laws of nature, a miracle.

Now then, as it is rational to expect this evidence of a revelation, so we find this is the evidence pretended by those who would press on us the Christian religion: We are then to examine, whether the Christian religion has this evidence or not. And in this search we ought to be very careful, it being certain that if this is the evidence to be expected, this is the evidence that counterfeits will claim to be in possession of.

In order then, to find whether the laws of nature were changed at the promulgation of the Christian religion, we are to examine,

1. Whether the pretended facts are changes in the laws of nature.

2. Whether there really ever were such facts.

Now, to know whether the pretended facts are really changes in the laws of nature, we must explain what we mean by the *laws of nature*.

That constant, regular, uniform way, by which bodies are determined to motion or rest, and the constant, regular connections betwixt certain known causes and effects, we call laws of nature.

And when certain bodies at rest, move without any external force; when certain bodies in motion, move in a different manner from what they were ever known to move; when certain known causes produce different effects, from what they have been ever known to produce; different from what themselves can produce the next moment, and different from what all others of a like nature with themselves can ever produce; then we may justly and properly say that the laws of nature are changed; that something is effected which could not be effected naturally.

A miracle then being a change in the laws of nature, in order to know that there is really a miracle, it is necessary first to know the laws of nature; and it is impossible to prove the laws of nature are changed, unless we first know what are these laws. Particularly, should we see a new appearance in the heavens, we could not say that the laws of nature were changed; we know not all nature, nor all the laws or powers of bodies; and this might be a constant, regular effect of a certain cause, for any thing we can say to the contrary. And time may bring us to a knowledge of the cause of this effect, as it has to a knowledge of the cause of eclipses, which have been, and perhaps yet may in some places be ignorantly reputed miracles.

It is evident then, that we must be fully acquainted with the constant, regular, uniform determination of certain bodies; the constant, regular connections betwixt certain known causes and effects; the powers of certain causes to produce certain effects, and their natural inability to produce certain other effects, before we can say that the laws of nature are changed; that there is not a natural connection betwixt cause and effect, that is, that there is a miracle.

Those who carry this matter farther, and say we know not all the laws of nature, the laws and powers of bodies, and consequently cannot say that ever the laws of nature are changed, argue not justly.

It is not necessary that I know all the laws of nature, nor even all the laws and powers of any one body, nor all the effects of certain causes, to say that the laws of nature are changed. There may be many powers in bodies, and even in those which we are most acquainted with, yet undiscovered; and there may be many effects not known by us, which may proceed from certain causes: but then all bodies of the same nature will be moved by the same laws, and the same causes will regularly and constantly produce the same effects. But when bodies move contrary to those laws, by which all bodies of the same nature move, and contrary to those by which themselves have hitherto moved; and when certain known causes produce new effects in single instances, and such effects in which naturally there is no connection betwixt cause and effect; then we may justly say that the laws of nature are changed.

And now having seen what is a change in the laws of nature, and that such a change is the evidence to be expected of a revelation, we proceed to examine the pretended facts, and to see whether there were changes in the laws of nature.

And no sooner do we examine, but we find the pretended facts given in evidence of the Christian religion, are of this sort; and allowing the facts, they are really changes in the laws of nature.

To instance, the laws of nature were changed, when the *sick, lame, withered, blind, deaf, dumb,* were cured of all those maladies by the speaking of a word, by the touching of clothes, or by an ointment made of spittle and clay; here was no natural connection betwixt cause and effect, a word, a touch, spittle and clay will not naturally, by any power of their own, restore health, limbs, eyes.

The laws of nature were changed, when *Peter* walked upon the sea; the sea will by no power of its own support walking persons, and in that instance acquired a new power.

The laws of nature were changed, when *Jesus* raised *Lazarus* from the dead by the speaking of a word; a word will not naturally restore life, nor do we know any cause, except the divine power, equal to that effect.

The laws of nature were changed, when *Jesus* showed Himself alive after His crucifixion.

The laws of nature were changed, when persons spoke languages they never learned.

But I need not instance farther; it is very evident, that if there really ever were such facts as these above-mentioned, they were changes in the laws of nature.

We proceed then to the next thing to be enquired after, which is, what is our evidence of the facts?

In the first place, then, we are to consider, what is the evidence to be expected? Now a miracle being a change in the laws of nature, it must be of the essence of a miracle, that is to give evidence, not to be frequent. The reason is, we know nothing of the laws of nature *a priori*; and our whole knowledge of these laws must arise from long observation and experience, from seeing the constant, regular, uniform determinations of bodies, the powers of certain causes to produce certain effects, and the inability of such causes to produce certain other effects. Had we not then a long experience of the constant regular determinations of bodies, powers of causes, etc. we could say nothing of a miracle. And were interruptions to the laws of nature frequent, we could not tell what were the laws of nature; and consequently could not say that these interruptions were miracles.

(By the way we may remark, that if God would reveal Himself to man soon after He had created him, miracles would not then be an evidence to him of a revelation; and if the Supreme Being would early communicate His mind to man, He must do it by vision and immediately speaking to him. And as this was the way, according to the Christian scheme, that God did at first communicate His will to man, it reflects credit upon that scheme.)

It is plain then, that it is of the very essence of a miracle, that is to give evidence, not to be frequent; and if so, then historical evidence is all the evidence that some persons can ever have, that there really were any miracles. The question then is, whether we have this evidence? Whether we have reason to believe that the history of *Jesus* and His apostles is a true history; that the persons who relate and bear testimony to this history, had full knowledge of what they relate and bear testimony to. And,

I. Were not deceived themselves.

II. Were men of integrity, and did not deceive others.

In the first place, if persons relate and bear testimony to a history of facts, and pretend to be themselves present at, eyewitnesses of, and concerned in, those facts, and if the pretended facts are of such a nature as to have lasting, visible effects; then it is demonstration that such persons must have full knowledge whether there ever were, or were not such facts, and consequently could not possibly be deceived themselves.

[Secondly,] if the same persons have been never known to falsify, or deceive in other instances; if they have no blot in their characters; and to deceive us in this instance is entirely contrary to their interest; then we have reason to think they do not deceive us in it, but faithfully relate what they have knowledge of.

We are then, in the first place, to examine whether the persons who relate and bear testimony to the history of *Jesus* and His apostles, pretend to be themselves present at, eyewitnesses of, and concerned in, the facts which they relate, and bear testimony to, and whether the professed facts had such lasting visible effects, that they could not possibly be mistaken concerning them, nor deceived themselves.

And here we find that these persons do actually claim to be themselves present at, concerned in, and eyewitnesses of, the facts which they relate and bear testimony to; and the pretended facts had lasting, visible effects; so that they could not possibly be deceived themselves, and not know whether there ever were, or were not such facts.

Thus *Matthew* and *John* give us a history of facts, and pretend to be themselves present at, concerned in, and eyewitnesses of, those facts; and the pretended facts had lasting, visible effects; it is evident, then, that these persons must have full knowledge whether there ever were, or were not, such facts.

Again, two other historians, called *Mark* and *Luke*, give us the same history; and *Luke* besides, publishes another history of facts, in which, *Peter, James, John, Paul,* and other disciples of *Jesus,* were the chief actors. This account he publishes, whilst these persons were yet alive, and must have denied the facts, if there had been no such, or themselves not parties in the deception.

Further, though *Matthew, Mark, Luke*, and *John*, only were the direct historians of the life and actions of *Jesus* and His apostles, *Peter, James, John*, and *Jude*, according to the relation of the above-named historians, were constant attenders of *Jesus*; and these persons themselves refer to the related facts, in their several Epistles to different churches; and the whole that they write is grounded upon a supposition of the facts.

We must reckon, then, as attesters of the history of *Jesus, Matthew, John, Peter, James, Jude, Mark, Luke*; the five first of which pretend to be themselves to be present at, eyewitnesses of, and concerned in the facts which they relate, and bear testimony to; and attesters of the history of the apostles - *Luke, Peter, James, John*, and *Paul*.

And as one part of the *Christian* history depends on the other part of it (and *Jesus'* disciples, according to their own account of things, acted by His authority and commission), it is evident, that if they did not the actions which they pretend they did, neither did He the actions which they ascribe unto Him; and if He did not the actions which they ascribe to Him, neither did they the actions which they claim they did; but it is impossible for persons to be deceived in their own case, and not know whether they really do, or do not, make the lame walk, the blind see, the dead come to life, etc. consequently all these persons must be grand cheats if there were no such facts.

As to the common objection of enthusiasm, it can have no weight here, the things testified by these persons, being of that nature, that they could not be possibly deceived concerning them: and though a warm imagination may be so far imposed on, as to apprehend visions and revelations when there are really no such things; yet no persons in their senses, no persons who can deliver to the world a consistent scheme of morality, can be so far deceived, as to imagine that they make the blind see, the lame walk, the dead come to life, or that they speak in languages which they never learned, if there were no such facts.

It is then beyond contradiction evident, that the persons who relate, and bear testimony to the history of *Jesus* and His apostles, had full knowledge whether there ever were, or were not such facts as they relate and bear testimony to, and consequently were not deceived themselves.

The next thing then to be enquired after, is, secondly, if they were ever known to falsify or deceive in any one instance; and if it was contrary to their interest to deceive.

1. In the first place, then, they were never known to falsify or deceive in any one instance; they had no blot in their characters; and their very worst enemies could not reproach them with immorality.

2. Secondly, it was against their interest to deceive. That to deceive, was contrary to their interest in this world, is evident, because persecution and death were the consequence of the imposture, if it was one. And that it was contrary to all future prospects is evident, because it is not possible for human nature to have so absurd notions of the Deity, as that his favor is to be purchased by inventing a lie, and persevering in it. Possibly, indeed, persons may have lied for God, that is, they may have supported a cause which they apprehended to be His, with falsehood; but then, they thought it was really His cause, and nobody has been so absurd as to imagine, that the favor of the Deity is to be purchased by inventing a lie concerning Him, by asserting that to be His cause, which they certainly know to be not so, which is not lying for, but against, in opposition to Him.

If it be said, that though it is true these persons acted contrary to worldly interest, yet they might have another notion of things at first, and that particularly *Jesus*, the ringleader of this sect, designed making Himself a King; and that after His decease His disciples acted upon the same worldly motives, I answer, it nowhere appears that *Jesus* designed making Himself a King; on the contrary, He constantly disclaimed whatever tended that way, and declared that His kingdom *was not of this world*. And as to His disciples, whatever notion they at first might have of worldly advancement, yet the repeated declarations of their Master, His ignominious death and sufferings, and their own cruel treatment in the world, fully apprised them of what they were to expect on Earth, and that *bonds, persecution, hatred of all men,* and *death,* were to be the only portions they were in this world to expect.

Again, what view to worldly advancement had Paul, a learned and ingenious man, in good repute in his own nation, and who well knew what fate the spreaders of *Christianity* were to expect, from the part he had acted towards them?

But to put this matter out of question, whatever prospect of worldly interest persons may have living, they can have none dying: these persons sealed their testimony with their blood, and laid down their lives to confirm the truth of what they delivered.

Now the question is, what could make them behave after this manner? Our reasoners tell us, that every effect must have a necessary cause, and a cause suited to the effect. Let them then tell us what is the necessary cause to this effect, and what could be the motive to so many persons to suffer not only persecution, but death, for the sake of a known falsehood. Here they renounce Earth; and if they have a thought of Heaven, they renounce this too. In this case they must choose pain, as pain, and renounce pleasure as such; which yet it will not be allowed that any man is capable of doing.

If it is said that they were Atheistic persons, disbelieved a God, and consequently had no future prospects; then I ask, what made them renounce this world? If it be said they believed a God, and their own future existence, then I demand how they came to renounce His favor for nothing; how they came knowingly and purposely to purchase misery in the next world, with misery in this?

If it be yet objected, that after they had once published their story, (whatever was their motive of doing it) pride made them resolutely adhere to it. I answer, when we argue that a certain behavior is the effect of pride, we should either show from a nature of pride that it may have such an effect, or give examples where there really has been such pride in the world. But if we can do neither of these, (as most certainly in the present case we cannot) then we cannot argue that the behavior of these persons was the effect of pride.

It is true that many persons have laid down their lives for erroneous opinions, but then it must be remembered, that these suffered for error as truth; but we find no instances where several persons have agreed to lay down their lives to maintain a known cheat and falsehood, without any prospect of interest or gratification to themselves. Criminals will die with a lie in their mouth, but it is in the hopes of saving their lives, their reputations, or estates; and they do not persevere in a cheat, without a motive to it.

And what yet strengthens the evidence that these persons were not deceivers, is the great number of them; and if it is irrational to think that one person would lay down his life to maintain a known falsehood, it is yet more irrational to think that many persons should agree to do it; that they should be true to falsehood, and to each other. And indeed considering the nature of mankind, their desire of life, aversion to pain, and love of pleasure, it is no less than demonstration that these persons did not die to maintain a known cheat.

To conclude this head, no greater evidence can be given of any proposition, than the nature of that proposition will admit; and when a proposition has the highest evidence that can be given to it, it ought to be received as truth, or all propositions of the same nature that have only the same, or a less evidence, to be rejected as falsehood. No higher evidence can be given that any persons are persons of integrity, and do not deceive us, than we have that those who relate and bear testimony to the history of *Jesus* and His apostles, are men of integrity, and do not deceive us. Consequently, we cannot rationally receive any history, and reject that which they delivered to us.

As to the point, whether those who relate and bear testimony to the history of *Jesus* and His apostles, did give this evidence of their integrity, and lay down their lives for the sake of what they delivered; this is out of question with all: and the sufferings and death of the founders of *Christianity*, was so open, and public, so circumstantiated, has suffered so many reproaches, and stands in so many records, that the greatest opposers of this religion have not been hardy enough to deny it: and it can no more be doubted that the founders of *Christianity* suffered and died for it, than it can be doubted whether there were such emperors as *Tiberius, Nero, Trajan,* etc. in whose times they suffered, etc.

We have then the highest evidence the nature of proposition will admit, that the persons who relate and bear testimony to the history of *Jesus* and His apostles, had full knowledge of what they relate and bear testimony to, and were not deceived themselves; and also that they were men of integrity, and did not deceive others. Then it follows, that the history which they delivered ought to be received as a true one.

But further, we have not only the testimony of these persons for the truth of the facts, but we have likewise other collateral evidence and circumstances.

Thus those who dispute the facts, and pretend that they were not true miracles, acknowledge the facts.

Those who ascribe them to diabolical power, acknowledge the facts; here then is the testimony of enemies.

Again, the pretended facts were of such a nature, and had such lasting visible effects, that everybody who lived at the time when they were pretended to be done, had opportunity to inform themselves concerning the truth of them. Thus the meanest person, if he had not himself been present, might easily have informed himself whether *Jesus* opened the eyes of the blind; raised *Lazarus* from the dead; and whether *Peter* and *John* had made a cripple, who had lain a long time at the Gate of the Temple, walk. They might have had the testimony of a thousand people, if they had not had that of their own eyes, that one had been blind, another lame; and could themselves examine how far these cures were wrought, and if *Lazarus* had been dead, and was then alive.

And since it is of the essence of a miracle that is to be an *evidence* to us, that the laws of nature be changed in such instances, where we have a full knowledge of the laws of nature, it is evident that cheats are liable to be discovered; and the most illiterate person knows the laws and powers of some bodies, and causes; particularly, he knows that spittle and clay will not open the eyes of the blind; nor the speaking of a word raise the dead to life, consequently has it in his powers to examine whether there be a miracle or not.

Again, the great number of converts to *Christianity* in the time of the apostles, is an evidence of the facts.

That there were a vast number of these early converts, is by none disputed; and it is incredible that so many persons should embark in a religion contrary to all worldly interest, if they had not thoroughly examined the facts on which this religion was founded. True, vast numbers of converts have been made to false religions, but with this difference from the present case; these religions had the support of worldly power, and the embracing of them suited worldly interest. But there are no instances, where a vast number of persons embarked in a religion contrary to both these; a religion which proposed no other worldly preferment to its followers, than bonds, stripes, and death;

which gave no relief from *persecution in one city*, but *flight into another*; and which stood charged with this frightful motto, *Take up your cross and follow me*. It could be only the evidence of this religion, which made so many persons engage in it under such disadvantageous circumstances.

Again, no instances of cheat or imposture being found with regard to the pretended facts, it is an evidence on the side of the facts.

We do not say, that the not discovering of a cheat, is an evidence that there is no such; for then it would follow, that there could be no such thing as a cheat undiscovered; but we say, and justly, that when many persons are engaged to search out a cheat, their not finding any is a probable argument that there is none to find.

Here was the Jew, to the last degree tenacious of his Law and modes of worship, which everyday were losing ground by the increase of Christianity; the new converts, whose discovery of a fraud would have restored them again to the world, and whatever was dear in it; and the Pagan, utter enemy to the setting up of what he called new gods; all endeavoring to detect the imposture. One argument for the facts then is, they stood the examination of a vast number of persons, whose interest it was to detect them.

Lastly, considering the selfish, and worldly views of all impostors, and the corrupted state of natural religion at the time when the Gospel was delivered, it seems utterly impossible that this Gospel should come from such persons.

This is certain, impostors have always worldly and selfish views when they endeavor to impose on mankind. And the particular motives to the deceits of every impostor, who has yet appeared in the world, may be traced out *a posteriori* from his religion.

But from the religion given us by *Jesus* and His apostles, no worldly, or selfish views are to be traced out in its founders. All is agreeable to the divine attributes; and from the end of this religion, its doctrine and precepts, we ascend to the divine wisdom and goodness, the only causes that appear equal to such an effect.

And when we consider how illiterate these persons were; how low their station in the world; and their want of opportunities to deceive; this argument will receive farther weight.

Again, a consideration of the corrupted state of natural religion at the time when the Gospel was delivered, gives us farther reason to believe that this Gospel came from God.

The teachers amongst the Jews had very much corrupted natural religion by their traditions. They laid a great stress on the ceremonials of the Law, and neglected that, for which alone the ceremonials were instituted. They made a gift to God stand in the room of their natural duty to their parents; and a punctual payment of tithes in trifles, excuse a neglect of the weightier matters of the Law , *judgment, justice*, and *mercy*.

Thus stood the case with the teachers: how then must it be with the taught? Could the illiterate, when their natural notions were corrupted, when led backward from truth, understand more than those who sat in *Moses'* chair? This can hardly be thought possible. Consider the state of the Jews, when *Jesus* appeared, and read the Sermon on the Mount, and then judge whether this was the performance of a man, who had all His teaching from the Scribes and Pharisees.

We have then the highest historical evidence, which is all the evidence we possibly can have in the present case, of the truth of the pretended facts; and we must, if we are consistent with ourselves, either receive this evidence, and acknowledge the facts, or receive no historical evidence, and acknowledge no facts, but what ourselves are witnesses of.

I now but put the Christian history, as to evidence, equal with other histories, which we everyday receive as true ones, and act upon the supposition of their being such; but we may fairly carry the argument farther, and say, that we have no history which has such testimony, which was delivered, and witnessed by so many persons, present at, and concerned in the facts which they deliver, and bear testimony to; and where the historians and witnesses gave such evidences of their integrity; and which besides is confirmed by so many collateral evidences.

Section X

OBJECTIONS

Objections to the Christian Religion

So far then the Christian religion is right as to the matter which it contains, and as to the manner in which it is delivered; it at present stands worthy of God, and is supported by the best historical evidence; but still we find objections against it, which come now to be considered.

And *First,* it is objected that *Jesus,* the Author of this religion pretends to be prophesied of in the *Jewish* Books; that He says: the *Scriptures*[452] *testify of Him,* that *Moses*[453] *wrote of Him,* that had the *Jews had believed Moses, they would have believed Him, for he wrote of Him;* but, that it does not appear that the *Scriptures testify of Him,* that *Moses wrote of Him*: consequently He is an impostor.

Now then, we so far agree with the objector, as to acknowledge that *Jesus* pretends to be prophesied of in the *Jewish* Books; and that if it appears that these Books do not foretell Him He is not to be received as a teacher from God. We proceed then to examine this point, whether He is really foretold in the *Jewish* Books or not; and in order to it must little consider the nature, end, and evidence of prophecy.

When the divine Being, by the mouth of a person is pleased to foretell future events, the foretold events are called prophecies, and

---

452   John 5:39
453   John 5:46

the person who foretells them a Prophet.

If the divine Being is pleased to instruct a person to foretell future events, that is, to prophesy, it is for some good end, either for the sake of the generation when the prophecies are delivered, or that when they shall be fulfilled.

If prophecies are designed for the sake of the generation when they are delivered, then must the evidence of them attend their delivery, and God give His people assurance, that what is then spoken shall surely come to pass. As thus, if God designs to comfort a nation in distress, or sorrow, by foretelling future ease and deliverance to them, or their posterity; then does He give that people assurance that the things promised or foretold shall certainly come to pass.

If prophecies are designed for the sake of the generation when they shall be fulfilled, then must the evidence of them attend their completion, and the event agreeing with antecedent descriptions of it, must give evidence to those descriptions that they came from God, and that it was by Him that the event was foretold.

Now, though all future events can only be known, or foretold by God, yet it will not follow that all events which agree with antecedent descriptions of them, give those descriptions the evidence of prophecy. Many persons from a knowledge of causes, may foretell future events; not certainly, because there are future contingencies which no man can foresee, but probably, and what they foretell frequently comes to pass; and also antecedent descriptions of events, when it is in human power to fulfill them, may come to pass from a belief that they are prophecies; the actions of men being greatly affected by their imaginations, and a belief that a thing will arrive, being often a means to make it do so; or, they may come to pass from a desire to have them received as prophecies; and persons may fulfill them, because they would be accounted to be foretold by God.

But though there are cases in which an event agreeing with an antecedent description of it will not give evidence to that description that it came from God, yet in many others it will, and particularly, it will in the following ones.

First, if the event foretold depends not on natural causes, but comes to pass contrary to the course of nature, we are sure that the foretelling of it was prophecy: for as no being can change the laws of nature but the Lord of it, so can no being foretell these changes but

Him. In this case there is the highest evidence of prophecy.

Secondly, if the event foretold depends on natural causes, yet if foretold long before it arrives, and it is not in human power upon a knowledge of the antecedent declaration to bring it to pass; then that antecedent declaration is to be looked on as a prophecy, since no Being but Him who was the Framer of nature, and who gave to all beings, and things existence, can foresee a train of events to come, and what shall be brought to pass according to the course of nature.

Thirdly, if foretold events depend on natural causes, and it is in human power to fulfill them, yet if the time for those events is limited, and the persons who fulfill them are ignorant of them, then the foretelling such events is to be received as prophecy: future times, and seasons, and the order of events to come, being only known to Him who appointed successions of events, and allotted to every thing that exists, its duration, and particular place in the succession of beings or things.

Fourthly, if several events are foretold which concur, and suit with each other, in order to some visible end or design, the foretelling such events must be acknowledged to be prophecy; since that Being alone who framed, and fitted beings, and things to each other, in order to the preservation or happiness of the whole system of created beings, can foretell concurring events.

And now having a little considered the nature, end, and evidence of prophecy; and given some instances wherein events give evidence to antecedent descriptions of them that they came from God, we proceed to see whether *Jesus* makes out His claim, and fulfills prophecies.

And first, we are to observe that as prophecy may be given for the sake of the generation when it is delivered, as well as for that when it shall be fulfilled, it follows that if *Jesus* only answers descriptions in the *Jewish* Books, though such as considered singly would receive no evidence from their completion, He makes out His claim to Gentile as well as Jew, and ought to be received by both, as that person He pretended to be.

The case is, He had the evidence of miracle and wanted no other; but He must answer antecedent descriptions in the *Jewish* Books because He says He does; if then He answers such descriptions, His evidence from His miracles is in full force, and on their account alone

He ought to be received as a teacher from God by all men.

Secondly, if He answers descriptions in the *Jewish* Books, though such as considered singly would receive no evidence of coming from God from their completion, yet then has He to the *Jews*, who acknowledge these descriptions divine, the evidence of prophecy.

For, as these descriptions must belong to that person whom they suit, if the *Jews* acknowledge they are prophecies, then they also must acknowledge the person who fulfills them foretold by God.

Thirdly, if He answers antecedent descriptions, which receive evidence that they came from God, from their completion, then has He the evidence of prophecy to all men; and if that which is foretold concerning Him be above the power of nature, then has He the highest evidence of prophecy.

And now having given some instances in which *Jesus* must be allowed to make out His claim, we proceed to examine whether He does really make it out; that is, we proceed to an examination of the *Jewish* Books, and as He particularly claims to be foretold by *Moses*, *Moses* we will in the *first* place examine.

Here we find that *Moses* declares that a Prophet will arise with these characters,

A Man raised up amidst his brethren[454]
And like unto[455] *Moses*

That He should have this office, to be in the place of God, and speak the words of His mouth:

I will [456] *put my words into his mouth, and he shall speak unto them all that I shall command him.*

And also that a punishment should attend the not hearkening to Him,

---

454   Deut. 18:15
455   Ibid.
456   Deut. 18:18

And it shall [457]*come to pass, that whoever will not hearken unto my Words which he shall speak in my Name, I will require it of him.*

And that the evidence which should be given Him whereby the people should know that what He spoke was really the Words of God, should be this, speaking in the name of the Lord, and having the thing which He speaks follow and come to pass.

When a prophet [458] *speaketh in the Name of the Lord, if the thing follow not, nor come to pass, that is the Word which the Lord hath not spoken.*

We are then to observe concerning this Prophet.

1. That he was to deliver something of great importance, what he was to deliver being called the *words of God's mouth*, and a penalty being annexed to the not hearkening to it.

2. That a particular evidence was to be given to Him.

3. That the particular evidence to be given to Him was to be given for a specific end and intent, namely, as a mark by which the people should know that what had been delivered to them by this Prophet was really the words of God.

And if thou say [459] *in thy heart, How shall we know the word which the Lord hath not spoken? When a prophet speaketh in the name of the Lord, etc.*

4. That something new, something which had not been delivered before, was to be delivered by this Prophet, there being no need of any particular evidence, or any evidence at all to be given to

---

457   Deut. 18:19
458   Deut. 18:22
459   Deut. 18:21

what had been before delivered by *Moses*; this having already the evidence of a miracle. Neither would the people ask, or God promise to give any more evidence to this.

It follows then, that the Prophet described by *Moses* could not possibly be, as some imagine, only certain persons who were to tell what was become of the lost goods, etc. because,

1. There manifestly was no need of any evidence to be given, whereby the people should know, that certain persons were able to tell them what was become of their lost goods, but their really telling what was become of them, the thing proving itself. And to suppose that any other evidence was promised to such persons, is to suppose that an evidence was promised which could not possibly be of any service to those to whom it was promised: for if upon their applying to a certain person to restore to them their lost goods, this person did restore them, there wanted no evidence of his ability to do it; and if he did not restore them, no evidence would persuade them that he did, or that he was a proper person to be applied to on such occasions. And to suppose that the only evidence promised whereby the people should know, that certain persons, were able to restore them their lost goods, was really restoring of them, appears from God's answer to it an impossible supposition: For in that case, the enquiry put by God into the mouth of the people would be this, *How shall I know who shall be able to tell me what is become of my lost goods?* God's answer, *He that does tell you what is become of them is able to do it.*

2. It was to be required of them if they did not hearken to this Prophet, which could not possibly have been the case, if his business had only been to tell what was become of lost goods; it being manifestly no crime not to seek to, and hearken to this sort of persons, who at best were only tolerated by the true God to keep His people from seeking false ones.

3. The timing of this promise, as well as the penalty annexed to the not receiving the words of this Prophet, *as the words of*

God's mouth, shows, that what he was to deliver was of much more importance to mankind, than only telling them what was become of their lost goods.

Thus, when the people were frightened at the manner in which God had delivered the Law, and said,

[460]*Let me not hear again the voice of the Lord my God, neither let me see this great fire anymore, that I die not:*

God answered,

They have [461] *well spoken that which they have spoken.* (Their request is what I approve of). *I will raise them up a Prophet from among their brethren, like unto thee, and will put my words in His mouth, and He shall speak unto them all that I shall command Him.* (When I again deliver *new* commands unto the people, I will speak unto them in the person of a man like unto thee.) *And it shall come to pass that whosoever will not hearken to my words, which He shall speak in my Name, I will require it of him.* (Whoever does not hearken to the words of this Prophet as to the words of God, I will punish his disbelief.) *But the prophet who shall presume to speak a word in my Name, which I have not commanded him to speak, or that shall speak in the Name of other gods, even that prophet shall die.* (An impostor, one who shall presume to give laws in my Name without my commission; or one who shall draw my people into idolatry, shall be put to death.) *And if thou say in thy heart, How shall we know the word which the Lord hath not spoken?* (If God will require it of me if I don't hearken to this Prophet, or if I hearken to a deceiver, you must tell me how I may infallibly know the one from the other.) Why, thus shall ye know an impostor: *When a prophet speaketh in the Name of the*

---

460   Deut. 18:16, Exodus 20:19
461   Deut. 18:17, etc.

Lord, if the thing follow not, nor come to pass (if God does not bear him witness by some extraordinary sign) *that is the thing which the Lord hath not spoken.*

Now then that the thing which was to follow or come to pass was some extraordinary sign, something miraculous, is certain; otherwise the Prophet, which was to be hearkened to; could not have been distinguished from an impostor; and if thing which was to come to pass could be affected by human power, an impostor might pass for the Prophet.

It is evident then that the Prophet, who should be hearkened to in all that He should deliver, was to have the evidence of miracles, the evidence which *Moses* had, whom it was promised He should resemble.

Now then we are to see, whether *Moses'* characters of a Prophet, and the promised evidence meet in *Jesus,* and whether we have reason to think him that Prophet whom *Moses* describes.

He is *raised up from amidst his brethren.*
He resembles *Moses* in the working of miracles.
He delivered a doctrine worthy of God and suitable to His nature.
And *He spake in the Name of the Lord, and the things which He spake, followed and came to pass;*
He worked miracles.

What hinders then that *Jesus* is not acknowledged as the Prophet foretold by *Moses?*

See His own claim and argument:

The works that I do [462]*bear witness of me that the Father hath sent me. The Father* [463] *that sent me, beareth witness of*

---

462   John 5:36
463   John 8:18

me. The works that I do in [464]*my Father's name, they bear witness of me. If I do not the works of my Father,* [465]*believe me not. But if I do, though ye believe not me, believe the works, that ye may know and that believe that the Father is in me, and I in him. Believe me for the very* [466]*works sake. If I had* [467]*not done among them the works which none other man did, they had not had sin.* (If my miracles, my evidence from God, had not been more clear, more convincing than any other man's, who has ever yet appeared in the world, their infidelity had not been so unpardonable.) Again,* [468]*do not think that I will accuse you; there is one that accuseth you, even Moses in whom ye trust; for had ye believed Moses, ye would have believed me,* etc.

Here then, in *Jesus*, is the very Prophet *Moses* describes, and in His miracles the very evidence *Moses* promised; both character and attestation answer in every point and circumstance; and He has a right to be acknowledged as that Prophet which *Moses* foretold.

We see, not only *Jesus* applies this Prophecy to himself, but also [469]*Peter* and [470]*Stephen* apply it to Him, and argue with the *Jews* that it is fulfilled.

If it should be said, false prophets may do signs and wonders, or work miracles, otherwise the *Jews* could not have been cautioned not to be deceived by such means, and consequently, that whatever can be a possible character of a false prophet, cannot be the evidence of a true one:

I answer, false prophets can never work miracles; and no being can change the laws of nature without the consent of the Lord of it; so cannot He consent to the changing of His laws to give evidence to

464   John 10:25
465   John 10:37-38
466   John 14:11
467   John 15:22-24
468   John 5:45-46
469   Acts 3:22
470   Acts 7:37

falsehood, for that would be to act in opposition to Himself.

[471] But impostors may to some persons appear to work miracles; they may by a knowledge of certain powers of nature, of which the vulgar are ignorant, seem to them to do things above the power of nature; and on that account there is need of caution against them.

If it is yet urged that these words of *Moses* are not applicable to *Jesus* only, but to all other prophets who work miracles; I answer, they are in all parts only applicable to *Jesus*, as appears not only from the *Jewish* history, but also from the confession of one of their own prophets in the time of [472]*Ezra,* since which there is no pretense that any person has appeared like unto *Moses.*

But granting the thing, granting that these words were in all parts applicable to other persons besides *Jesus,* yet it would not lessen the evidence which they give Him. Suppose God Almighty should distinguish a succession of persons from the rest of mankind by particular characters, and foretell them by these characters, it would not lessen the evidence of any particular person amongst them, that others were foretold also. When a person appears, and answers descriptions which only could be foretold by God, we are to receive him as witnessed by prophecy; and if another appears and answers the same descriptions, we are to receive him also as foretold by God, and our receiving him will not lessen the evidence of the first; it will not, unless God cannot endue two persons with equal powers.

Putting then a case which our opposers would desire, and which certainly is not the true one; that is, that these words of *Moses* are applicable to other persons who worked miracles, yet it will not lessen the evidence which they give *Jesus;* and whilst He works miracles, and teaches a doctrine worthy of God, He has a right to be received as foretold by *Moses.*

If it is said that those words of *Moses* are no prophecy at all, but are only a criterion whereby to try a Prophet from an impostor, I answer they cannot be only such a criterion, for they directly foretell the appearance of a Person

471   See *Traité sur les Miracles* by Mr. Jacques Serces, 1729
472   Deut. 34:10

[473] *And the Lord said unto me, They have well spoken that which they have spoken. I will raise them up a Prophet like unto thee, and I will put my words into His mouth, and He shall speak unto them all that I command Him,* etc.

We find then upon an examination of *Jewish* Books that *Jesus* fulfills prophecy, and also that He has the highest evidence of it; He answers antecedent descriptions, which could only be given by the Lord of nature.

And we might go on to show that *Jesus* not only fulfills this prophecy of *Moses*, but also many others in the *Jewish* Books; and that there are many descriptions in these Books, of a Person who was to appear and be a blessing to mankind, with several circumstances which were to attend His appearance, and also the time of it, which were fulfilled in *Jesus*, and at His appearance: But of these I shall speak afterwards; it being evident that from this prophecy alone *Jesus* has made out His claim, and has a right to be received as foretold by God.

Proceed we then to answer another objection; and it is urged,

Second, that *Jesus* not only pretends to be the *Prophet* foretold by *Moses*, but also the *Messiah* of the *Jews*, a Person expected under another character besides that of a Prophet; but He is not this person; consequently, an impostor.

I answer, if *Jesus* has a right to be received as the Prophet foretold by Moses, then has He the right to be received as the *Messiah* of the *Jews*; since that Prophet has a right to be hearkened to in whatever He should deliver, and *Jesus* declares [474]Himself to be this Person.

But, say the *Jews,* or others for them, the *Messiah* was to appear under a different character than that which *Jesus* appeared; consequently, *Jesus* is not this Person.

Let then the objector make out this point; let him give clear, and express characters of a *Messiah* in the *Jewish* Books, and then show that these do not belong to *Jesus:* let him, I say, give clear and express

473   Deut. 18:17-18
474   John 4:26

characters of a *Messiah*; otherwise we cannot regard the objection, and we cannot set doubtful interpretations and uncertain meanings against a testimony supported by both miracle, and prophecy.

But, upon an examination of the *Jewish* Scriptures, we find that the *Jews* can do no such thing; on the contrary, several acknowledged characters of the *Messiah* are found in *Jesus*. Particularly, he is of the tribe, family, and town, of which the *Jews* confess that the *Messiah* was to be born; and He appeared at a time when they themselves expected Him; and during a period in which, unless their own Books are imposture, He must have appeared, as will be seen afterwards.

But, say the *Jews*, according to these Scriptures the *Messiah* was to be a temporal Prince, and to reign visibly over the *Jews*. Let then the *Jews* produce their evidence for such an assertion; let them produce plain and express testimony out of their own Books that the *Messiah* was to be a temporal Prince, and at his first appearance on Earth to reign visibly over the *Jews*: but the *Jew* cannot do this, nor is there any such testimony concerning the *Messiah* in his Books: On the contrary, if we search the *Jewish* Books we shall find that those very texts, on which the *Jews* ground their expectation of a temporal *Messiah*, relate only to a spiritual one, such a one as *Jesus* claimed to be. And if the *Jews* say, that the following texts, and others of the same nature, are not the grounds on which they expect a temporal *Messiah*, they must produce those that are, and show that what they produce really do relate to the *Messiah*, and cannot possibly belong to any other Person.

In that[475] Day shall the Branch of the Lord be beautiful and glorious.

[476]Unto us a Child is born, unto us a Son is given, and the government shall be upon His shoulder; and His name shall be called Wonderful, Counselor, the mighty God, the everlasting Father, the Prince of Peace. Of the increase of His government and peace there shall be no end, upon the throne of David and upon His

475   Isaiah 4:2
476   Is. 9:6-7

kingdom to order it, and establish it with judgment and with justice from henceforth even for ever; the zeal of the Lord of hosts will perform this.

But [477]*thou*, Bethlehem Ephrata, *though thou be little among the thousands of* Judah, *yet out of thee shall He come forth unto Me, that is to be Ruler in* Israel, *whose goings forth have been from of old, from everlasting.*

[478]*There shall come forth a Rod from the stem of* Jesse, *and a Branch shall grow out of his roots. And the Spirit of the Lord shall rest upon Him, the Spirit of wisdom and understanding, the Spirit of counsel and might, the Spirit of knowledge and of the fear of the Lord; and shall make Him of quick understanding in the fear of the Lord, and He shall not judge after the sight of His eyes, neither reprove after the hearing of His ears; But with righteousness shall He judge the poor, and reprove with equity, for the meek of the earth: And He shall smite the earth with the rod of His mouth, and with the breath of His lips shall He slay the wicked. And righteousness shall be the girdle of His loins, and faithfulness the girdle of His reins.*

And in [479]*mercy shall the throne be established, and He shall sit upon it in truth, in the tabernacle of* David, *judging and seeking judgment and hasting righteousness.*

Behold [480] *a King shall reign in righteousness,* etc.

Behold, the days come, saith the Lord, that I will raise

477   Micah 5:2
478   Isaiah 11:1-5
479   Is. 16:5
480   Is. 32:1

unto David *a righteous Branch, and a King shall reign and prosper, and shall execute judgment and justice in the earth. In His days* Judah[481] *shall be saved, and Israel shall dwell safely: and this is His name whereby He shall be called,* The Lord our Righteousness.

Behold My [482]*Servant whom I uphold, My Elect in whom My soul delighteth: I have put My Spirit upon Him, He shall bring forth judgment unto the Gentiles. He shall not cry, nor lift up, nor cause His voice to be heard in the streets. A bruised reed shall He not break: and the smoking flax shall He not quench: He shall bring forth judgment unto truth. He shall not fail, nor be discouraged, till He has set judgment in the earth: and the isles shall wait for His law. Thus saith God the Lord, He that created the heavens, and stretched them out, He that spread forth the earth, and that which cometh out of it, He that giveth breath unto the people upon it, and spirit to them that walk therein: 'I the Lord, have called Thee in righteousness, and will hold Thine hand, and will keep Thee, and give Thee for a covenant to the people, for a Light to the Gentiles: To open the blind eyes, to bring out the prisoners from the prison, and them that sit in darkness out of the prison-house. I am the Lord, that is My name, And My glory I will not give to another, neither My praise to graven images.*

Behold, My [483]*Servant shall deal prudently; He shall be exalted and extolled, and be very high. As many were astonished at Thee, (His visage was so marred more than any man, and His form more than the sons of men) so shall He sprinkle many nations, the Kings*

---

481   Jeremiah 23:5-6
482   Isaiah 42:1-8
483   Is. 52:13-15

shall shut their mouths at Him: for that which had not been told them shall they see; and that which they had not heard, shall they consider.

I saw [484] *in the night visions, and behold, One like the Son of Man, came with the clouds of heaven, and came to the Ancient of Days, and they brought Him near before Him. And there was given Him dominion and glory, and kingdom, that all people, nations, and languages should serve Him: His dominion is an everlasting dominion, which shall not pass away, and His kingdom that which shall not be destroyed.*

[485]*Rejoice greatly, O daughter of Zion; Shout, O daughter of Jerusalem: behold thy King cometh unto thee: He is just, and having salvation, lowly and riding upon a donkey, and upon a colt the foal of a donkey. Sing* [486]*and rejoice, O daughter of Zion: for lo, I come, and I will dwell in the midst of thee, saith the Lord. And many nations shall be joined to the Lord in that day, and they shall be My people: and I will dwell in the midst of thee, and thou shalt know that the Lord of hosts hath sent Me unto thee. And the Lord shall inherit* Judah *His portion in the Holy Land, and shall choose Jerusalem again.*

[487]*And the Lord shall be King over all the earth, in that day there shall be one Lord, and His name one.*

In that [488]*day there shall be a Root of* Jesse, *which shall stand for as an ensign of the people; to it shall the Gentiles seek, and His rest shall be glorious.*

---

484   Daniel 7:13-14
485   Zechariah 9:9
486   Zech. 2:10-12
487   Zech. 14:9
488   Isaiah 11:10

And He will [489]*destroy in this mountain, the face of the covering cast over all people, and the veil that is spread over all nations. He will swallow up death in victory, etc.*

Say to them [490]*that are of a fearful heart, Be strong, fear not: behold your God will come with vengeance, even God with a recompense; He will come and save you. Then the eyes of the blind shall be opened, and the ears of the deaf shall be unstopped; then shall the lame man leap as a hart, and the tongue of the dumb sing: for in the wilderness shall waters break out, and streams out of the desert.*

And the [491]*glory of the Lord shall be revealed, and all flesh shall see it together: for the mouth of the Lord hath spoken it.*

And the [492]*Gentiles shall come to Thy light, and kings to the brightness of Thy rising.*

I will [493]*also give Thee for a Light to the Gentiles, that thou mayest be My salvation unto the ends of the earth.*

The [494]*Spirit of the Lord God is upon Me, because the Lord has anointed Me to preach good tidings unto the meek, He hath sent Me to bind up the brokenhearted, to proclaim liberty to the captives, and the opening of the prison to them that are bound. Seventy weeks are determined upon thy people, and upon thy holy city, to finish the transgression, and to make an end of sins,*

---

489   Is. 25:7-8
490   Isaiah 35:4-6
491   Is. 40:5
492   Is. 60:3
493   Is. 49:6
494   Daniel 9:24

and to make reconciliation for iniquity, and to bring in everlasting righteousness, and to seal up the vision and prophecy, and to anoint the Most Holy.

[495]*And in the days of these kings shall the God of heaven will set up a kingdom, which shall never be destroyed: and the kingdom shall not be left to other people, but it shall break in pieces, and consume all these kingdoms, and it shall stand forever.*

[496]*So the Lord will reign over them in Mount Zion from now on, even forever.*

[497]*And all thy children shall be taught of the Lord, and great shall be the peace of thy children.*

Now we say, that either these characters and circumstances of a King and Kingdom, with others of a like nature are the grounds, on which the *Jews* found their expectation of a temporal *Messiah*, or they are not: If they are, then we can prove (and it is evident to every impartial enquirer who considers these texts) that they can only relate to a Spiritual King and Kingdom, such a King as *Jesus* pretended to be, and such a Kingdom as He pretended His was; and that it is impossible to apply them to a temporal one. If these are not the texts on which the *Jews* found their expectation of a temporal *Messiah*, they must produce those that are; and before we acknowledge that the *Messiah* was to be a temporal Prince, contrary to the evidence of miracle and prophecy, we must see clear and express testimony that He was to be such; it must be proved from words that admit no other possible meaning; but, as has been observed, the *Jew* has no such clear and express testimony that the *Messiah* was to be a temporal Prince, nor any expressions concerning His being such which admit no other possible meaning: then *Jesus* is the *Messiah* for any thing yet found in the *Jewish* Books to be contrary.

---

495   Dan. 2:44
496   Micah 4:7b
497   Isaiah 54:13

We pass on then *thirdly*, to another grand Jewish objection which is this,

The *Jews* were commanded to observe their Law *forever:* but *Jesus* and His apostles abolished this Law; therefore *Jesus* and His apostles are impostors.

The question then is, whether God required of the *Jews* a perpetual observation of their whole Law, and whether the expressions concerning the duration of this Law, can have but one possible meaning; which is, that it was God's will that it should be observed *forever*, and never give way to another dispensation.

In order to resolve this point, we must remember that in a divine revelation no one part can contradict another, and particular texts must first be reconciled betwixt themselves, before any thing can be advanced from any of them.

Now *Moses* and other prophets commanded the *Jews* to observe *forever* the Law given to them by God.

Moses likewise assures them, that a Prophet should arise *like unto himself,* who should *speak to them the Words of God,* and to whom if they *did not hearken,* it would be *required of them.*

And the calling of the Gentiles is foretold by many of the prophets.

Those texts then which require a perpetual observation of the *Jewish* Law; and that particular one which commands, that *a Person who speaks in the Name of the Lord, and the thing which he speaks, follows and comes to pass, should be hearkened to*; and those which foretell the calling of the Gentiles, must have all such meanings as are consistent with each other.

When then a Person appears with the promised evidence, the *Jews* were to hearken to him, and to receive him as the promised Prophet. But when this Person, or those who act by His authority and commission, abolish the Law of *Moses,* then were the Jews to examine the expressions concerning the duration of their Law, and to see whether these expressions can possibly be understood according to the sense put on them by those who abolish this Law; whether this Law may give way to another dispensation.

This is the true point to be considered here: for if the expressions concerning the duration of this Law can be understood in a limited sense, and do not strictly mean a perpetual duration; then we ought to understand them in that sense which is put on them by Those who have the evidence of miracle and prophecy.

And upon examination of these texts we immediately find that they are not only capable of being understood in a limited sense, but that really they can have no other; the calling of the Gentiles being inconsistent with a perpetual observation of the Law of *Moses,* some part of this Law consisting in a separation of the *Jews* from other nations.

Upon the whole then, the true state of the matter seems to be this: the Law was to be observed as long as it was a Law, till the Power who made should abolish it; till the Prophet should arise Who should be as a God to the people and give them a new dispensation; till the happy time when the Gentiles should be called, and all nations serve the Lord.

The *forever* does not relate to the Law but to the people's duty; they were to observe it *forever,* that is, as long as it was a Law.

And in this sense is the expression *forever* understood when it relates to laws promulgated by a human legislator. The people are required to observe them *forever,* that is, as long as they are laws; but the legislator does not by this expression preclude himself from annulling these laws, if he thinks fit so to do, nor do the people understand the expression in this sense.

Suppose that God, when He gave these laws, designed they should be abolished, and give way to another dispensation; would He not, think we, have commanded the *Jews* to observe them forever? Doubtless He would have done this, it being their indispensible duty to do so; to observe them as long as they were laws, and until He pleased to abrogate them. We cannot suppose He would acquaint them with the designed change, which would have been a probable means to lessen their esteem for that which it was their duty to observe.

Yet again, we may and ought to conclude that several of the expressions concerning the duration of the *Jewish* Law related only to the moral part of it; and as to this, it is very evident that *Jesus* according to His own Words, might properly be said to *come not to destroy the Law, but to fulfill.*

And we may yet farther observe that the expression *forever* is often used in a limited sense in the Jewish Scriptures; thus an everlasting Priesthood is promised to [498] *Aaron and his sons.*

Again, from God's own expressions concerning this Law we have reason to think it was only occasional, and given for a time: thus He says, *He gave them*[499] *statutes which were not good*, etc.

Again, from the nature and office of the Person foretold by *Moses*, and the particular evidence which was to be given Him, it is evident that He was to be Author of a new dispensation

In a word, the Jew must, to make the expressions in his own Books concerning the duration of the *Jewish* Law any objection against *Jesus*' being the Prophet foretold by *Moses*, or the *Messiah* of the *Jews*, show that these expressions can have only one possible sense, which is, that this law was to be observed as long as the world should last, and never give way to another dispensation; but, as has been seen, the *Jew* cannot possibly do this, therefore the expressions in the *Jewish* Books concerning the eternality of the *Jewish* Law, can be no objection against *Jesus*' being the Person He pretended to be.

Fourthly, it is objected that *Jesus* and His apostles applied many places of Scripture to themselves, which did not belong to them; consequently are impostors.

Before we examine into the truth of this charge, we may remark that it is very strange, that the persons who were in possession of the very best evidence which could be given them, miracle and prophecy, and who had craft enough to deceive us thus far, should yet be so weak as to invalidate their own evidence by misapplications. We might rather expect they would have let their cause rest upon a good footing, when they had once got it there, and not have taken the most probable step to the ruin of it. But be this as it will, certain it is that only impostors can misapply: the question then is, whether the texts applied by *Jesus* and His apostles, are misapplications.

Now if *Jesus*, or His apostles, affixed a sense to words which they could not possibly bear; if they applied characters to themselves which could not belong to them, if they pretend to be spoken of when they are not spoken of, then they are guilty of misapplications, and are impostors.

498   Exodus 40:15, Numbers 25:13
499   Ezekiel 20:25

But we must observe, that nothing but their affixing impossible meanings, can be called misapplications; and as they were in possession of miracle and prophecy, they have a right before all other persons, to interpret difficulties; and a possible sense supported by miracle and prophecy ought to be received before that which is only the product of human judgment.

We are then to proceed to an examination of the objected places, and in order to this, think it proper to take a view of the Jewish dispensation.

The Jewish dispensation consisted of many *rites, ceremonies,* and *sacrifices;* which seem in their own nature to have no worth or excellency in them, and to have nothing to commend them but the commands of the legislator.

Again, the Legislator Himself places no worth or excellency in them, tells the *Jews* that He gave them [500]*statutes which were not good*: and assures them that most punctual observation of these statutes would be to no purpose, nor render them acceptable to Him, if they were deficient in other duties.

This is the *Jewish* Law as we find it. Now let us see the Gospel account of it.

And this acquaints us that these *rites, ceremonies, sacrifices,* and whole Law, were preparatory to, and symbolical of, the dispensation by *Jesus;* that they were given *only for a time,* and *because of transgression,* and until the dispensation should arrive, *promised to Abraham four hundred years before the giving of the law,* in which *all the families of*[501] *the Earth were to be blessed,* in which *Jesus appeared to bless us, in turning*[502] *every one of us from our iniquities.* Thus wrote the author to the Hebrews,

> *Being* [503]*made perfect, He became the Author of eternal salvation unto all them that obey Him.*

> *By* [504]*His own blood He entered in once to the holy place,*

500   Ezekiel 20:25
501   Galatians 3:8,17
502   Acts 3:26
503   Hebrews 5:9
504   Heb. 9:12b

having obtained eternal salvation for us.

Once [505]*in the end of the world, hath He appeared to put away sin by the sacrifice of Himself.*

Now in what manner the first dispensation was symbolical, and representative of the second, the author in several chapters sets before us. He says, that the

> *Priests under the law serve as an* [506]*example and shadow of heavenly things, that the high* [507]*priest went alone, once every year, into the Holy of Holies, the Holy Ghost this signifying, that the way into the holiest of all, was not yet made manifest while as the first tabernacle was yet standing: which was a figure for the time then present, in which were offered both gifts and sacrifices,* etc.

And speaking of the *rites, sacrifices,* and *sprinklings* under the *Law* by the *blood of calves and goats:* he says,

> *It was therefore necessary* [508]*that the patterns of things in the heavens should be purified with these, but the heavenly things themselves* (represented by those patterns) *with better sacrifices than these. For Christ is not entered into the holy places made with hands, which are the figures of the true, but into heaven itself, now to appear in the presence of God for us.*

This is the Hebrew author's account of the *Jewish* dispensation; and those strangely mistake things who say that these places in the *Hebrews* are only *allusions* or *accommodations.* He plainly tells us, that the *priests, high priests, tabernacles, sacrifices,* and *Law* were *shadows,*

---

505   Heb. 9:26b
506   Heb. 8:5, 9:24
507   Heb. 9:7-8
508   Heb. 9:23-24

patterns, figures, examples of the *dispensation* by *Jesus*. And *Jesus* Himself says, that *the Law* [509]*and Prophets prophesied until* John. *That He* [510]*came to fulfill the Law and Prophets; and that till Heaven and Earth pass, one jot or tittle shall in no wise pass from the Law till all be fulfilled*; that is, the Law should in no part be abolished till that dispensation should arrive, of which the Law was only a resemblance. Again *Jesus* says, *He* [511]*will not eat any more of the Passover till it be fulfilled in the Kingdom of Heaven*: that is, till the Lamb is sacrificed, which this *Paschal Lamb was to represent.*

Now then, this being the account which *Jesus* and His apostles give us of the *Jewish* dispensation, the question is, whether it is a possible one? If it is, it will follow that it ought to be received as a true one, being supported by miracle and prophecy.

And upon the first view we find that this is not only a possible account of the *Jewish* dispensation, but likewise the most rational and consistent one that can be given of it; and if it was suitable to the Divine Wisdom to give *Jesus* to live and die for the sake of mankind, it is reasonable to expect that a mode of worship, which He Himself would institute, should bear resemblance to this great propitiatory sacrifice; that the whole *Jewish* dispensation should show forth His death before He came, after the same manner as that sacrament which He Himself instituted, does show forth His death since He is come.

The *Jews* cannot object to the reasonableness of such an institution, they who were commanded to express their deliverances by symbols of them, who yearly offered up the [512]*Passover lamb, the firstlings of their flocks,* and who observed *the Feast* [513]*of Tabernacles.*

And other nations cannot object to it, it being a common practice with them, as may be shown from many instances taken from different countries, to celebrate great deliverances by symbols of those deliverances.

But, as before, not so much as this is wanted in the present argument; and if the account given of the *Jewish* dispensation by *Jesus* and His apostles is only a possible one, it ought to be received as a

---

509   Matthew 11:13
510   Matthew 5:17-18
511   Luke 22:16
512   Exodus 7-8
513   Leviticus 23:34

true one.

And if it ought to be received as a true one, many of those difficulties, which arise from certain applications made by these persons, will vanish, as will appear from a consideration of them.

Farther, as God might make the Law symbolical of the Gospel, so might He, if He pleased, purposely make some events under the first dispensation, resemble others under the second; the reason why He should do this may be considered afterwards; all we at present want is, that it be allowed possible for Him to do it But it must be allowed possible for Him to do it, there being nothing in this way of acting disagreeable to His attributes.

Again, it is likewise possible for God, that is, it is not unsuitable to His nature, to give the *Jewish* nation signs of temporal deliverance which should bear resemblance to a greater deliverance, the appearance of the *Messiah*. As He often pointed out temporal deliverances by signs of them, as may be shown from many instances, it could be no contradiction to His attributes to make these signs, if He pleased, signs also of that great deliverance.

Yet once more, if the first dispensation was given for the sake of the second, and only added *for a time because of transgressions*, as from a view of both dispensations it is rational to think it was, then we may expect that the prophets under the first should be full of descriptions of this last; that what they deliver should tend to something farther than the present state of things, and to draw the people's attention to the great deliverance designed for them.

We now proceed to examine some applications made by *Jesus* and His apostles, in order to see whether they are impossible ones.

We will divide the applied texts into two sorts; and first speak of those which seem to be indeterminate, neither applicable to the present circumstances of affairs at the time of delivery, or to the person of the prophet who delivered them.

Secondly, of those which seem determinate, that is, which at first view appear to relate to the person of the prophet, present times, or state of things.

Of the first sort are the following ones:

All ye [514]shall be offended because of me this night: for it is written, I will smite the Shepherd, and the sheep of the flock shall be scattered abroad. And he [515]was numbered with the transgressors, etc.

These places are applied to *Jesus* by Himself; now the question is, what is the evidence that they related to Him?

First, they exactly in all parts and circumstances correspond with the character of Jesus.

Secondly, there is the evidence of miracle and prophecy that they do relate to Him.

But we want not so much as this in the present argument; and if it cannot be proved that these texts could not possibly relate to *Jesus,* then it cannot be proved that He has misapplied them: but it cannot be proved that they could not possibly relate to *Jesus,* then it cannot be proved that He has misapplied them.

[Also,] the following texts from the manner in which they are delivered, at first view seem to relate to the person of the prophet, time of delivery, or the then state of things.

Behold, [516]a virgin shall conceive, and bear a Son, and shall call His name Emmanuel.

When [517] Israel was a Child, then I loved Him, and called my Son out of Egypt.

They [518]gave me gall for my meat and in my thirst they gave me vinegar to drink.

514   Matthew 26:31, Zech. 13:7
515   Mark 15:28, Is 53:12
516   Matt. 1:23, Is. 7:14
517   Matt. 2:15, Hosea 11:1
518   Ps. 69:21, Matt. 27:34

[519]They part my garmens among them, and cast lots upon my venture.

They [520]weighed for my price thirty pieces of silver. And the Lord said unto me, cast it unto the potter: a goodly price that I was prized at of them. And I took the thirty pieces of silver, and cast them to the potter in the House of the Lord.

[521]I will declare the decree: The Lord hath said unto Me, Thou art My Son, this day have I begotten Thee. Ask of Me and I will give Thee the heathen for Thine inheritance, and the uttermost parts of the earth for Thy possession.

[522]I have set the Lord always before me; because He is at my right hand, I shall not be moved. Therefore my heart is glad, and my glory rejoices; My flesh also shall rest in hope. For Thou wilt not leave my soul in Hell, neither wilt Thou suffer Thy Holy One to see corruption. Thou wilt show me the path of life; In Thy presence is fullness of joy, and at Thy right hand there are pleasures forevermore.

These, and many other places which at first view seem to relate to the times in which they were spoken, or the person of the speaker, are produced, and differently applied by *Jesus*, and His apostles.

The point we are next to examine then is, whether the applications made by these persons are possible ones.

And no sooner is this point examined, but we find that though some of these texts do at first view seem to relate to the times in which they were spoken, or the person of the speaker, yet that they really

519   Matt. 27:35, Ps. 22:18
520   Matt. 27:9, Zech. 11:12
521   Psalm 2:7-8
522   Ps. 16:8-11

do not, but must relate to other persons, or times. Thus, of those cited, *Thou art my Son, this day have I begotten thee. I will give thee the heathen for thine inheritance, and the uttermost parts of the Earth for thy possession.* These were circumstances never applicable to *David*, and consequently, he could not in these places speak of himself. So the words cited out of the sixteenth Psalm could not relate to *David*; he could not call himself the *Holy One*, this term being unsuitable to his character, and to that humility which appeared in his writings.

And those particular expressions, [523]*They gave me gall for my meat, and in my thirst they gave me vinegar to drink,* [524]*they part my garments among them, and cast lots upon my venture,* which were applied to *Jesus* by one of His apostles, we have reason to think from *David's* history, were circumstances that never happened in his life.

Now, then if these characters and circumstances delivered by *David* could not relate to himself, they must relate to some other Person; and if they do this, He has the best right to them whom they suit, and who can give the evidence of miracle and prophecy that they really relate to Him.

But *secondly*, as for those texts which directly suit the circumstances of affairs when delivered, the person of the prophet, or the then state of things, the answer is direct; and if it was not unsuitable to the wisdom of God, to let some events under the first dispensation resemble the great events under the second; if it was no contradiction to His attributes sometimes to give His people a sign of temporal deliverance, which should bear resemblance to the greatest deliverance they were capable of receiving: then could it be no misapplication to apply the words of the first event to the second, of the sign to the thing signified, they being directly according to the will of God fulfilled in both cases.

To instance, supposing God when he gave *Ahaz* a sign from *Pekah*, and *Remaliah*, likewise intended that this should be a sign of that great future deliverance of mankind, by a Child born of a virgin; then, when *Jesus* was born of a virgin, might *Matthew* properly say, *Now all this was done that it might be fulfilled, which was spoken of the Lord*

---

523   Ps. 69:21, Matt. 27:34
524   Matt. 27:35, Ps. 22:18

by the Prophet (that it might be fulfilled which was spoken of the Lord by the Prophet, when he gave a sign which prefigured the birth of the Messiah,) *Behold a virgin shall be with child*, etc.

Thus again, supposing God when He sent His people into *Egypt*, designed sending His own Son thither, and intended that one event should prefigure the other, then, when *Jesus* came out of *Egypt*, might *Matthew* again justly say, *That it might be fulfilled, which was spoken of the Lord by the Prophet, saying*, (that this event might come to pass according to the will of God, and the expression of the Prophet concerning a former one that prefigured it,) *out of* Egypt *I have called my Son.*

But not so much as this is wanted in the present argument; it is not necessary that the sign given to *Ahaz* should be a sign of the birth of the *Messiah*; or the event of *Israel's* being called out of *Egypt* prefigure the calling of the *Messiah* from thence, to make *Matthew's* application just. For if a *Messiah* was intended, the whole manner and circumstances of His life and death must be also predetermined by God. Well then might *Matthew* when *Jesus* was born of virgin, or when he came out of *Egypt*, upon a consideration of God's determinate counsel and knowledge, say, *Now all this was done, that it might be fulfilled which was spoken of the Lord by the Prophet*, (that this event which God has long ago determined should come to pass, may now do so, according to the expression of the prophet,) *Behold a virgin shall be with Child*, etc. *out of Egypt I have called my Son.*

But we need not seek for many solutions of the above proposed difficulty; one possible one is sufficient, as has been before observed.

The whole mistake concerning these applications seems to be taking them in a wrong view, and imagining that *Matthew* brings them as proof that *Jesus* is the *Messiah*. He offers at no such thing, nor is it his business in this place. He is only telling a plain narrative, the history of *Jesus*, and by the way remarks upon several events in which the will of God was fulfilled according to the expressions of the prophets.

In short, unless it can be proved, that the texts applied by *Matthew* could not possibly relate to *Jesus*; that God could not, if He pleased, make events under the first dispensation resemble others under the second; give signs of temporal deliverance which should be signs also of deliverance by *Messiah*; and that the manner and circumstance of the appearance of the *Messiah*, was not predetermined by God; it cannot be proved that he has been guilty of misapplication; but neither of the above mentioned particulars, (much less all of them) can be proved; then it cannot be proved that *Matthew* has been guilty of misapplication.

But *secondly*, another mark of falsehood is objected against the Christian religion and that is, *Matthew* makes a false quotation, and says, *He [Jesus]* [525]*came and dwelt in a city called Nazareth: that it might be fulfilled which was spoken by the prophets, he shall be called a Nazarene.*

This objection is almost too slight to answer. Suppose the Jews had a tradition, which arose from the mouth of some of their prophets, that the *Messiah* was to be a *Nazarene*; this is a much more easy supposition than that *Matthew* should make a false quotation, which would manifestly have been an injury, and could not possibly have been any way an advantage to his cause. As then we are sure, that if *Matthew* was not an impostor, he could not, and as we have reason to think that if he was one, he would not make a false quotation, we ought not to look upon it as such, notwithstanding we cannot, at so great a distance of time, find whence it is produced.

But another objection yet remains, and that is, *Elijah* was to come before the coming of the *Messiah*; but *Elijah* is not come; consequently, *Jesus* is not the *Messiah*.

The argument stands thus. The followers of *Jesus* do not pretend to say that *Elijah* is come, if *John the Baptist* is not *Elijah* (proof his [526]own words), then Elijah is not come.

Now the account given by *Jesus* of this matter is this, that *John the Baptist was the* [527]*Elijah which was to come*; that he was the person promised by the prophets under the name of *Elijah*.

The query is, whether this is a possible account of the matter, whether this assertion of *Jesus'* concerning *John the Baptist* is consistent with *Jewish* prophecy, that is, whether the calling one person by the name of another whom he resembles, whose character he takes, and by *whose spirit and power* he acts (which is the account given of *John the*

525   Matthew 2:23
526   John 1:21
527   Matthew 11:14

Baptist by the angel [528]*Gabriel*) is agreeable to *Jewish* Scriptures.

This way of speaking is certainly agreeable to *Jewish* Scriptures, where we often find the characters and offices of persons given us in their names, and the same person called by different names. Instances of the first kind are frequent; of the second, the following one is sufficient. It is said, that David, *the Son of* David, *and the Lord shall reign over the House of* Jacob *forever.*[529]

It follows then, that provided *John the Baptist* acted *by the spirit and power of* Elijah, acted as *Elijah* would have himself acted, if he had been upon Earth; it was not unsuitable to *Jewish* prophecy to foretell him under the name of *Elijah;* but *John the Baptist* did *act in the spirit and power of* Elijah, act as *Elijah* would himself have acted, if he had been upon Earth, for which we have the evidence of miracle and prophecy; then it was not unsuitable to *Jewish* prophecy to foretell him under the name of *Elijah.* And if it was not unsuitable to *Jewish* prophecy to foretell *John the Baptist* under the name of *Elijah,* then *Jesus'* assertion that *John the Baptist* was the promised *Elijah,* was not unsuitable to *Jewish* prophecy; and if *Jesus'* assertion concerning *John the Baptist* is neither unsuitable to *Jewish* prophecy, nor is an impossible one, then it ought to be received before any other whatsoever, having the evidence of miracle and prophecy, and *John the Baptist* ought to be received as the promised *Elijah.*

That the speaking of persons under the names of others, whom they resemble, is common to other nations besides the *Jews*, is too well known to need instances.

---

528   Luke 1:17
529   Ezekiel 37:25; Jer. 33:17-21; Micah 4:7

Section XI

※※※※※※※※※※※※※※※※※※※※※※※※※※※※※※※

The Implications for the Jewish Scriptures if Jesus is not the Messiah

And now having shown that the *Christian* religion has the evidence of miracle and prophecy; that the *Jews* cannot consistently; with a belief of *Moses*, reject *Jesus* as not being the *Messiah*, the Person He pretends to be; and having seen the insignificancy of the objections commonly urged against Him, I proceed to show that the *Jews* are so far from being able to prove *Jesus* not the *Messiah*, that on the contrary, their own books are imposture, if He is not this Person.

I pass by all those repeated promises above produced of a *King* and *Kingdom, deliverances, blessings,* etc. which if not fulfilled in *Jesus,* are yet unfulfilled, and consequently are justly suspected of never coming from God; and only insist on the following ones.

God in a particular manner calls *Abraham* from his kindred and his country, and three times solemnly assures him[530], *That in him and his seed all the nations of the Earth should be blessed.* Now there is no pretense that all the nations of the Earth have been really blessed in *Abraham,* or in any person descended from him, unless it be in *Jesus;* and though we were to understand the words according to the sense which some put on them, (which doubtless is not the obvious and literal one) that is, that *Abraham* should be a standard of blessedness to mankind, and people should say when they bless, *God make you* as Abraham, they are even in this sense unfulfilled; *Abraham,* or any of his descendants, having never been a standard of blessedness to

---

530   Genesis 12:3, 18:18, 22:18

any nation, (unless perhaps a short time to the *Jewish*) much less to all; and the seed of *Abraham*, but in the fourth or fifth generation from him, fell into bondage and slavery, recovered but short-lived prosperity, came again into distress, and have continued many ages in a condition that is the reverse of blessedness.

This promise is then yet unfulfilled, or fulfilled in *Jesus*; if it is unfulfilled, then there is a mark of falsehood in the *Jewish* religion, it being impossible for God to promise and not to perform in due time.

If it be replied that this promise is yet to be fulfilled, and that *a thousand years with the Lord are as one day;* I answer, that though *a thousand years with the Lord are as one day*, yet they are not so with man; and that when the Supreme Being condescends to communicate Himself to man, He must act with him according to his nature, as well as His own; He cannot then give so solemn a promise of such a nature to *Abraham*, and not fulfill it in above three thousand years, and besides let the seed of *Abraham* continue for many generations in such a distressed and dispersed condition, that all hopes and human prospect of its being ever fulfilled, ceases.

If the *Jew* yet tells us, that according to our account of things, this promise was not fulfilled until near two thousand years after it was given, and that what might for wise and good reasons be deferred so long, might for as wise and good ones be deferred longer; I again return, that though the promised blessing was so long deferred, yet by constant revelations from God, the prospect of its being fulfilled increased, and God kept up the hopes and expectations of the *Jews* by other prophecies, which pointed out the time, manner, and circumstances of this blessing; He renewed and confirmed it to them by the mouth of His prophets. But now as all prophecy has ceased for above two thousand years, there is no prospect of its ever being fulfilled, and it stands as a mark of imposture in the *Jewish* religion, if *Jesus* is not the *Messiah*.

This is the plain and direct view, in which this text is to be considered; and those strangely mistake things, who considering it simply, give it in evidence of the *Christian* religion. *Jesus* must be first proved the *Messiah*, before we can apply the blessedness; and those who deny his being the *Messiah*, deny the blessedness. Yet this text affords a strong argument to the *Jew*, that *Jesus* is the *Messiah*; and as he cannot pretend that it is fulfilled in any person if not in *Jesus*, he is driven to acknowledge, either that God promised and did not perform, or that *Jesus* is the *Messiah*.

Secondly, Jacob blessing his sons, declares, that *the scepter*[531] *shall not depart from* Judah, *nor a lawgiver from between his feet, until* Shiloh *come*. Here then is a remarkable Person foretold to come into the world before a certain period; the question then is, whether the Person foretold is the *Messiah*, or some other person: but the *Jews* cannot possibly apply this prophecy to any other person; it is yet unfulfilled, or fulfilled in *Jesus*. If it is yet unfulfilled, then there is a mark of falsehood in the *Jewish* religion, the period being manifestly past before which *Jacob* declared that this person should appear.

Thirdly, Moses' promise to the people, that God would send them *a Prophet like unto himself*, who should be in the place of God, and *speak the words of his mouth*, etc. is fulfilled, or not fulfilled. If it is not fulfilled, there is another mark of falsehood in the *Jewish* religion; if it is fulfilled, that it can be fulfilled in no other Person than *Jesus*, is evident, from the Jewish accounts of their own prophets, none of whom were like unto *Moses*, and from the direct confession of one of them, *and there arose not a prophet since in* Israel *like unto* Moses.[532]

Fourthly, all those promises to *David* of *establishing his* [533] *throne forever, letting his seed remain as long as the Sun and Moon endureth*, etc. must be fulfilled in *Jesus*, or are delusion and imposture. Ten tribes were rent from *David* in the second generation after him, and all government has been taken from his family for above these seventeen hundred years: shall we then assert that God promised and did not perform; or that these promises may yet be fulfilled, notwithstanding there has been so long an interruption to all dominion in the House of *David*? The point is evident; either these promises are *Jewish* forgeries, or they are fulfilled in *Jesus*.

Indeed it seems as if God by taking ten tribes from *Rehoboam*, purposely designed to show the people that it was not a temporal Kingdom which was to be established in the House of David, and these promises had another signification. And if we consider the last

---

531   Genesis 49:10
532   Deut. 34:10-11
533   Psalm 89

Words of the son of *Jesse*, we have reason to think that he himself understood as much.

> [534]*The Spirit of the Lord spoke by me, and His word was in my tongue. The God of* Israel *said, The Rock of* Israel *spoke to me, He that ruleth over men must be just, ruling in the fear of God: And he shall be as the light of the morning, when the sun riseth, even a morning without clouds; as the tender grass springing out of the earth by clear shining after rain. Although my house be not so with God; yet He hath made with me an everlasting covenant, ordered in all things and sure: For this is all my salvation, and all my desire, although He make it not to grow.*

Fifthly, the fifty-third chapter of *Isaiah* relates to the *Messiah,* or it does not relate to Him; if it does not relate to the *Messiah,* then the *Jew* must show to whom it does relate, and who that person is that is so great, *that kings shut their mouths at him,* yet *is led like a lamb to the slaughter wounded for our transgressions; bears the sins of many; makes intercession for his transgressors; see his seed, and prolongs his days, after his soul is make an offering for sin;* let them show who this person is, if it be not the *Messiah.* If they cannot do this, then there is another mark of falsehood in the *Jewish* religion, the time for the appearance of this person being so limited by the prophet *Daniel,* (as will appear presently) that he must be already come, if *Daniel* is not an impostor. For that *Isaiah* and *Daniel* describe the same person, is evident from comparing the characters given by each of them.

Sixthly, the following remarkable prophecy is fulfilled in *Jesus,* or the person who delivered it is an impostor:

> [535]*Seventy weeks are determined upon thy people and upon thy holy city, to finish the transgression, to make an end of sins, and to make reconciliation for iniquity,*

534   2 Samuel 23:2-5
535   Daniel 9:24, 26

and to bring in everlasting righteousness, and to seal up vision and prophecy, and to anoint the Most Holy, etc. And after threescore and two weeks shall Messiah *be cut off, but not for Himself: and the people of the prince that shall come, shall destroy the city, and the sanctuary, and the end thereof shall be with a flood, and unto the end of the war desolations are determined.*

Now this prophecy cannot possibly be applied to any person who has yet appeared in the world unless it be *Jesus*: and though the *Jews* and some persons for them, would fain apply it to one of their own high-priests, yet it is so impossible they should do this, given the character of the Person, and the work He was to perform as *finishing transgression, making an end of sins, bringing in everlasting righteousness, sealing up vision and prophecy,* etc. being no way applicable to any such person.

If then this prophecy cannot possibly be applied to any person who has yet appeared in the world unless to *Jesus*, then it is fulfilled in Him, or is unfulfilled: but it cannot possibly be unfulfilled, unless *Daniel* who delivered it, is an impostor; because according to him this person was to appear before the destruction of the *city* and *sanctuary*, and both these have been destroyed seventeen hundred years.

That this prophecy is applicable to *Jesus* in all its parts, is confessed by the adversaries of *Christianity*, when they take pains to show that it is a *Christian* forgery.

If we consider this prophecy rightly, we shall not need to be critical in a calculation of *Daniel's Seventy Weeks*; it is enough that it was to be fulfilled before the destruction of the *city* and *sanctuary*: so that these being destroyed, it must be fulfilled, or *Daniel*, who delivered it, an impostor.

The true end of this remarkable prophecy (like the fifty-third chapter of *Isaiah*) seems to be, to take off objections which might arise on account of a suffering *Messiah*, and to confirm and establish the weak in future ages.

Thus, as *Abraham* had been assured *that in his Seed all the families of the Earth should be blessed; Moses* had told the people that *God would raise them up a Prophet from amidst their brethren, who would speak to them the words of God, and to whom they should hearken,* and *Nathan, Isaiah, Jeremiah,* and other prophets, promised that *the throne of* David *should be established forever;* that a King *should rule in righteousness,* etc. and were full of descriptions of this *King* and *Kingdom,* lest the *Jews* might from hence conceive hopes of a temporal prince and worldly prosperity and grandeur, God kindly guarded them against so dangerous a mistake, and let them know by His prophet *Isaiah,* that the Prince who was to be their Deliverer, was to have *no outward from or comeliness, but to be a man of sorrows, and acquainted with grief;* that the evil He was to deliver them from, was *their sins;* and that the manner in which He was to do it, was by *wounds, sufferings, stripes, death;* and again, He by *Daniel* confirms this, perhaps unacceptable, truth, and fixes a *period,* namely, the destruction of their *city* and *sanctuary,* before which, He assures them their Prince should be thus treated and cut off.

Seventhly, the time is so limited for the fulfilling of another remarkable prophecy, that it must be fulfilled, or the person who delivered it an impostor,

> [536]*The Lord whom you seek, shall suddenly come to His temple: even the Messenger of the covenant, whom you delight in: Behold, He shall come, saith the Lord of hosts.*

Now there is no pretense, nor can be any, that this text is fulfilled, if not in *Jesus* (in His being the *Messiah,* and in person in the temple) and if it is not fulfilled, then neither can it ever be; the temple being destroyed. And if it neither is, nor can be fulfilled, unless *Jesus* is the *Messiah,* then it is either fulfilled in Him, or is delusion and imposture.

So again, those other texts[537] *I will shake all nations, and the desire of all nations shall come, and I will fill this house with glory, saith the Lord of hosts. The glory of this latter house shall be greater than of the former, saith the Lord of hosts,* can in no sense be true, according to the best accounts of both temples, if *Jesus* is not the *Messiah.*

---

536   Malachi 3:1
537   Haggai 2:7,9

Again, lastly, there are several prophecies concerning the calling of the *Gentiles*, which are yet unfulfilled, or are fulfilled by the calling of them to the *Christian* religion. If they are yet unfulfilled, then we cannot reconcile with the wisdom and justice of God His suffering so remarkable and amazing a conversion of *Gentiles* to a false religion, which was a direct way to draw the *Jews* into error by an application of this event to their prophecies; if they are fulfilled, that they can only be fulfilled in the conversion of the *Gentiles* to *Christianity*, is evident.

Now if one remarkable text standing for many ages unfulfilled, raises suspicion of falsehood, several texts doing so, and some of them such as now never can be fulfilled, are evident proofs of it.

We can have no greater certainty of a revelation than we have, that God cannot deceive; that He will not require our assent to His will without giving us sufficient evidence that it is such; that He will deal with us according to our nature, etc.

He cannot then promise to *Abraham, that in his Seed all the families of the Earth should be blessed,* and yet defer this *blessedness* above three thousand years; to *Moses, that He would raise up a Prophet like unto himself, who should speak the Words of God,* yet never send any such person; to *David, to establish his throne forever,* yet immediately rend ten tribes from him, and let his seed be scattered seventeen hundred years together over the face of the Earth; *to come suddenly to His temple, and fill it with glory,* yet let the temple be destroyed so that it is impossible He should do this; *to make an end of sins, to make reconciliation for iniquity, and to bring in everlasting righteousness, and to seal up the vision and prophecy,* yet never send any Person on such an errand.

These are direct impossibilities, and I must conclude, according to my proposition, that the *Jewish* religion is imposture, if *Jesus* is not the *Messiah*.

It is remarkable, and worth observing, that the evidence to a *Jew* of *Jesus'* being the *Messiah,* increased with the difficulties which arose against it; and that every circumstance was guarded, which might be an occasion of stumbling to them. This seems to be the wisdom of God.

Thus, when *Jesus* appeared and preached the true God; gave the most perfect system of morality, and worked miracles; He ought to have been received as a teacher from God, on account of His miracles, and also as the Prophet foretold by *Moses*.

And accordingly, as has been observed, He expects their conviction upon this evidence, *Believe me for the very works sake*, etc. *If I had not done among you the works which no other man did*, etc. And again, when *John* sent two of his disciples to ask Him, [538]*Art Thou He that should come, or do we look for another?* He only answers by recounting His works, *Go and show* John, says He, *those things which ye do hear and see: The blind receive their sight, and the lame walk; the lepers are cleansed, and the deaf hear, the dead are raised up, and the poor have the gospel preached to them. And blessed is he whosoever shall not be offended in Me.* (The number and nature of My works, My miracles, are full evidence that I am the promised Prophet, and blessed is he, who not prejudiced by worldly views, can receive this evidence, and be My disciple).

Here then, the works of *Jesus*, His miracles, were full evidence that He was the Prophet *Moses* foretold, and the promised *Messiah*. But when He came to suffer, then had the *Jews* a stumbling-block, owing to their own prejudices and worldly attachments. Now was the hour come, when *blessed was he who was not offended at a suffering* Messiah. Now was it time for the *Jews* again to look into their Books to which *Jesus* over and over kindly refers them. Here *Isaiah, Daniel,* and *Zechariah*, set them right by telling them, that the *Messiah was to be a Man of sorrows, and acquainted with grief; that He was to pour out His soul to death; that after threescore and two weeks He should be cut off, but not for Himself; and that the sword should awake against a Man that was fellow to the Lord of Hosts.*

Again, when persecution arose, which was another bar to the flesh and blood, then were those remarkable prophecies concerning the calling of the *Gentiles*, fulfilled, and fulfilled under this extraordinary disadvantageous circumstance, that the conversion was to a persecuted Church.

When the city and temple were destroyed, then had the *Jews* demonstration that the *Messiah* was to come, or that *Daniel*, who told them that the *Messiah* should be cut off before this period; and *Malachi* and *Haggai*, who had promised that *the Lord should come suddenly to His temple*, and that *the glory of the second House shall be greater than that of the former*, were impostors.

And at this day the dispersed and distressed condition of the *Jews*, as well as their unfulfilled prophecies, is an evidence against them.

Though it is not necessary that God, after He has once revealed Himself, should give fresh evidences to His revelation in different ages, yet it is necessary that He does not mislead and give grounds for hope of deliverance, yet not let this deliverance ever arrive; and further let an impostor arise to whom the characters of the promised, and expected Person, are so suitable, that by that means He draws multitudes into error. In this case the people favored with a revelation, are in a worse condition than all others, one part of them being deceived by an impostor, the other left to languish in fruitless hopes and expectations.

But, if the *Jewish* religion advances inconsistencies and impossibilities, if *Jesus* is not the *Messiah*; on the contrary, change the prospect, and, if He is this Person, the whole of it is rational and consistent.

In the first place, it is rational to expect that the *Messiah*, a Person who was *to speak the words of God*, to be hearkened to *in all things*, and to be the Author of a new dispensation, should be foretold by *Jewish* prophets, particularly by *Moses*, this being a connecting evidence, an evidence that the Author of the first was the Author of the second dispensation; that the very God who brought the people out of *Egypt*, and gave them their Law, also sent them that Person who abolished it. And as it is rational to expect that the *Messiah* should be foretold in the *Jewish* Scriptures, so in *Jesus* we find a concurrence of all the prophetical characters of the *Messiah*; He is truly the *blessing* promised to *Abraham*, and in the Savior of the world *all the families of the Earth are blessed*; the Prophet *Moses* describes, *He* delivered a doctrine worthy of God, and *spoke in His Name, and the thing which He spoke followed and came to pass*; He had the divine attestation that (according to His own declaration) *He did not speak of Himself, but* [539]*whatever the*

Father commanded, that He spoke; he is the King promised to *David, Isaiah,* and *Daniel;* in His divine nature truly *reigns over the House of* Israel *forever; does not judge after the sight of His eyes, neither reprove after the hearing of His ears, but with righteousness judge the poor, and reprove with equity; and His Kingdom is such as shall not pass away, nor be left to other hands, but shall stand forever;* He is the Man of sufferings *Isaiah, Daniel,* and *Zechariah* describes; he is born of the *tribe, family,* and in the *town* foretold, he appeared at the promised, and what's more, at the expected time: When therefore all things concur, when miracle, prophecy, and prophetical characters all meet in *Jesus,* where is the ground for infidelity? Why is not *Jesus* acknowledged the *Messiah* of the *Jews?*

One thing we must observe, and that is, that in a dispute betwixt a *Jew* and a *Christian* who both acknowledge the divinity of the Old Testament, the *Christian* evidence, the evidence that *Jesus* is the *Messiah,* increases with time, and consequently the *Jewish* cause grows everyday worse and worse. And as by the confession of the *Jews,* their prophecies are unfulfilled, if not fulfilled in *Jesus,* they have everyday more reason than other to believe they are fulfilled in Him, or are imposture.

On the other hand, every independent argument for the divinity of the *Jewish* religion is a proof of *Christianity.*

As to the *Deist,* the evidence to him that *Jesus* is the *Messiah,* the Person He pretended to be, in short is this: *Jesus* appears and teaches a doctrine worthy of God, and worked miracles to confirm His divine mission. Whilst *Jesus'* miracles are not invalidated, He has a right to be received as a Person sent by God. But He also pretends to fulfill prophecies, and to be spoken of in a certain Book, He must then fulfill prophecies, and be spoken of in this Book. By this Book then, which He appeals to, He must be tried; and if it appears that He made an impossible claim, He is to be rejected. But no sooner is this examined, but we find that He does not make an impossible claim; on the contrary, such a Person, as He appears to be, is exactly described and foretold in this Book. And further we find that He has the highest evidence of prophecy.

If any *doubt* yet remains concerning the meaning of certain texts, it must be remembered that a possible sense supported by miracle and prophecy, ought to be received before any other whatsoever.

Conclusion

Hitherto we have considered several applications made by *Jesus* and his apostles, as not vacating the evidence of miracle and prophecy: we now proceed to look on them in another view, and to examine how far they may be reckoned to give evidence, and be judged rational parts of a great design.

And *first,* though these characters and circumstances might not singly be sufficient to prove a revelation, yet joined with miracle and prophecy, they give additional evidence, and form a threefold cord not to be broken.

Miracle alone was sufficient evidence that *Jesus* was sent by God; His fulfilling prophecies proved Him to be the *Messiah* of the *Jews*; and the prophesied characters and circumstances come in as it were over and above, to guard against those prejudices and unreasonable doubts of mankind, which might possibly arise at the manner of His appearance and sufferings. And surely, it is not only probable that the *Christian* religion is a divine revelation, which would be sufficient to determine every rational enquirer to embrace it; but it is no less than demonstration, that miracles, clear and express prophecies, and a number of prophetical characters, and circumstances, cannot meet in an impostor.

Secondly, as some of the prophetical characters and descriptions of the *Messiah* might be given to remove offences, which might arise from His mea appearance and sufferings; so might others which describe His grandeur, offices, and kingdom, be delivered wholly for the sake of that generation to which they were given, to keep up the hopes and expectations of the people, and make them have a constant eye to this great Deliverer.

Thirdly, if *Jesus* be the Person He pretends to be, the Deliverer of us from our sins, then the dignity of His Person, and importance of His errand, make it reasonable to expect that the prophets who lived before Him should be full of characters and descriptions of Him; and these characters and descriptions may teach us in what manner we should receive and honor Him.

Fourthly, as the making the ceremonies and sacrifices under the *Jewish* Law resemble the sacrifice by *Jesus* was a proper mode of worship for God to institute, because in these was the death of *Jesus* the great sacrifice constantly shown forth; so was it reasonable God should make the first dispensation a pattern of the second, that the *Jews* might be inclined to part with the first, give the shadow for the substance, when the perfect dispensation should arrive.

This is one view of the author to the *Hebrews* in his showing a resemblance betwixt the Law and the Gospel; and they strangely mistake things, who say that this author is proving *Christianity* by typical arguments. He is so far from attempting to prove *Christianity* at that time, that he declares he will not do it, that *leaving the* [540]*principles of the doctrine of* Christ, *he will go on to perfection.* And he gives a reason why he will not do it, namely, because he looked on it as an impossible work to *renew again by* [541] *repentance, those who had once been enlightened* and were fallen off; he could not hope to offer new arguments which might convince such apostates. Writing then as to believers, he goes on to set before them the difference betwixt the Law and the Gospel; the *imperfection of the one,* and *the perfection of the other*: He shows them how unable the Law was to do what they wanted of it, *take* [542] *away sins,* but that in the dispensation by *Jesus, their*

---

540   Hebrews 6:1
541   Heb. 6:4-6
542   Heb. 10:4

[543]*sins and iniquities would be remembered no more. That the* [544]*Law could make nothing perfect, but the bringing in of a better hope did;* that under the first dispensation, *the High Priest,*[545] *who offered for the sins of others, himself wanted a sacrifice;* that under the second, we had a [546]*High Priest who was holy, harmless, undefiled, separate from sinners, who after He had once offered one sacrifice for sins, forever sat down on the right-hand of God; that* the dispensation by *Moses* was only a *pattern, example, shadow, figure,* of the dispensation by *Jesus.* From the *imperfection* then of this dispensation, this *first covenant* as he calls it; from its being *unable to take away sins;* its being only a *shadow, pattern, figure* of the second; as well as from God's promise to the *Jews* to *give them a new* [547]*covenant,* this author proves that God never intended that it should remain always, but that *as it grew old, it should vanish away,* that *there should be a* [548]*disannulling of the commandment going before, for the weakness and unprofitableness thereof;* and that the *Priesthood being* [549] *changed, there was of necessity a change also of the Law.*

Fifthly, if some events under the first dispensation were made to resemble others under the second, it was of great use to the *Jews* to reconcile them to difficulties under this last, and was a training of them up to believe the mysteries of the Gospel.

Thus, if they should make a difficulty of believing that *Jesus* bore their sins on the cross, this difficulty would rationally be removed when they remembered that the scape-goat bore their sins into the wilderness.

If they should object to the possibility of *Jesus'* Resurrection after lying in the grave three days, they might remember that *Jonah* was delivered from the belly of the whale after lying there an equal time.

If they doubted of salvation by looking to a crucified Savior, *Moses* would put them in mind that the *Israelites* were healed of bodily disease by looking on the serpent.

---

543   Heb. 10:17
544   Heb. 7:19
545   Heb. 7:27
546   Heb. 7:26, 10:12, etc.
547   Heb. 8:6-13
548   Heb. 7:18
549   Heb. 7:12

Thus could not the *Jews* rationally object to the second dispensation, on account of any difficulties it contained, when they were used to believe equal difficulties in the first.

To conclude, if God was pleased to give signs of deliverances and blessings under the first dispensation which resembled others under the second, which pointed to the great Deliverer *Jesus*; He by this, lets us see the insignificancy of temporal felicity considered abstractedly and by itself, and that there is but one deliverance of importance to mankind, the deliverance by *Jesus* the Redeemer.

F I N I S.

FOLLOW

@SarahREnterline

sarahrenterline.com
noapologiesbook.com

FOR UPDATES AND NEWS ABOUT
UPCOMING BOOKS AND ARTICLES

CPSIA information can be obtained
at www.ICGtesting.com
Printed in the USA
LVHW032135231220
675033LV00020B/307